Fighting for Jobs

SUNY Series
The Sociology of Work
Richard Hall, editor

FIGHTING FOR JOBS

Case Studies of Labor-Community
Coalitions Confronting Plant Closings

BRUCE NISSEN

STATE UNIVERSITY OF
NEW YORK PRESS

Published by
State University of New York Press, Albany

© 1995 State University of New York

Printed in the United States of America

For information, address the State University of New York Press,
State University Plaza, Albany, NY 12246

Production by Bernadine Dawes • Marketing by Theresa Abad Swierzowski

Library of Congress Cataloging-in-Publication Data

Nissen, Bruce, 1948–
    Fighting for jobs : case studies of labor-community coalitions
    confronting plant closings / Bruce Nissen.
        p.   cm. — (SUNY series in the sociology of work)
    Includes bibliographical references and index.
    ISBN 0-7914-2567-3 (acid-free paper). — ISBN 0-7914-2568-1 (pbk.
    : acid-free paper)
        1. Plant shutdowns — United States — Case studies.   I. Title.
    II. Series.
    HD5708.55.U6N57   1995   94-34608
                                                                  CIP

    1 2 3 4 5 6 7 8 9 10

To Karen, Jared, and Leif; and to
my friend, Lynn Feekin

CONTENTS

ACKNOWLEDGMENTS

As typically happens with social science case study research, my debts are many. In my case, the list is so long that I will not attempt to thank everyone individually, but my gratitude is nevertheless very real.

A few individuals and institutions, however, must be mentioned. Indiana University granted me a sabbatical leave that provided the opportunity to begin this entire project. The International College of Hospitality Administration (ICHA) in Brig, Switzerland, provided a beautiful setting in the Swiss Alps to complete the final chapters of the book while my wife taught there.

David Fasenfest of Purdue University read an earlier version of the manuscript and provided insightful reactions that led to rearrangement and rewriting of much of the material. My debt is enormous. Anonymous reviewers for SUNY Press also provided helpful criticisms and suggestions. Mamie Anderson typed one of the chapters; and I thank her.

Finally, I owe an incalculable debt to the men and women of the board and staff of the Calumet Project for Industrial Jobs. In particular, former director Lynn Feekin has been an inspiration and a teacher. And the men and women who fought the battles depicted in this book have my highest admiration and gratitude.

In the late spring of 1987 I was asked to get involved in a campaign to re-open a closed steel mill in northwest Indiana. My subsequent involvement was to have far-reaching consequences for both my research and my community activities for years to come.

As a labor studies professor at the Gary campus of Indiana University, I am constantly in contact with local trade unionists who make up the majority of the students in my classes. Perhaps for that reason, I was asked to address a meeting of dislocated workers from a recently closed local steel mill who were attempting to reopen the mill. Following my talk the participants asked me to facilitate a session where they organized themselves into action teams to undertake the various tasks needed to accomplish their goal.

Since one of my former students was leading the effort, I was doubly interested in this campaign to reopen the mill and to save employment. I went to that meeting and was so impressed by what I saw that I continued to volunteer my services to that campaign, which was to continue for more than a year and a half.

I also became more and more fascinated by the organization that was spearheading the effort to build broad-based support for the workers' efforts. It was an unusual group known as the Calumet Project for Industrial Jobs. In mid-1988 I agreed to serve on its board of directors and have continued to serve every year since except during a sabbatical leave. In addition to being on its board, I have involved myself in a number of its issues, which extend considerably beyond plant closings.

This increasing involvement with the Calumet Project reoriented my research interests also. This book is one result of my ever-growing interest in labor-community coalitions and the dynamics of public struggles over what will be the final outcome in potential or real plant closing situations.[1]

The struggles described in the following pages are important for a number of reasons. First, plant closings have had a major negative impact on industrial communities in the past 15 years; tools to deal with this impact are rare but sorely needed. Second, the labor-community coalition approach to dealing with plant closings and larger related economic development issues is relatively untried yet potentially rewarding for embattled unions and declining industrial communities. Third, the Calumet Project's many campaigns seemed to me to offer an unusually rich mix of experiences, providing a "living laboratory" that was somewhat distinctive in its combination of many factors only partially replicated elsewhere.

Finally, I have been quite impressed with some of the personal transformations of individuals and the alterations in local public policy debates as a result of the Calumet Project's campaigns. I am convinced that, on a minor scale, a "social movement" has been started in northwest Indiana that has changed both the local political and social environment and those participating in it. As such it has drawn my attention; I hope the reader finds it equally interesting.

The Blaw-Knox Closure

1968	White Consolidated Industries (WCI) acquires Blaw-Knox foundry.
1970s	WCI acquires many firms, primarily in home appliances.
1980–85	WCI sells off many businesses, other than home appliances.
1980	U.S. Army begins to phase out M-1 tank (foundry's main product).
May 1984	Calumet Project researcher reads business press speculation that WCI will sell Blaw-Knox.
Summer 1984	Calumet Project convinces USWA Local 1026 to take action.
Late Sept. 1984	Local 1026 president sends memo alerting others to possible closure.
Late Oct. 1984	WCI announces plans to sell Blaw-Knox.
31 Oct. 1984	Blaw-Knox Steering Committee formed.
Nov.–Dec. 1984	Steering Committee begins work; seeks funding for a feasibility study.
11 Feb. 1985	A. D. Little (ADL) named to do feasibility study.
March–April 1985	Calumet Project and union prepare plans; host public meeting.
1 May 1985	ADL gives midterm report.
3 May 1985	ADL reports to workers; is criticized for lack of contact.
May–June 1985	Calumet Project and union prepare for campaign once ADL report is issued.
12 July 1985	ADL presents draft of final report to Steering Committee.
19 July 1985	ADL presents final report to workers and press. Report details plans for conversion to nonmilitary production.
24 July 1985	WCI informs Steering Committee that plant will be sold.
July–Sept. 1985	Steering Committee leadership refuses to consider Calumet Project proposal for an activist role; cancels meetings while awaiting news of sale.
Late Sept. 1985	WCI announces Blaw-Knox sale.

Oct. 1985	Steering Committee effectively disbanded.
Nov. 1985–Feb. 1986	Company and union fight over contract issues.
24 Feb. 1986	Plant manager reconvenes steering committee; asks it to petition and write letters for more tank orders.
Mid-March 1986	Community representatives refuse to ask for more military orders; plan collapses.
March–April 1986	Steering committee divides into sub-committees, which fail because company refuses to commit to anything. Sub-committees stop meeting.
March–July 1986	Politicians attempt to get more tank orders; fail.
28 Oct. 1986	Plant closes.

The Combustion Engineering Closure

1964	East Chicago plant loses research and design capabilities; company considers closing it but decides not to.
Late 1960s	Plant's product line narrowed to one item.
1972	Company plans to shut down East Chicago plant; changes mind because of pension liabilities.
26 May 1972	Ten-week strike over union contract comparability with "basic steel" contracts.
1972–1981	Boom years for the plant.
2 June 1975	Five-week strike, again over comparability.
31 May 1978	Sixteen-week strike, again over comparability.
July 1981	Contract bargaining conducted locally; settled peacefully.
1983	"Boom" market slows down; minor layoffs at plant.
1983–86	Rapid plant management turnover and instability.
1983–88	Parent company expands rapidly and loses millions in new product markets (not served by East Chicago plant).
5 Nov. 1984	Company requests an Industrial Revenue Bond (IRB) for new machinery; promises to retain eighteen jobs.

Jan. 1985	Company road show proclaims "new era" of labor-management relations; no subsequent real changes.
Early 1986	East Chicago plant's product market drops precipitously; major layoffs hit.
April 1986	Plant officials mislead city officials about prospects for the plant during an annual meeting.
10 May 1986	USWA Local 1386 officers attend Calumet Project early warning training class; begin activity concerning potential shutdown.
29 May 1986	Company announces it is considering shutdown.
5 & 12 June 1986	Company announces shutdown.
14 July 1986	Union and Calumet Project staffers meet with mayor; request action against company for breach of faith on IRB.
21 July 1986	Economic Development Commission (EDC) hearings on IRB issue; union and Calumet Project personnel testify.
4 Aug. 1986	EDC legal council recommends against legal action; recommendation followed.
25 Aug. 1986	Calumet Project and union host meeting with congressman and others; demand "settlement terms."
26 Aug. 1986	Congressman writes company requesting settlement terms.
29 Aug. 1986	Company responds to congressman; avoids the issue.
9 Sept. 1986	Congressman's aide meets with company in Washington, D.C.
15 Sept. 1986	Top corporate officer flies to East Chicago; meets with congressman, union officials, and Calumet Project staffers.
25 Sept. 1986	Company agrees to limited set of conditions.
26 Sept. 1986	Plant closes.

The Stratojac Closure

| Late 1970s to early 1980s | Aging Stratojac owner Louis Winer unsuccessfully looks for a successor. |
| 1 Jan. 1984 | Winer sells to Mesirow Finance; Indiana state subsidized funds aid the purchase; Steve Sakin named company president. |

1984	Sakin runs company long distance from New York; overproduces merchandise and alienates New York sales manager; company turns profit only through accounting gimmick.
1985	Sakin hides steep price discounts causing losses from creditor bank.
Sept. 1985	Deception is discovered; bank demands repayment.
Sept.–Nov. 1985	Plans devised to save company, including move to Amsterdam, New York.
Nov. 1985	Seasonal layoffs; all appears normal to workers.
Early Dec. 1985	Union accidentally discovers plan to move.
Dec. 1985–April 1986	Company requests and receives large public subsidies in Amsterdam.
Jan.–April 1986	Union attempts to reopen Hammond plant; fails.
April–May 1986	Sakin gives press exaggerated employment claims at Amsterdam site.
May–July 1986	Union looks for buyers for Hammond plant; attempts to pressure mayor to help with reemployment effort.
5 Aug. 1986	Union disbands.
Oct. 1986	Sakin resigns as Stratojac president.
Dec. 1986	Hammond workers win Trade Adjustment Act retraining money.
Nov.–Dec. 1988	Company in Amsterdam deeply in debt; brings in crisis management firm.
March 1989	Creditors files for involuntary liquidation.
April–May 1989	Bankruptcy status changed to voluntary; reorganization attempted unsuccessfully.
6 July 1989	Stratojac label bought.
Oct. 1989	Remaining Amsterdam equipment sold.

The LTV Bar Mill Closure

Mid-1970s	LTV buys Jones & Laughlin Steel, including the Hammond plant.
1984	LTV merges with Republic Steel, creating company overcapacity in bar-making facilities.
1984–85	Company attempts to "whipsaw" Gary and Hammond union locals into concessions; Hammond local successfully resists.
July 1986	LTV declares bankruptcy; idles Hammond mill.
3 Nov. 1986	Idling turned into permanent closure.
Nov. 1986– Jan. 1987	Union local works with Calumet Project; forms Alternative Ownership Committee (AOC).
Late Feb. 1987	Union local requests steelworkers district to fund "quick look" feasibility study; files grievance over closure.
Early March 1987	Steelworkers hire Locker & Associates to do feasibility study.
March 1987	Mayor attends union local meeting; pledges to help.
March– June 1987	Union local requests international union legal department to file in bankruptcy court to prevent removal of equipment; request denied.
Late April 1987	Congressman pressures LTV president to reopen or to sell to owner who will.
8 May 1987	Feasibility study released; pessimistic conclusion.
July–Sept. 1987	Union sounds out Chicago management consultant who had expressed interest in buying; turns out to be unreliable and a union-buster.
July–Sept. 1987	Union proposes ESOP; LTV gives offer no credibility.
30 July 1987	Canadian steel company Union Drawn Steel expresses interest in buying; agrees to AOC/Calumet Project terms.
Sept. 1987	AOC hires legal council to file in bankruptcy court to prevent key equipment removal; attempt abandoned in November.
24 Sept. 1987	Public meeting on issue attended by over 150.
28 Sept. 1987	Hammond city council calls for a legal lien on property, exploration of eminent domain proceedings, etc.

8 Oct. 1987	Plant tour by Union Drawn president postponed when LTV insists key equipment will be withdrawn before sale.
Oct.–Nov. 1987	Congressman and LTV president exchange letters on the issue.
23 Oct. 1987	AOC press release accuses LTV of breaking promises.
12 Nov. 1987	LTV meets with AOC and Calumet Project; agrees to consider proposals and cooperate.
23 Nov. 1987	Picket line and rally prevent Ohio contractor from removing key equipment; all-day negotiations result in agreement allowing equipment removal in exchange for LTV's commitment to co-operate in sale of remainder of plant.
Dec. 1987	Union Drawn withdraws its interest in buying.
Late Dec. 1987	Mayor requests LTV to honor its commitments.
12 Jan. 1988	LTV responds to mayor's letter; LTV denounced at public meeting for failure to honor its commitments.
22 Jan. 1988	LTV writes mayor complaining of false accusations and bad press.
Feb.–May 1988	Massive community outreach effort by AOC/Calumet Project.
30 April 1988	Deadline for finding a buyer passes.
Mid-July 1988	LTV announces sale of remaining equipment.
Fall 1988	Steel tubing company plans to buy plant; agrees to AOC/Calumet Project conditions.
Early Nov. 1988	LTV announces site contamination.
Late Nov. 1988	Hammond city council passes resolution supporting AOC/Calumet Project campaign.
Dec. 1988	LTV meeting with newspaper editorial board results in pro-company editorial.
11 Jan. 1989	LTV announces contamination widespread; tubing firm pulls out.
12 Jan. 1989	Community meeting; LTV denounced on employment and environmental grounds.
1989–1991	Under pressure, LTV cleans up site.
May 1991	New steel company buys site; agrees to AOC conditions for receiving public subsidy; later opens up, hiring the few ex-LTV workers desiring employment.

The LaSalle Steel Struggle

30 Dec. 1981	LaSalle Steel acquired by Houston-based Quanex Corporation.
Feb. 1984	Three-day strike by the independent LaSalle union over concession demands; fewer granted than in comparable plants elsewhere.
Fall 1986	Quanex terminates employee pension plan and replaces it with an annuity and a new plan; pockets $12 million "excess" in old plan.
Early 1987	Contract negotiations result in wage freeze, temporary two-tier wage structure.
Feb.–March 1990	Thirty-two-day strike over pension, cost of living, and two-tier pay issues.
Fall 1990	Rumors in the mill that the key "turning and grinding" department will be shut down and relocated.
27 Oct. 1990	Four LaSalle workers attend Calumet Project early warning training session; rumors discussed.
Early Nov. 1990	Union joins Calumet Project; begins campaign to save department.
16 Nov. 1990	LaSalle plant manager Richard Treder writes union president about rumors and unrest.
26 Nov. 1990	Union president replies; insists on being part of decision.
30 Nov. 1990	Treder replies; agrees to meet and gives thirty-day notice of closure.
Late Nov. 1990	Union members send letter to Quanex CEO exposing bogus quality reports used to discredit turning department.
3 Dec. 1990	Quanex CEO replies; refers issue to Treder.
6 Dec. 1990	Press conference on danger of relocation.
7 Dec. 1990	Treder meets with union leaders, angry over press reports; rescinds thirty-day notice.
10 Dec. 1990	Public meeting on the issue attended by many public officials.
11 Dec. 1990	Union letter to Hammond mayor opposing a public subsidy "bidding war" with another municipality and putting conditions on any subsidies given.

20 Dec. 1990   Hammond city council Economic Development Committee chair writes Quanex CEO about the issue.

Late Dec. 1990   Union executive board decides not to take further action at this point, despite Calumet Project urging to maintain the initiative.

4 Jan. 1991   Quanex CEO replies to Economic Development Committee chair; refers matter to Treder.

Mid-Jan. 1991   Bogus "buyer" appears; tries to convince union to work with him because he will soon own the plant.

25 Jan. 1991   Treder notifies union of tentative decision to relocate turning department and an additional production line.

29 Jan. 1991   Plant-wide educational sessions.

Early Feb. 1991   Attempts to involve the United Steelworkers, which represents workers at a nearby facility likely to be affected, fail.

12 Feb. 1991   Treder shares comparative cost data on different sites with union.

Mid-Feb. 1991   Union and Calumet Project mail document to public officials, community leaders, and the press; document calls on LaSalle to postpone decision and cooperate with a feasibility study on retaining employment.

14 Feb. 1991   Daily newspaper editorial rebukes LaSalle and supports union/Calumet Project proposals.

15 Feb. 1991   Calumet Project reveals to the press that LaSalle received tax abatements on the very equipment it planned to move; Treder refuses to speak to press from this point on.

Mid-Feb. 1991   City attaches conditions to any public subsidy.

20 Feb. 1991   Treder sends letter defending his position.

25 Feb. 1991   Hammond city council president writes to counterpart in city of potential destination, requesting no public subsidies at a new site.

26 Feb. 1991   Hammond mayor writes to Treder supporting workers.

Late Feb. 1991   Hammond mayor writes counterpart, opposing subsidies at new site.

28 Feb. 1991   Calumet Project sends Quanex CEO press clips and a document; request support of union/Calumet Project position.

5 March 1991   Treder reverses relocation plan; refuses to speak to press.

May 1991   Treder retires.

1991–93   LaSalle develops extensive employee involvement program; claims success due to cooperation with the union.

1
INTRODUCTION

In the 1980s plant closings became a major public policy issue in the United States. As entire industries went through wrenching restructuring that included closing plants in successive waves and as industrial regions of the country experienced continuing decline, the issue became increasingly important. Legislative measures to provide early warning of closures and to regulate shutdowns in a variety of ways were introduced in over thirty state legislatures, culminating in a national plant closing law that took effect in 1989.

Not surprisingly, plant closings have also been the subject of a growing body of literature.[1] This literature has examined plant closures from a wide variety of angles: the emotional and health effects on dislocated workers, legislative requirements for prenotification, unemployment duration and reemployment experiences, worker retraining issues, collective bargaining clauses and issues, employee ownership and other alternatives to shutdown, and others.

However, the literature on plant closing struggles is relatively sparse.[2] This book attempts to partially fill the gap by examining five cases of battles over plans to partially or completely shut down facilities in northwest Indiana. Between 1985 and 1991 the Calumet Project for Industrial Jobs spearheaded labor-community coalition efforts to alter outcomes.

Chapters 2–6 contain five comprehensive case studies of real or threatened full or partial plant closures and the resultant campaigns to save jobs. Chapter 7 contains a comparative analysis of the cases, drawing conclusions regarding the role of early warning, labor-management issues, corporate strategy and structure, economic forces, and local government policy. Chapter 8 highlights the role of "problem definition" in determining the final outcome and the importance and determinants of alliance formation and mobilization for labor-community coalitions. It also examines the cases in light of existing theoretical and empirical literature and argues there is more promise here than some acknowledge.

The reader of the following case studies would benefit from an understanding of the context within which they occurred. The book's analytical framework should also be made explicit. Therefore the remainder of this introduction will address the context of the cases and the analytical framework that ties the cases together.

The two immediately following sections explain the economic and institutional features and trends of northwest Indiana during the 1980s. The third section then details the organizational characteristics and history of the Calumet Project for Industrial Jobs, the labor-community coalition organization that was involved in all the plant closing campaigns in this book.

The next section introduces the analytic framework for the cases that follow. That framework centers on five factors of potentially great import to plant closing outcomes: (1) early warning of the shutdown; (2) the role of labor-management relations in the plant; (3) the corporate structure and strategy of the owner; (4) the role of economic market factors; and (5) local government's role.

Against the backdrop of these five factors, I then introduce ways in which union and community activists can alter the usual configuration of forces to obtain more favorable outcomes. Analysis centers on the struggle over what will be the dominant definition of the problem in the local media and other centers of public opinion, plus the relative successes and failures of the Calumet Project in forging alliances and mobilizing constituencies. These last two factors — controlling the dominant problem definition and successful alliance formation and constituency mobilization — are the key to proactive intervention by workers and local communities in their economic affairs.

ECONOMIC CONTEXT

The Calumet Region of northwest Indiana, directly adjacent to the Illinois state line, the city of Chicago, and Lake Michigan, is a heavily industrialized area. Large integrated steel mills on the shore of Lake Michigan have historically dominated the economies of the two counties in this region, Lake and Porter counties. Well paying unionized jobs in the steel and related primary metals industries created above average per capita income: in the 1960s and 1970s it was approximately 110 percent of the national average.[3]

But the 1980s were devastating to the region. High-income jobs in steel and related primary metals dropped from approximately 32 percent of total employment to around 15 percent. Steel mill employment dropped 8.3 percent annually from 1979–84, and 3.7 percent annually from 1984–91. Over 45,000 jobs in durable goods manufacturing were lost from 1969–90. Steel jobs dropped 48 percent (down 31,300) while other durable good production jobs dropped 57 percent (down 14,600).

Nevertheless, the region fared better than other steel producing areas. The major U.S. steel producers consolidated much of their production in the Calumet Region because of its central location and lesser vulnerability to import penetration. While steel employment was halved, it did not disappear entirely, as it virtually did in other steel areas on the east, south, or west coasts. Growing wholesale, retail, trade, finance, insurance, and service jobs took up some of the slack, but this has been inadequate for two reasons. First, the new jobs do not pay as well as the old ones did, on the whole. Second, there have not been enough of them created to keep the region up to national averages. Total employment in the region grew at an annual rate of .5 percent during 1969–90, compared to a national annual rate of 1.9 percent. Figure 1.1 contains a graphic illustration of total employment, steel mill employment, and service industries employment in northwest Indiana.

Compounding this regional distress, the impact of the economic decline has been very unevenly distributed. The region is highly segregated — according to some studies it is the most highly segregated region in the nation. The three major cities of Gary, Hammond, and East Chicago contain close to 99 percent of all African-American and Hispanic residents in the region. They are also the cities most dependent on the disappearing manufacturing jobs.

The results are predictable: according to U.S. Census figures, while real per capita income in the United States increased 15 percent during the 1980s, it fell by 13.1 percent in Hammond, 14.7 percent in Gary, and 18.1 percent in East Chicago.[4] Unemployment rates in all three cities have remained high well into the 1990s despite massive population loss. Census figures reveal that Gary lost 23.2 percent of its population during the decade; Hammond and East Chicago lost 10.1 percent and 14.8 percent, respectively.

Plant closings played a major but not overwhelming role in the job loss of the decade. No usable government statistics exist on plant closings during this period, but the Calumet Project conducted a study in 1989 of seventeen regional plants that had closed in the past decade. There were at least double that number, but precise data are not available. A sizable percentage, but not a majority, of the employment loss was due to plant closings. Because of this significant impact, plant closings became a public issue in the 1980s in the region.

Figure 1.1. Northwest Indiana total employment, steel mill employment, and service industries employment, 1969–90.

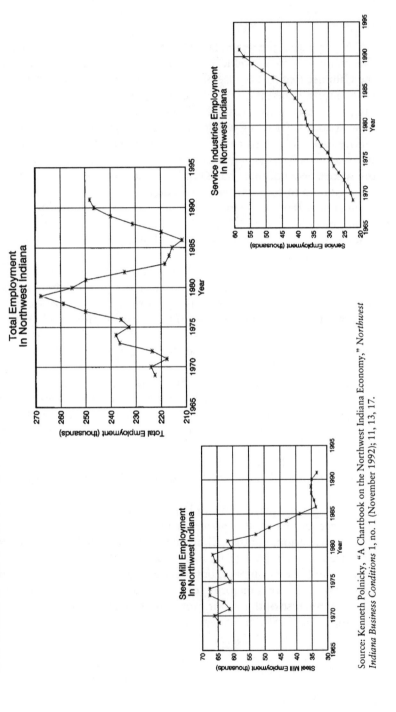

Source: Kenneth Polnicky, "A Chartbook on the Northwest Indiana Economy," *Northwest Indiana Business Conditions* 1, no. 1 (November 1992); 11, 13, 17.

INSTITUTIONAL CONTEXT

The institutions of northwest Indiana are closely intertwined with the demographic and racial characteristics of the region. Lake County, which abuts Illinois and which contains Gary, Hammond, and East Chicago, houses 98 percent of all nonwhite residents in the two county area. It has close to half a million residents, although it lost over 9 percent of its population from 1980 to 1990. Porter County to the east has no towns with over 30,000 (Lake County's Gary, Hammond, and East Chicago have about 120,000, 80,000, and 40,000, respectively); its virtually all-white population of close to 130,000 is mostly composed of rural and small-town residents. Its population grew 6 percent in the 1980s.

Since all of the plant closings in this study occurred in the more heavily industrialized Lake County, the remainder of this book will focus on Lake County alone. Its three major cities — Gary, Hammond, and East Chicago — account for approximately half its population. Gary is primarily African-American (81%); Hammond is predominantly white (85%); and East Chicago is heavily Hispanic (48%). The surrounding towns with one or two exceptions are over 99 percent white.

The extreme racial segregation of the area is complemented by a history of political corruption. The Democratic Party has controlled the county for decades, although the Republican Party has made real headway in the rural and wealthy suburban southern part of the county. Historically the Democratic Party machine has been plagued by corruption; periodically federal grand juries have indicted and convicted county and municipal political figures on a variety of financial corruption charges.

In 1968 Gary elected its first African-American mayor, Richard Hatcher. White flight, which had already begun, accelerated rapidly in the following decades. Many residents of Porter County or southern Lake County are former Gary residents. In East Chicago, although Hispanics are the largest ethnic group, the city remains under the control of a white-led party machine headed by Mayor Robert Pastrick that rivals Chicago Mayor Richard Daley's machine in the 1960s. Hammond has had a Republican mayor, but an overwhelmingly Democratic city council, for many years.

There is a long history of rivalry and hostility between municipalities in the region. Long-term Gary mayor Hatcher blamed the continuing decline of the city on racism; his relationship with (mostly white) politicians outside the city was often hostile. After twenty years in office, Hatcher was replaced by another African-American, Thomas Barnes, but the city has remained isolated from the surrounding population. East Chicago and Hammond have likewise remained rather isolated from the larger region. A proposal in the 1980s for a "uni-gov" structure providing for one overarching governmental entity for the region was immediately rejected on all sides.

There are few regional structures dealing with the economic health of the region. The Northwest Indiana Regional Planning Commission (NIRPC) channels federal money into research on regional issues but has mostly confined itself to transportation needs and plans. Even in transportation, regional cooperation has been lacking to such a degree that public transportation across city boundaries has been difficult to attain. There is a regionally based business group that functions somewhat like a "super Chamber of Commerce" for the region. Known as the Northwest Indiana Forum, it addresses economic development issues but is entirely private in character. Public policy remains firmly tied to individual policies of the cities in the region. County structures likewise play no significant role in economic policy.

The overall political and institutional structures in the Calumet Region are thus highly "Balkanized." Regional cooperation is difficult; individual cities jealously guard their own "turf," while mutual recrimination, suspicion, and charges of racism continue.

Within the business community, the Northwest Indiana Forum is by far the biggest and most important organization. It plays a major role as a business lobbying force to ensure that state legislation is positive for business interests within the region. In addition to lobbying heavily for state legislation to legalize casino gambling in Gary, the Forum has also conducted massive media (radio) advertising in Chicago in an attempt to lure businesses out of that city into northwest Indiana. Beyond the umbrella of the Forum, the most powerful businesses in local affairs are the local utility (Northern Indiana Public Service Company — NIPSCO) and USX (formerly U.S. Steel), which has singlehandedly dictated tax and other policies to the city of Gary for some time.

The region is relatively heavily unionized because of the dominance of large-scale steel production. Lake County has an estimated 35 percent of its workforce under union contract. The United Steelworkers of America (USWA) is by far the dominant union; USWA District 31, which covers northwest Indiana and some adjacent areas in Illinois, is one of the largest districts within the parent union. Despite its size, District 31 lost more than half its members in the 1980s. As of 1993 it had approximately 50,000 members, down from about 110,000 in the late 1970s. There are also important concentrations of union members in the building trades craft unions, and smaller numbers in the teachers (AFT); Oil,

Chemical, and Atomic Workers (OCAW); Teamsters (IBT); Service Employees (SEIU); Clothing Workers (ACTWU); public sector (AFSCME); Machinists (IAM); and Communication Workers (CWA) unions.

Despite its size, the labor movement has not been a major player in public policy issues in the region outside of those issues directly related to its immediate institutional interests. The local political structure is careful to cultivate labor support and can usually be counted on to support organized labor's most narrow, "special interest" concerns, but it has not included the unions in broader political affairs. The labor movement itself is neither extraordinarily active nor inactive in public affairs. Like the bulk of the labor movement in post–World War II United States, it has been content to play an important but secondary role in political affairs, primarily through support of the local Democratic Party.

CALUMET PROJECT FOR INDUSTRIAL JOBS

The severe contraction of jobs and income in the Calumet Region provoked a number of responses. One of them was the creation of the Calumet Project for Industrial Jobs. It was initially formed in 1984 as a joint effort by the Midwest Center for Labor Research (MCLR), a union-oriented research group based in Chicago, and the United Citizens Organization (UCO), a church-based community organization located in East Chicago, Indiana.

Despite the union and church connections of its parent organizations, the Calumet Project initially was a less effective coalition than it would be if it directly developed its own structure, membership, fund-raising capacities, and institutional base of support. Therefore, in the second half of 1988 it separated from its two parent organizations and organized its own Board of Directors, bylaws, organizational members, and funding. It is incorporated as a nonprofit organization, and has employed a staff of between 1½ and 4 employees.

The Calumet Project's twofold mission is to preserve well-paying industrial jobs in the region and to empower worker and community constituencies in the economic development decision-making process. Countering the usual tendency to leave economic development to the business community and their political allies, the Calumet Project aims to inject labor and community institutions into the center of public policy debates and decisions.

Its structure follows from this mission. Membership consists of unions, churches, community organizations, and individuals. Over twenty organizations are members, a majority being unions, followed by a smaller number of churches and community organizations. A board of directors with between fifteen and twenty-one members is elected from the various constituencies; six seats are reserved for labor unions, with three apiece reserved to church and community representation. Task forces open to all interested parties carry out the programmatic work; committees primarily composed of board members conduct organizational business, such as program planning, membership, or fund-raising.

Over half of the Calumet Project's budget (which has fluctuated between $50,000 and $195,000) comes from private foundation and religious grants, but membership dues, local fund-raising, contributions, and occasional fees for research are also important parts of the budget.

The Calumet Project conceives of itself as a labor-community coalition; it takes an organizing approach to all areas of programmatic work. The goal is to see that its labor, church, and community constituencies shape and work for their own solutions to the problems facing them. Although it encompasses the entire Calumet Region, the Calumet Project has concentrated most of its work within the three cities most in need: Gary, Hammond, and East Chicago.

Chronologically, the work of the Calumet Project can be divided into three stages:

> Stage 1. Publicizing and calling attention to plant closings and the plight of dislocated workers (mid-1984 through 1985);
> Stage 2. Creation and use of a plant closing "early warning system" and the running of specific campaigns to save endangered plants (from 1986 on); and
> Stage 3. Development of public policy initiatives to address job retention and economic development from a labor and community perspective (from 1990 on).

Each of these stages can be seen to logically flow from the earlier work of the project. Each stage is an attempt to broaden the range of concerns and the influence of labor and community constituencies beyond that of the previous stage.

The case studies in this book all concern plant closings, which fall within the confines of Stage 2. Thus, they do not present a full picture of the work of the Calumet Project. Rather, the attempt is to use these in-depth case studies to determine which ingredients are necessary for a labor-community coalition to obtain and exercise power and to demonstrate how even seemingly "narrow" struggles over the fate of an individual plant raise fundamental questions involving public policy. Some of the broader questions that the Calumet Project has subsequently addressed in its public policy work (Stage 3) are raised in the subsequent chapters of this book.

ANALYTICAL FRAMEWORK

The cases in the following chapters highlight certain central issues. The interplay of factors is different from case to case, but all exhibit similar dynamics at work. The analysis in the book isolates five issues as central to the background within which the plant closing struggles took place:

1. *Early Warning.* Were there "early warning" signs that the plant may be closing? Did the workforce or the local government notice any that were present? What should the workers and the local government do if they wish to obtain advance notification? What do these cases tell us about early warning signs and how they can best be read?

2. *Labor-Management Issues.* Did labor-management issues play a role in the closing decision? What role, if any, did labor relations play in determining the ultimate outcome? Can labor-management innovations help prevent plant closures? Alternatively, can unions through traditional labor relations mechanisms exert an important influence to prevent or reverse shutdown decisions?

3. *Corporate Strategy and Structure.* How important is corporate structure and strategy to determining ultimate outcomes? What corporate structures make a closing more likely? Which corporate structures are more vulnerable to influence by labor-community coalitions? What role do corporate strategies play?

4. *Economic Factors.* How important is the state of the product market? How large of a role do import penetration, production overcapacity, need for massive reinvestment, and similar economic factors play in determining a shutdown? How important are they in thwarting or aiding efforts to avert a closing or to reopen a facility?

5. *Role of Local Government.* What role did local and regional government officials play? Who did they primarily respond to? Would an alternative course of action have produced different results? Which roles were most and least successful in preserving employment?

These five issues have received varying amounts of attention in the plant closing literature. The cases in this book extend our understanding of all of them.

Early Warning

Advance notification to the workforce of impending shutdowns became a major national issue in the United States in the 1980s. Surveys by the U.S. Bureau of Labor Statistics (BLS) and the General Accounting Office (GAO) in the middle of that decade revealed that most employers provided either no notice or less than two weeks notice.[5] It is widely recognized that advance notification is beneficial to both the workforce and the local community because it allows for planning in making adjustments.[6] Numerous studies have shown beneficial public effects from advance notice.[7] Opposing arguments have relied heavily on neoclassical free-market economic theory but have been short on empirical evidence.[8]

It is also widely agreed that advance notice is important, and perhaps critical, for any attempts to avert a shutdown. Long lead times are needed for any realistic effort to lower production costs, restructure the production process for greater efficiency, develop new product lines, sell to a new owner, change management teams, employ new technology, or do whatever else may be necessary to salvage a plant that is endangered but potentially viable.

In 1988 the federal Worker Adjustment Retraining and Notification (WARN) Act was passed, mandating sixty days advance notice to the workforce and to local and state government from employers with one hundred or more employees. The law contains many loopholes and fails to cover many workers because of the one hundred employee cutoff point. Further, the sixty days is an absolute minimum amount of time to set up even the barest of adjustment programs for displaced workers (e.g., job search training, skills training). It is definitely insufficient time, in most circumstances, to alter a plant closing decision or to arrange an alternative future for the facility and its workers where this could be a realistic possibility.

Therefore sixty days advance notice is inadequate for those attempting activist strategies to save jobs. By most accounts, a minimum of six months is necessary for any successful intervention strategy, usually even more than this. This means that activist workers, unions, or communities must rely on "early warning" signs that a closure may be coming if the company does not, as a matter of policy, provide prenotification of six months or longer. Early warning systems of various types have been employed by state governments, local governments, unions, and community groups in the 1980s.[9]

A number of the early warning systems employed by state and local governments consist of nothing more than a computerized economic database on particular industries or regions, "word of mouth," or self-reports from plant managers or owners. Most of the systems utilized by community groups or unions rely on worker reports on conditions in and around the plant, as well as publicly available financial information about the corporation. However, most are unsystematic and are not ongoing systems that conduct monitoring over a sustained period of time.

The Calumet Project has an ongoing early warning system based on worker monitoring of conditions within the plant, supplemented by collection and review of public financial data on corporations. Perhaps the only systematic ongoing early warning system of this type in the nation, it has been in effect since the second half of 1986. A fuller report on this effort has been written elsewhere.[10]

Because of the existence of the early warning system, and due to the extensive amount of data collected on each case, the following chapters will document a number of early warning signs. They also contain lessons concerning the usefulness and importance of early warning to those interested in intervention efforts. The general results confirm the prevalence of early warning signals preceding a shutdown, indicate the nature of those signals, validate the usefulness and accuracy of the Calumet Project's "early warning scorecard," and demonstrate the severe limitations of most local government- or business-based forms of early warning, compared to systems based on in-plant monitoring by workers.

Labor-Management Issues

The degree to which labor-management relations influence plant closing decisions is little understood. Anecdotal evidence supports the view that bad labor relations, a unionized labor force, or inflexible work rules contribute to plant closings. So the issue is: do labor issues cause plant closings and can they help prevent them? Can labor relations play an important role in either preventing closure or in reversing closure decisions?

It is widely thought that unionization contributes to the chance that a plant will close. Yet this impression is apparently the result of confounding separate factors by failing to control for other variables (such as age) that often accompany unionization. The best evidence indicates that unionization per se has no impact on the probability of closure. On the basis of a well-conceived quantitative analysis, Howland concludes that "there is no indication that plants situated in a unionized labor market are more likely to close than plants located in a nonunion area," and Freeman and Kleiner find "virtually no union effect" on the rate of plant closures or the likelihood of business failure.[11] This contradicts the perspective of many scholars from right to left on the political spectrum, but it is the best evidence we have. Howland also finds that neither the level nor rate of change in wage levels has any statistically significant impact on closure rates.[12]

However, this does not prove that all labor relations issues are irrelevant to closure decisions or to the prevention of closures. More detailed factors or patterns not captured by data on mere unionization or wage levels may be at work. The five cases in this book provide limited evidence for a few conclusions.

My general results indicate that labor relations usually play a subsidiary or nonexistent role in plant closing decisions, although there are clear exceptions. I also draw conclusions concerning the limitations of traditional collective bargaining relationships as a means of providing influence over "capital" decisions about investment and plant location, indicate exceptions where conventional labor relations channels are effective, and indicate structural features of unions that make them more or less effective in shutdown situations.

Corporate Structure and Strategy

Previous literature contains both theoretical arguments and empirical evidence that the owner's corporate structure and strategy influence the likelihood of a plant closure. Likewise, the susceptibility of a company to pressures to alter or reverse a closing decision may also be influenced by its structural characteristics and strategic focus.

Many authors cite both theoretical reasons and empirical evidence showing that branch plants and subsidiaries are more likely to shut down than are single plant firms or corporate headquarters. Reasons include wider potential investment choices, corporate "hurdle" profit rates for individual plants that have no counterpart in single plant companies, "paper entrepreneurialism" and/or poor management by multiplant conglomerates, and others.[13] Four of the five cases studied here fit into this category; the latest and best statistical documentation confirms the speculations that this is a category especially at risk of a plant closure.[14]

The case studies confirm the prevailing wisdom of the literature and also go beyond mere structural features by relating the plant closings to corporate strategic orientation. The results show that workers, unions, and communities need to pay close attention to the overall corporate strategies of their corporate employers. The evidence supports the claims of Bluestone and Harrison and others that corporate institutional and structural features and their strategic orientation are integral to most decisions to close a particular plant.

Economic Factors: Product Market and Capital Needs

Pure neoclassical economic theory would see plant closures as inevitable responses to market forces. Institutional factors such as those considered in the previous section are ignored as irrelevant from the larger perspective. Thus, most plant closing interventions are seen as impediments to economic efficiency that ultimately cost jobs, rather than saving them.

Empirical studies do not validate the predictions of pure theory: least efficient and least profitable plants do not always close first. Therefore the most interesting studies of plant closings within the neoclassical tradition posit "market imperfections" as a way of incorporating institutional factors.[15]

The case studies contained in this book are not written according to such a neoclassical paradigm. Nevertheless, the degree to which purely economic forces made the closings inevitable, or to which they made attempts to save or reopen a plant absolutely utopian, is important to assess. Each case study examines economic conditions in the industry of the closing plant, and chapter 7 contains a comparative analysis of the cases of four economic factors: (1) market decline (or lack of it), (2) import penetration, (3) overcapacity in the industry, and (4) industry profit rate.

The results indicate that economic market factors have an importance but not the iron necessity attributed to them by the neoclassical paradigm. The results also indicate a role for such factors in determining the *timing* of shutdowns and an influence over the ability of the industry to attract managerial talent and other prerequisites to saving or reopening an endangered plant.

Role of Local Government

Local government officials played an important role in determining the outcomes of these five cases. Public officials assume political responsibility for the economic health of the community. Aside from the private owner of the company, they also have the most legitimacy and greatest institutional power base from which to act in the event of a threatened or real shutdown. Public officials also help "set the context" within which private actors (e.g., owners, workers, unions, community groups) make choices. Although the actual power of local governments — particularly in relation to massive corporations — is severely constrained, they are nevertheless important local players.

Analysis of local government role centers on two focuses: public policy prior to the announced (or effected) shutdown and the government's actual response to the plant closing. Both individual case studies and a comparative analysis in chapter 7 examine and critique standard government preshutdown policy of tax incentives and government subsidies to create a "good business climate."

After announced closure, government responses fall into three patterns. The local government can play (1) a "bystander" role, (2) an "offset" role, or (3) a "player" role.[16]

A *bystander* role calls for the government to be passive: stand aside and allow private market mechanisms to determine the outcome. An *offset* role calls for the government to leave all the major decisions to the private decision makers but to attempt to offset the effects if those decisions result in undesirable local outcomes. The offset approach can take either a "financial offset" or a "labor offset" direction. In the former, the government attempts to help the company through financial assistance, technical assistance, a feasibility study, or the like. In the latter, the government provides worker retraining, job search assistance, and so on to the affected workforce.

A *player* role calls on the government to insert itself into the decision-making process. Here the government plays the largest of the three possible roles: it becomes an integral "player" in the situation. Ideologically, the player role could range from right (corporate) to left (populist). Corporate player roles are extremely rare in the United States; they call for major government intervention in key economic decisions, but the intervention is dominated by the corporation. U.S. business tends to be ideologically opposed to such a major government role; hence even massive government assistance (such as with the federal government bailout of the Chrysler Corporation around 1980) tends to be confined to an offset role. Populist player roles mean government intervention allied with labor or community interests, rather than the corporation. Often the corporation opposes such intervention.

The Calumet Project was seeking a populist player role from the government in the cases studies in this volume, in addition to offset measures. A comparative analysis in chapter 7 draws a number of conclusions about its successes and failures in this regard. The results show both obstacles and possibilities — possibilities that, in turn, depend on the ability of community forces to break the local government out of standard roles and into a more proactive stance.

The five background factors given above set the stage for the key points in the book, which concern the ability of labor-community coalitions to address the problems created by plant closings and corporate disinvestment. Here analysis centers on two issues that are addressed in the cases themselves and more systematically and comparatively in chapter 8. These issues are:

- *Problem Definition.* How was the main issue or the central problem defined? What criteria or what authorities were relied upon to substantiate the way the problem was defined? When differing definitions were articulated, what factors determined which definition became dominant? How important was problem definition to the final outcome?
- *Alliance Formation and Mobilization.* How successful was the Calumet Project at mobilizing key constituencies or in building powerful alliances? Who exerted real power? What determined success or failure in these efforts to build a "social movement?" In turn, did the more developed social movements achieve greater results?

Definition of the problem — What is it that needs a remedy? — is crucial to any program of action. In the cases presented in this volume, the Calumet Project's labor-community coalitions struggled to have their understanding of the problem become widely accepted and acted upon. Such a process is not automatic: contending definitions are offered by other interested parties, and political struggle ensues over whose definition will prevail. This is a crucial battle, for it is a truism that framing the original question or setting the terms of the political debate is at least as important to victory as is one's subsequent argumentation or performance.

Problem definition has three components: (1) a standard by which to judge if there is a problem, (2) a causal explanation for the problem, and (3) a remedial action plan to correct the problem.[17] The case studies in chapters 2–6 and the comparative analysis in chapter 8 reveal that the Calumet Project and its allies differed from their corporate and political opponents on all three dimensions.

In general, the Calumet Project's standard by which to judge a situation as satisfactory or unsatisfactory was that of community welfare. A Calumet Project self-description states, "Economic decisions for the region must be guided by one question: how does this effect the community and workers in the area?"[18] In contrast the standard employed by corporate and political opponents was private company profitability or the local area's good business climate, which they tended to see as identical to the public's interest. Antagonists battled over which standard was appropriate.

Causal explanations also varied. The Calumet Project's labor-community alliances usually found corporate mismanagement, corporate misbehavior (such as public subsidy abuse or lack of good faith in dealings with government or the workforce), disinvestment and "milking" of the facility, and the like as primary causes of the shutdown decision. Corporate decision makers and some politicians usually saw the cause as strictly economic: market and competitive conditions beyond the control of the company or the local government.

Remedial action plans were likewise divergent. Corporate interests called for strictly private market mechanisms to resolve all problems (occasionally supplemented by government offset measures as long as they were beneficial to the corporation's profitability). The Calumet Project's alliances called for a variety of remedial measures, most of them involving a populist player role for the government and corporate recompense to the workforce and the community.

Chapter 8 argues that the standard corporate definition of the problem forces communities and workers to accept as unalterable givens many "facts" that are in reality social contrivances or constructions, and that these constructions force communities to make unnecessary choices. But these "facts" can only be changed if the community organizes to alter the political and social landscape within which the various actors are operating.

Thus alliance formation and mobilization become the key to success or failure of labor-community coalitions of this type. The case studies and a comparative analysis in chapter 8 outline the various attempts to forge broad community alliances and to mobilize constituencies into effective public and political action. Six major lessons regarding effectiveness are drawn from the analysis of the cases.

The book concludes by placing the cases within two broad theoretical perspectives: the resource mobilization framework and the class conflict perspective.[19] Resource mobilization theory analyzes social movements according to their ability to mobilize significant resources, constraints on the use of those resources, and the environmental confines shaping the movement's ability to act effectively.[20] This is an especially useful framework for movements depending heavily on external resources and support, like those in this volume.

The class conflict framework is also appropriate because these struggles pitted working class communities and institutions (unions) against employers, usually multinational companies. Much of the literature in this tradition is written at a high level of abstraction beyond the direct concerns of this book. However, the notion of "class capacities" is useful because it examines the relationships within a class that enable or prevent its successful pursuit of class interests.[21] Working-class structural capacities develop from features of work and home life that unite or disunite workers. Organizational capacities depend on the effectiveness of worker organizations, primarily unions.

In the concluding section of this book I will use these two frameworks (especially the resource mobilization framework) to analyze the potential and the limitations of labor-community coalitions. Addressing "class" vs. "community" controversies, and comparing these cases to others, I will argue that labor-community coalitions have some potential to empower both working-class institutions like unions and industrial communities. Contrary to the pessimism of some of the literature, the limitations on this form of struggle are not absolute.

My goal in writing this book is twofold: to deepen our analytic understanding of the power dynamics of labor-community coalition efforts and of plant closing struggles, and to expose labor and community activists to the possibilities and the limitations inherent in such an approach to union and community empowerment. If I am successful in all that I have attempted, the book will have both academic and practical value.

The cases in the following five chapters are arranged in roughly chronological order. The final two chapters analyze the cases from comparative and broadly contextual perspectives. The generalizations drawn in these two chapters should be subject to further verification and refutation, both by academic researchers and practitioners.

MILITARY CONVERSION AND THE SHUTDOWN OF THE BLAW-KNOX STEEL FOUNDRY

The following case study concerns a foundry producing primarily for the U.S. military. The parent company chose to "milk" the facility for remaining profits when the primary military product market dried up, rather than reinvesting and converting to a civilian product market.

The case highlights the early warning signals of the forthcoming shutdown that were detected and followed by an extended campaign to save the plant. It also analyzes in detail the corporate structure and strategy of the parent company and their relationship to the vulnerability of the facility.

The extremely dependent role of most local government and economic development officials is also analyzed and shown to be a consequence of their notion of what is a "good business climate" and how to achieve it. In the end this self-chosen role is seen to be counterproductive.

The campaign to save the foundry was characterized by sharp struggles over problem definition, pitting "good business climate" officials against labor and community activists upholding a standard of community welfare and corporate accountability. The ultimate failure of the campaign stemmed from weaknesses in forming an effective alliance to challenge the corporate plan and in mobilizing the forces necessary to alter the local government's normal passive stance.

In the following section, I relate the historical and economic background to the closure of the Blaw-Knox foundry in northwest Indiana. Following that, I describe a two-year campaign to save the facility. Finally, I analyze the forces at work and summarize the possible sources of power for unions and communities in plant closing situations of this type.

BACKGROUND

The Blaw-Knox steel foundry in East Chicago, Indiana, began as the Hubbard Steel foundry in 1911. Located near the giant U.S. Steel mill in Gary, it produced castings for the local steel industry. Shortly before World War II it was purchased by the Continental Roll and Steel Foundry Company; during the war it produced military tank hulls and turrets to supplement civilian production. After the war it was purchased by the Pittsburgh-based Blaw-Knox Corporation. Blaw-Knox then shifted production back to making steel mills and mill equipment.[1] The postwar years were good ones worldwide for steel mill construction, and the Blaw-Knox foundry was well positioned to do a substantial part of the work.

In 1968 the Cleveland-based conglomerate, White Consolidated Industries (WCI), acquired the Blaw-Knox parent company. White Consolidated was aggressively acquiring subsidiaries at the time, primarily in the home appliance industry but also in the industrial equipment, machinery, metal products, and home or office product fields.

Press statements addressed fears that the local plant might be sold or have its operations reduced. President R. J. Sherlock stated, "We have in the past spent more on the East Chicago plant than on others. We'll continue. This is our policy."[2] Plant manager Frank J. Satek assured the community that the 1,400 employees were secure: "We are the only millbuilder in the Midwest. So as the steel industry grows, so do we."[3] They also claimed to be investigating new product lines for the plant, which never materialized.

In the 1960s and 1970s White Consolidated grew rapidly by absorbing other firms. In 1967, the year before it acquired Blaw-Knox, WCI had net sales of $172.7 million, which grew to more than $1 billion by 1974 and over $2 billion by 1979. During the same period net income grew from $11.25 million to $38.5 million and to $62.9 million, the last excluding an extraordinary item.[4] Much of this growth was attained through the aggressive acquisition of competitors, particularly in the home appliance division.

Most of WCI's growth was in the home products division, even though this line of business did not generate the most operating income. From 1974 through 1983, this division grew from 54 percent of total sales to 77 percent; during the same period its share of operating income grew from 48 percent to 97 percent. Consolidated figures for the years 1974–83 are given in table 2.1.

Table 2.1 shows that in the early period the Home Products Division consistently generated less income per dollar of sales than did the other two divisions: 59 percent of sales but only 44 percent of earnings.

Income per sales in the Machinery and Metal Casting Division (to which Blaw-Knox belonged) was about average until the 1981–83 period, when it dropped precipitously.

Of the three divisions, Home Products was the favored one for expansion. The company's business plan stressed "balance" between con-

Table 2.1. White consolidated operating performance, 1974–1983

Division	Sales		Earnings	
	1974–78	1979–83	1974–78	1979–83
	(percent of total)			
Home Products	59	69	44	66
Machinery & Metal Castings	26	19	27	6
General Industrial Equipment	15	12	29	29

Source: Computed from WCI *Annual Reports,* 1974–1983.

sumer and industrial products but was firmly and strategically wedded to the home appliance industry. Overall capital expenditures and acquisitions demonstrate the same pattern: from 1976 to 1983, the book value of all assets in the Home Products Division increased 49 percent, compared to a 25 percent increase in the Machinery and Metal Castings Division and a 34 percent increase in the General Industrial Equipment Division.[5]

Therefore the parent company was expanding most rapidly in the home products field and was expanding least rapidly in Blaw-Knox's division, machinery and metal castings. In addition, Blaw-Knox's main commercial customer, the steel industry, was ordering very little in the way of new mills or equipment. Although profitable through 1981, the division was not growing.

In 1980 WCI began to aggressively divest itself of businesses. Within three years it would shed more businesses than it had in its entire prior history; a trend that only accelerated in the mid-1980s. Virtually all of these sales were in the two divisions other than Home Products. In 1982 WCI engaged the management consulting firm of McKinsey and Co. to do a comprehensive analysis of the company to formulate or redefine long-term objectives and strategic plans. A goal was to streamline operations, which produced more candidates for divestiture.[6]

The 1983 WCI Annual Report revealed three new strategic objectives. The first goal was an overall 20 percent return on stockholders' equity, that is, 20 cents of profit on every $1 invested in the company. The second goal was to obtain a net profit of at least 5 cents on each $1 of sales, that is, a "net margin" of at least 5 percent. The third goal was to produce a minimum of $1.60 in sales for each $1 in book value of assets, which is an "asset turnover ration" of 1.6:1. Businesses that failed to meet these three "hurdles" would be candidates for divestiture, consolidation, or closure.[7]

Table 2.2. White consolidated income/sales ratios by division, 1974–1983

Division	Time Period	
	1974–78	1979–83
	(percent)	
Home Products	7.6	6.2
Machinery & Metal Castings	11.0	1.6
General Industrial Equipment	19.2	16.2

Source: Computed from WCI *Annual Reports*, relevant years.

Data to calculate return on equity figures by particular subsidiary or division are not publicly available. However, it is possible to roughly measure the performance of WCI's three major divisions regarding the second two goals. Figures for "net" income are not available on a division basis, but "operating income" figures are. Assuming that the ratio of operating income/sales is roughly proportional to the net income/sales ratio, we can learn the relative standing of the three divisions on the latter ratio. Percentages for 1974–83 are given in table 2.2.

From the table, it is apparent that the General Industrial Equipment Division companies as a whole clearly met WCI's second "hurdle" of 5 percent net income on sales. Home Products was marginal but was generally meeting this goal (in 1983, even if all general corporate expenses, interest expense, and an "unusual item" had been charged to this one division, it would have met the goal of 5 percent net income on sales). Machinery and Metal Castings, the Blaw-Knox division, had definitely met this goal prior to 1981 but had rapidly deteriorated in 1982 and 1983. Both were years where it lost money on an accelerating basis, both proportionally and absolutely.

From the above, it would appear that, as of 1984, the most likely candidates for divestiture or shutdown would come from the Machinery and Metal Castings division. The third goal, $1.60 sales for every $1 in assets, pointed in the same direction. Performance on this measure is given in table 2.3.

Table 2.3 demonstrates that the Home Products and General Industrial Equipment divisions were each meeting the third goal, but the Machinery and Metal Casting division was not and never had. Again, this division continued to deteriorate after 1981.

Historically the East Chicago Blaw-Knox foundry produced primarily steel mills and rolls. In 1969 plant manager Satek estimated that mil-

Table 2.3. White consolidated sales, 1976–1983

Division	Average Dollar Sales Per $1 of Assets	
	1976–79	1980–83
Home Products	1.68	2.06
Machinery and Metal Castings	1.44	1.25
General Industrial Equipment	1.77	1.64

Source: Computed from WCI *Annual Reports,* relevant years.

itary tank orders accounted for only 15 percent of production at the foundry.[8]

In the 1970s the foundry shifted heavily toward production of the M-60 tank for the U.S. Army and U.S. military allies. By the mid- to late 1970s the plant was producing 4–5 tanks a day, working three shifts and employing approximately 2,500 workers. Meanwhile domestic construction of steel mills began to decline and foreign competition for mill work increased. The plant constructed its last steel mill in 1983. Occasional commercial work for the foundry's extraordinarily large castings was obtained, but nonmilitary work was estimated to be less than 20 percent of business by the early 1980s.[9]

By the early 1980s the product mix was the reverse of what it had been in 1969: military tank production up from 15 percent to 85–90 percent of the total product. Steel mill construction had plummeted from being the "main thrust" of production to a virtual phaseout.

A U.S. government decision in 1980 to replace the M-60 tank with the M-1 led to an end of all orders by the end of fiscal year 1981. From then on the steadily decreasing M-60 tank orders were from U.S. allies. From four tank hulls a day in the mid-1970s, production dropped to one and a half per day by 1984. Blaw-Knox could not convert to production of the newer M-1, because it did not require the huge plate castings needed for the M-60.

Employment in the mill also declined. In 1978 there were 2,278 employees; by 1983 this figure had dropped by one half to 1,137. Table 2.4 gives employment figures for the 1978–85 period.

Table 2.4. Employment at Blaw-Knox East Chicago foundry, 1978–1985

	Total Employment	Hourly	Salaried
1978	2,278	1,997	281
1979	1,540	1,348	192
1980	1,668	1,479	189
1981	1,462	1,266	196
1982	1,353	1,172	181
1983	1,137	966	171
1984	992	830	162
April 1985	812	684	128

Source: A. D. Little, *Reuse of the Blaw-Knox Casting and Machinery Mill.*

THE CAMPAIGN TO SAVE THE BLAW-KNOX FOUNDRY

In May 1984 Calumet Project researcher Tom DuBois noticed, in an article in *American Metal Markets,* speculation that White Consolidated may sell Blaw-Knox. At the May annual meeting Roy Holdt, WCI chairman and chief executive officer, had stated that White would move "as quickly as is possible" out of some of its steel mill machinery and steel processing businesses.[10] At the same meeting, WCI President and Chief Administrative Officer Ward Smith confirmed that steel-related businesses were prime candidates for divestiture despite their past history of profitability.[11] Analysts considered the Blaw-Knox Foundry and Mill Machinery Company (with four plants including the East Chicago foundry) and the Aetna-Standard Engineering Company (one plant), which produced finishing equipment for the steel industry, to be the most likely candidates for a sale.

In late September 1984, following a series of meetings and consultations with the Calumet Project, Steelworkers Local 1026 President Clarence "Buck" Martin sent a memo to eleven individuals about imminent layoffs and a possible shutdown of the facility. The memo went to the top district and national officers of the United Steelworkers Union, the congresswoman from the region, the governor, the mayor of East Chicago and his director of business development, an aide to the state's two senators, three key local and regional economic development officials, and a local minister chairing an East Chicago task force on economic development.

The memo noted the speculation that WCI would sell Blaw-Knox and pointed out that company officials refused to confirm or deny this. It also stated that tank orders were due to run out sometime in the coming months and that no replacement orders were visible. The conclusion drawn was harsh:

> This seems to be an obvious case of disinvestment and "milking" of what has been a profitable operation, or at least one with a high cash flow. White Consolidated says in its annual report that parts of the conglomerate which have not shown large profits have been useful to the parent because "positive cash flows were usually produced through increased financial control. These profits and cash flows have been available to invest in our business and to support our development activities." (1983 Annual Report)[12]

Martin also noted that the machine shop, the second largest in the Midwest, was due for complete shutdown by the end of the month (over 150 were already laid off from the machine shop). A shutdown of the roll shop also was imminent; employment had declined from sixty to thirteen and the union believed (correctly, it turned out) that the roll shop equipment would be shipped out shortly after shutdown.

Martin called for (1) a meeting to consider responses, (2) investigation of company plans, (3) possible use of a court injunction or a feasibility study to save jobs, (4) a determination of the viability of employee ownership, (5) investigation of alternative product possibilities, and (6) utilization of the expertise of others previously undertaking "conversion" efforts.

This unusual memo prompted an immediate response. Local economic development officials promised to help, while White Consolidated denied any intent to sell the plant:

> An official of White Consolidated Industries Inc., which owns the foundry, said he knows of no plans to sell the Northwest Indiana plant. "As far as I know, tank production will continue through 1985," said Charles Conlin, White's vice president of industrial relations.[13]

Within two weeks WCI announced that it was selling all of its foundry, steel machinery, and printing equipment businesses, including the East Chicago foundry.[14] Ronald G. Fountain, White's treasurer and vice president, expressed hopes of selling to someone wanting to keep the foundry running because, "It's worth more that way," but he refused to promise to hold out for a buyer committed to keeping the facility open.[15] Buck Martin responded to the sale plans negatively:

> I can only feel the company came in when it was profitable, worked
> it until it no longer served a purpose for them and now they're going to
> sell it. . . . It isn't right to milk a company and then leave the member-
> ship high and dry.[16]

These sentiments reflected the feelings of many foundry workers; the
ensuing campaign was based on this bedrock of worker sentiment.

On 31 October, United Steelworkers District 31 Director Jack Parton
called a meeting attended by the East Chicago mayor and his two top
economic development aides, state and regional economic development persons, aides to state political figures, and union and community representatives. A permanent Blaw-Knox Steering Committee was formed to save
the plant. Its first goal was to raise the money to finance a feasibility
study to determine what could be done to preserve employment and keep
the facility running. Everyone agreed that this required retooling for commercial market production as tank orders disappeared.

November and December of 1984 were busy months. The local congresswoman requested Department of Defense aid in attempting conversion to nonmilitary production, representatives from the Department of
Defense came to East Chicago for a meeting, funds for a feasibility study
were sought, plans were laid for a possible Economic Development Administration (EDA) grant and/or Urban Development Action Grant
(UDAG) to follow up, the potential for employee ownership was explored, the East Chicago mayor wrote the state commerce department
requesting $60,000 for the feasibility study,[17] the steering committee took
a guided tour of the plant, and requests for proposals to do the feasibility study were mailed.

Funds for a $50,000 feasibility study were raised by contributions
from the Indiana state Department of Commerce, the Steelworkers Union,
the United Citizens Organization (the Calumet Project's "parent" community organization), and the city and Economic Development Commission of East Chicago. Congressman-elect Peter Visclosky requested
WCI funding. WCI did contribute a sum that was reported as confidential.[18] Since the other contributions totaled approximately $40,000, White
Consolidated's "confidential" sum must have been about $10,000.

Meanwhile union and community activism grew. On December 13 the
union local, the Calumet Project, and the United Citizens Organization hosted a meeting of approximately one hundred workers and community residents. Representatives of the state's two Republican senators, an aide to
outgoing Democratic U.S. Representative Katie Hall, and the incoming

Democratic Representative Peter Visclosky all attended and addressed the meeting. Audience interest was high, as was hostility toward the company. One union member launched into a tirade against the plant's industrial relations manager, who was present, accusing him and White Consolidated of lack of good faith in its dealings with the workforce.

On 27 December, United Steelworkers District 31 Director Jack Parton called a meeting in his office where Blaw-Knox Steering Committee members were requested to report on what they were doing. The union and community monitoring of and involvement in the effort to save the plant at this point were great.

In January and early February candidates to do the feasibility study were evaluated. On 11 February, the Blaw-Knox Steering Committee chose Arthur D. Little (ADL), a Massachusetts consulting firm with extensive foundry experience. The study was to be completed by summer, and ADL was required to give preliminary progress reports to the steering committee.

In March, the Calumet Project met with Local 1026 leaders to plan for an ongoing public campaign. The aims were to involve the membership of the local, to publicize the issues widely, to pressure politicians and economic development officials to continue to keep the *jobs* issue foremost, and to force WCI to reveal full information and to cooperate in transferring the facility to an owner committed to keeping it open. The Calumet Project and the union local made plans to hold a public meeting in conjunction with the United Citizens Organization, to speak on popular local radio talk shows, and to communicate with and involve laid-off workers.

These plans were at best only partially carried out. The local union president felt he could handle all the work; he was reluctant to actively involve the lower levels of leadership. Consequently communication with the membership and most forms of active involvement were missing. The local union never initiated anything after the original memo that started the whole process.

April union elections complicated matters. Buck Martin chose not to run for reelection as local union president for personal reasons and retired shortly thereafter. Tom Patterson, a thirty-year employee, ran unopposed for president and was elected along with a team that included many new officers. The leadership turnover made consistent union planning even harder. As president, Patterson took an even less activist role than had Martin. His main role was to express optimism to the press and to wait for the Blaw-Knox Steering Committee to take action.

Despite these problems, March through May were busy months. At a 19 March Steering Committee meeting ADL representatives gave a preliminary report of their study, and local plant manager Jon J. O'Connor reported that an order for 140 more tanks was likely — ensuring the plant would remain open through 1985.

United Steelworkers District Director Parton again called a meeting of the Steering Committee and other interested parties for 1 April. As usual for a meeting allowing attendance beyond the official membership of the Steering Committee, it was far from tame. Blaw-Knox workers in attendance lambasted White Consolidated, charging it with milking millions from the local plant and refusing to honor its responsibilities to the workers and the community. Economic development officials on the Blaw-Knox Steering Committee were being pressured strongly to keep an unrelenting focus on the number one goal of job preservation.

On 1 May, ADL gave the Blaw-Knox Steering Committee a midterm report. Two days later approximately one hundred workers and community residents attended a forum where the Little representatives again spoke. A. D. Little spokesman John Reed indicated the only hope for future long-term production was a major reliance on smaller commercial casting because military orders were disappearing and extraordinarily large castings had a very limited market.

Workers at the 3 May community forum criticized ADL for lack of consultation. Local 1026 member Vern Felton noted that the union had partially funded the study, but the workers had not been contacted, making for a "one-sided approach."[19] Workers also wanted ADL to criticize White Consolidated for past disinvestment and "milking" policies. Local 1026 treasurer Lynn Strong stated, "We're where we are today because White Consolidated did not want to reinvest." Reed refused to review past investment decisions of White Consolidated. "We're looking at the plant as it is now," he stated. "We're looking for a viable option that an investor from the outside can say, 'Yes, that makes sense.' We're looking at it from the point of view of an investor."[20] The workers in attendance were less committed to an exclusively investor-driven private market approach; to them long-term stability and job creation were uppermost. These opposing viewpoints were the cause of the clash at the forum.

While the Blaw-Knox Steering Committee was quiescent until a 12 July presentation of Little's findings, the Calumet Project and the union local prepared for the worst. If the findings were that the facility was not viable under any circumstances, they wanted to be ready to initiate a broad-based community campaign against White Consolidated. The purpose would be to develop a broad public consciousness of corporate misbehavior on WCI's part, and to force them into generous assistance for retraining, severance pay, pensions, and the like.

Calumet Project's case against White Consolidated claimed that the company had:

1. Dangerously narrowed the product line at the East Chicago facility, making it vulnerable to military demand trends;
2. Disinvested in the facility over the years, putting in only money procured from the defense department;
3. Made enormous profits off the plant, only to invest the cash elsewhere (i.e., treating it as a "cash cow");
4. Left the Blaw-Knox pension plans underfunded; and
5. Failed to pay its property taxes to the city for the past few years, hurting local services including the school system.

Available information supports most of these charges. WCI had narrowed the product lines at the foundry until military production became its only source of survival. Ex-managers claim the company abruptly cut off commercial customers when defense orders grew, not even giving them thirty days notice. When the military gravy train slowed down and then stopped, these previously spurned customers refused to consider Blaw-Knox as a supplier because they distrusted the company.[21] While the switch may have been a good business decision for the company as a whole, it jeopardized the facility and local jobs.

The disinvestment charge is harder to assess, but it appears to be correct. Divisional figures show that WCI expanded its Home Products Division at the expense of the other two. However, this growth was more the result of acquisitions than it was of uneven capital investment patterns in existing divisions. Table 2.5 shows the net investment (capital expenditures minus depreciation and amortization expenses) for the divisions from 1977 to 1983.

Table 2.5 does not show a clear pattern of "milking" one division to pay for capital expenditures in another. Blaw-Knox's Machinery and Metal Castings Division as a whole was not being "milked" to pay for investments elsewhere. It received proportionally *more* than other divisions, especially in the later years. Only in 1983 did net capital investment in the Machinery and Metal Castings Division turn negative. In that year WCI disinvested in the division in the amount of $276,000.

But much of the investment in the Machinery and Metal Castings Division during this period was going into White's machine tool line, including new flexible manufacturing systems and automated numerical control equipment, not its foundries. WCI did put approximately $30 million into its Blaw-Knox roll shop operations, but it all went to the Wheeling, West Virginia, facility, not the East Chicago one.

Table 2.5. White Consolidated Industries, net investment by division,*
1977–1983.

Division	Time Period	
	1977–79	1980–83
	(millions of dollars)	
Home Products	35.0	53.4
Machinery & Metal Products	25.2	55.0
General Industrial Equipment	11.2	13.1

* Capital expenditures minus depreciation and amortization expenditures.

Source: Computed from WCI Annual Reports, selected years.

The clear case for disinvestment is at the plant level. Virtually all of the machine shop equipment was 1950s and 1960s vintage — way out of date for modern competitive purposes. A former manager told me that basically nothing had been put into the plant at company expense for years; Department of Defense money had gone into some departments. Finally, near the end, WCI had invested a couple of million dollars, but when it was spent it was nothing compared to the needs at that point.[22] Perhaps this money was spent on the innovative "vacuum process" (V-process) equipment ($1.2 million) and a modernized electric furnace. Workers, the ADL report, and ex-managers stated that the company never learned to use the new V-process equipment properly, so even this expenditure was wasted and underutilized.

In any case, company investment in the foundry was minimal for well over a decade despite immense profitability. Ex-local union official Lynn Strong claims defense contracts were set at a cost-plus basis that guaranteed a minimum 15 percent profit on sales.[23] A former manager confirmed that the Department of Defense routinely negotiated more money whenever the foundry ran into a problem.[24]

Strong's estimate of 15 percent profit on sales is almost certainly too conservative. Precise figures on profitability of a particular plant are confidential, but considerable information has been obtained in this case. When WCI put the company up for sale in late 1984, a prospectus was issued by their investment banker Lehman Brothers, giving financial data for the East Chicago foundry. Data are given in table 2.6.[25]

These figures show that the facility produced a 22 percent gross profit on sales in 1984. Conservatively estimating that the profit rate was the

Table 2.6. Actual and projected financial data for the Blaw-Knox East Chicago foundry, 1980–1986. (in millions of dollars)

Year	1980	1981	1982	1983	1984*	1985**	1986
Net Sales	76.0	80.9	74.1	71.7	71.8	60.3	19.9
Net Sales from Tank Armor					64.5	49.9	0
Gross Profit					15.9	15.8	4.0
Profit / Sales *(percent)*					22	26	20

* Projections based on incomplete figures as of 31 August 1984.

** Estimates for 1985 and 1986 based on projected future tank orders and refurbishing the #2 commercial castings foundry.

Source: Lehman Bros. prospectus.

same in 1980–83 as it was in 1984, although it was probably higher, WCI reaped a gross profit of $82.53 million in profits during 1980–84 from this facility.

This was a highly profitable plant that easily exceeded WCI's three "hurdles": with total assets in 1984 of $34.4 million and profits of more than $15 million, the facility was far exceeding the required 20 percent net return on equity. Net profit on sales was 3 to 4 times the required 5 percent. And with a book value of $14.128 million, sales of $71.8 million meant $5.08 in sales per $1 book value, over 3.5 times the required $1.60 per $1 ratio.[26]

Steel foundries reinvested 4.7 percent of sales into plant and equipment from 1980 to 1982. Had WCI done the same for the 1980–85 period, it would have made capital expenditures of $17.6 million. Charges of disinvestment and treatment of the facility as a "cash cow" therefore seem justified.

It is also true that WCI had not fully funded its pension plans. The prospectus noted that White had unfunded pension liabilities of $58.3 million that it would retain in the event of a sale. Pension obligations also became an issue in the sale of the plant, as will be noted later.

Finally, Blaw-Knox was delinquent in its local property tax payments, as alleged. Property tax records in mid-1985 indicated that the company was delinquent in paying $107,516.53 in 1983 taxes payable 1984, and behind $115,813.93 in 1984 taxes payable 1985, for a total of $223,330.46.

The particulars of the Calumet Project's indictment of White Consolidated were basically correct. However, a public relations campaign against the company had doubtful prospects. Local politicians were firmly wedded to a "good business climate" approach to economic development. They stressed a cooperative and positive environment for businesses and wished to avoid any confrontation with corporate interests. Local economic development officials had a similar orientation and very likely would have dissociated themselves from a "negative" campaign against WCI. The Steelworkers Union was a more likely ally, but its main interest was a strictly pragmatic one: saving jobs and preserving union pattern wage rates. As with most of the American labor movement, the union was not accustomed to wide-ranging "social movement" approaches to achieving these goals. Unless a campaign had a very high likelihood of achieving fairly immediate results, the union leadership was not likely to devote much energy to methods that it considered unorthodox. A highly motivated leader of the union local who was determined to stand up to the company and who had a strong view of corporate accountability to the workers and the community could have changed this, but neither Martin or Patterson was such a leader.

Only certain active members of the union local (none of them on the crucial Blaw-Know Steering Committee) and allied community forces organized through the United Citizens Organization were activist enough in their orientation to be willing to immediately initiate and develop such a campaign. As it turned out, this approach was never tried; events intervened.

On 12 July 1985, Arthur D. Little presented a draft version of its final report to the Blaw-Knox Steering Committee. One week later Steelworkers District Director Parton called a meeting open to the press to make the findings public. At these meetings and in its 130-page report, ADL presented a mixed picture for the future of the facility.[27] It recommended that the foundry operations shift from the Department of Defense market to the commercial castings market. If this did not occur, the plant would close.

The report recommended consolidation of the small foundry and the large foundry because the latter was not viable standing alone. The market for extraordinarily large castings was small and depressed.

The key to ADL's recommendation was a modernized small castings foundry (less than one hundred pounds to approximately five thousand pounds). This would provide the stable market needed to keep the operation viable. ADL estimated that it would not be too difficult to capture 3–5 percent of the U.S. market in this size range, producing approximately 15,000–20,000 tons per year. Supplemented by five thousand tons per year in large castings work (8–15% of the U.S. market), the foundry should be quite viable. The small foundry would have to be a highly automated, state-of-the-art operation. Employment would drop drastically in the consolidated foundry to 100–200, considerably less than the 812 employed at the time of the study.

The cost would also be considerable: $3–5 million to upgrade the small foundry; $7–11 million total (including consolidation costs and minor upgrading of the large foundry).[28] Because of the depressed state of the small castings market and the low returns to producers, ADL estimated that $3–5 million of the $7–11 million total would have to come from public sources. With that degree of public funding, ADL thought there was a moderately good chance of finding a buyer. To keep costs moderate, the report recommended a 20 percent wage cut from the current $10.90 per hour average. To facilitate an ownership change, WCI should sell at a "nominal" price of the liquidation value and should assume pension obligations rather than carry them over to the new owner.

The study confirmed charges of disinvestment in the portions of the plant not devoted to tank production. The machine shop equipment was of 1940s to 1960s vintage. Not one major piece of equipment in it had been bought since 1968, the year WCI bought the company. The remains of the roll shop were close to useless; all of the best equipment had been moved recently to the Wheeling, West Virginia, plant in a consolidation move. ADL suggested scrapping most of this equipment or possibly seeking a local buyer.

A small satellite operation of machining work to supplement the basic foundry was considered viable and would provide 25–50 jobs. This would cost approximately $2 million in private funds plus $1–1.4 million in public financing.

In total, then, $9–13 million in private funds plus $4–6.4 million in public funds would be necessary to rejuvenate the foundry. ADL also recommended use of remaining buildings and space as a business "incubator" for other small companies and a parking lot. All this would require perhaps $9–11 million in private investment ($4 million for parking lots alone!) and $600,000 in public assistance.

In total, the ADL proposals promised three hundred jobs immediately and six hundred within a few years. Total cost would be $20–24 million in private capital and $4.6–$7 million in public assistance. The public costs look high for a venture that would immediately save less than one half the existing jobs. However, ADL's public cost-benefit analysis showed that savings in unemployment compensation costs ($1.9 million) plus savings in local public assistance and increased tax revenues plus the ripple effect on the rest of the local economy would generate enough tax savings and collections to almost cover these public expenses. With any grant money from the federal government, the state and local governments would indeed recover their expenditures in less than two years.

The ADL report had two unusual recommendations which reflected the public source of much of its funding and the pressure which union and community forces had exerted on the consulting firm. First, it recommended that the city and the Blaw-Knox Steering Committee should be actively involved in the transfer of ownership of the plant in order to protect the interests of workers and the community:

> The City and Blaw-Knox Steering Committee should play an active role monitoring the negotiations of White Consolidated Industries, Inc.'s disposition of the Blaw-Knox facilities in East Chicago. Efforts should be made to encourage its sale to a company that will reuse the facilities rather than run-out the current tank contract and liquidate the plant. (p. I-3)

Were it acted upon, this recommendation would have meant that the usual secrecy of sales negotiations would be broken. The public interest would be forcefully injected into a supposedly "private" affair within the private sector. Such a course of action would breach the normal "business climate" approach that is standard economic development practice in northwest Indiana and the United States today. Because of this the city and economic development officials were reluctant to carry out the suggestion.

Second, the report recommended that a public development corporation be set up to buy, manage, and market the plant:

> Consideration should be given to setting-up an overall agency to acquire the Blaw-Knox facilities, plan their conversion, undertake marketing, provide financing, oversee operation and eventual disposition of most facilities (excluding the incubator buildings). (p. VII-4)

This again was a rather unorthodox recommendation that injected public control over transactions normally considered to be exclusively in the private domain. East Chicago's director of business development Mary Kaczka immediately rejected this recommendation: "I think without a buyer we would not want to put ourselves in that position."[29]

Steering Committee monitoring of any possible sale of the foundry quickly became an issue. At a 24 July Steering Committee meeting to discuss implementation of the ADL proposals, plant manager Jon J. O'-Connor indicated that serious negotiations were underway to sell the company, although he declined to give details. The Steering Committee chair, an official of a regional economic development agency, requested that all steering committee members send in "scenarios" of what should be done in the coming months. Worried that the plant would be sold to a buyer interested only in running out the armor contract prior to liquidation, Calumet Project staff person Lynn Feekin (who was representing the United Citizens Organization on the steering committee) developed a memo with four common goals for all possible scenarios and suggestions based on different scenarios.[30] The four common goals were:

1. New buyer will provide stable business operations in East Chicago for an adequate period of time.
2. New buyer will reinvest sufficient monies in the East Chicago Blaw-Knox facility to ensure long term viability.
3. New buyer's operations will provide jobs for current Blaw-Knox employees.
4. New buyer will recognize the union.

The first scenario assumed that White Consolidated would sell Blaw-Knox. Feekin recommended that the steering committee contact the (potential) new owner to determine the intended use for the plant. If the owner planned to reinvest with financial aid from the city and/or state, the Blaw-Knox Steering Committee could set out the conditions under which the aid should be given, based on the four common goals. If the new owner planned to reinvest without public aid, the steering committee could meet with the owner to encourage conversion in line with ADL recommendations.

If the new owner had no reinvestment plan, the Blaw-Knox Steering Committee could push for suitable reinvestment. Failing in this, the memo suggests that the steering committee pose the possible use of "eminent domain" (involuntary sale to the government at reasonable compensation "for the public good"). ADL's "nominal cost" could be the basis for determining what was reasonable compensation.[31]

If White Consolidated did not sell the plant the memo suggested that the steering committee request the company to establish a reinvestment fund by setting aside a certain amount of money per tank produced, the specific figure to be determined later. This money, plus a newly created public development corporation, could be used to facilitate eventual transfer of ownership and reinvestment.

On 26 August, the United Citizens Organization's Board of Directors endorsed the four goals and unanimously passed a motion recommending that "No private deals (be) made on a financial package without the Blaw-Knox Steering Committee or the larger committee's involvement." In a letter to the executive director of the East Chicago Department of Redevelopment, UCO president Reverend Vincent McCutcheon noted the motion and continued,

> UCO is outraged that this union-initiated process, which initially comprised very broad-based representation, has been narrowed down to a select few.[32]

These suggestions from the UCO and the Calumet Project were not acted upon. The Blaw-Knox Steering Committee chairperson postponed two meetings, deferring to a company request to temporarily cease meetings pending an imminent sale. The economic development officials from the city were unwilling to confront White Consolidated to demand or even ask anything regarding the pending sale. Even the union local's leadership was unwilling to demand a real role in the sale; it was completely passive and gave no overt support to the UCO/Calumet Project recommendations. The company took a very dim view of any such "meddling" in its "private" affairs; an ex-manager in 1989 told me that he considered the Calumet Project staffer "nothing but a Goddamn Communist" for putting forth such suggestions.[33]

The Blaw-Knox Steering Committee awaited word on a new owner. In late September, WCI announced that it had sold seven companies to a group of private investors led by Robert J. Tomsich, chairman of Nesco, a Cleveland holding firm. One of the units sold was the East Chicago foundry. The new company was to be called the Blaw-Knox Corporation, headquartered in Pittsburgh. East Chicago manager Jon J. O'Connor stated that all nine plants would be kept open. "As far as East Chicago specifically, their desire is to follow up on the Arthur D. Little study" he told the press.[34]

The union greeted the news positively. Local 1026 President Tom Patterson stated he was "very pleased" with the news:

> I'm very optimistic that it's going to be something for the betterment of everybody. White had made it very clear that they don't want to be in the business we do anymore. Maybe the new company will.[35]

United Steelworkers District 31 Director Jack Parton also expressed guarded optimism:

> Right now, let's just say I'm happy the company has been bought by businessmen who say they want to keep operating the plant. It could have been worse; the facility could have been bought by U.S. Steel.[36]

The optimism turned out to be misplaced. Despite O'Connor's promises, the ADL recommendations were ignored. The Blaw-Knox Steering Committee did not monitor the sale or meet with the new management to force the company to reveal its intentions toward the plant. The chair of the steering committee refused to call any more meetings; in effect the steering committee disbanded. The UCO/Calumet Project proposals were never allowed to be discussed.

The new owners repeated to the press their intention to implement the ADL recommendations. They evaded any particular commitments. However they energetically pursued the ADL call for wage concessions by demanding wage cuts on 1 December for all other plants and on 1 March 1986 for the East Chicago facility (approximately the time the current armor contract would run out). The union demanded financial information before considering concessions; the company refused. The union and later the company filed unfair labor practice charges with the National Labor Relations Board.[37] The union also took a case to arbitration over early pension retirement issues. November 1985 to February 1986 was thus spent fighting over contractual issues. The contract was repeatedly extended 2 to 3 months at a time. The company made no move to upgrade or consolidate the foundry. Only the remaining tank orders, due to run out approximately in March, were being worked on.

The foundry's wages were roughly comparable with those of other foundries. In October 1986 production workers at ferrous foundries in the Great Lakes region averaged $11/hour, compared to $10.90 at Blaw-Knox.[38] The 20 percent pay cut recommended by ADL would have reduced Blaw-Knox wages to an average of $8.72 per hour — well below any regional standard, and even below comparably large firms (over 250) in the United States ($9.12 per hour).

Whether any wage reduction would have helped to make a refurbished foundry competitive was academic; the company never committed to upgrading the facility and never even put an offer to upgrade on the table as a bargaining chip to obtain concessions. Under the circumstances, the union refused to give any.

In early February, the Egyptian government announced that it was canceling a tentative order for more M-60 tanks. At this point Blaw-Knox management understood that tank production would end by summer or early fall; before the announcement they had counted on work into 1987 or possibly 1988.

New plant manager Gary Stanklus reconvened the Blaw-Knox Steering Committee, which had not met for almost six months. On 24 February, a restricted version of the steering committee met without representation from the union local or UCO/Calumet Project. Stanklus ran the meeting. His intent was to get help in obtaining more tank orders. Economic development officials and politicians obliged. City, regional, and national economic development personnel and politicians intervened with the Pentagon, the Egyptian ambassador, and the Army undersecretary to attempt to get more tank orders.

Congressman Visclosky's office was upset that union and community representatives had been cut out of the revived Blaw-Knox Steering Committee. They insisted that the entire steering committee membership be included in future meetings. On 14 and 18 March, expanded meetings were held with Stanklus chairing. His agenda called for a "public awareness campaign" whereby employees, concerned citizens, and others would write letters and sign petitions begging the Department of Defense for more tank orders. Stanklus even had draft letters already prepared (by the company) for people to sign. The model "employee letter" equated job preservation with continued tank orders, and relied heavily on patriotism and belief in the "American way":

> I believe in the American dream that if you work hard for a living, the rewards will come. But I feel as if my country is letting me down when the government says thanks for your efforts, but we no longer need you. . . . I need your involvement in helping to keep the doors of Blaw-Knox open with continued production of the M-60 tank. Your sincere efforts with regard to my plea for help may restore my concept of the "American way."[39]

The draft "taxpayer" letter relied on an alleged Soviet threat plus arguments that the M-60 tank was a better buy than the M-1:

> The ever-present military threat of the Soviet Union demands that we maintain our military readiness. It seems that the M-60 tank at one-third the price of the M-1 tank has a real place in this budgetary/military strength dilemma. Does it really make sense to completely eliminate the M-60 as an option to the more expensive, less reliable M-1?[40]

The draft "petition" argued that loss of the facility would harm the economic base of the local economy and that it would have a severe impact on the strategic industrial strength of the country. It claimed that more armor casting work would allow the company to "achieve stability and implement long term programs aimed at future operating and employment goals."[41]

The UCO, which had recently passed a resolution against wasteful military spending, refused to cooperate with this company effort to drum up more defense work. UCO demanded that the company live up to the ADL recommendations and convert to commercial casting production. The union also felt that the company had used and abused the steering committee, changing its entire intent. Union local president Tom Patterson stated:

> The steering committee has become a way for the company to manipulate political people and clout in the steering committee to their own use and has lost sight of what the intent was. The company has really taken it over.[42]

The company's "public awareness campaign" fell apart because of internal dissension within the steering committee. The letter writing and petition circulation did not materialize.

In March and April 1986, the Blaw-Knox Steering Committee divided into six subcommittees to work on all aspects of saving the plant (obtaining a new government contract, retaining government equipment, transitional operating costs, funding for facility conversion, employee matters, and developing commercial market plans). But the subcommittees were exercises in futility because the company never committed to anything. Even the business-oriented members of the steering committee began to get disgusted with the company. Richard Griebel, a $90,000+ executive with the Northwest Indiana Forum, was upset:

> What is the business plan? What is the alternative? What commercial applications are there? What alternative military applications are there? I found to my surprise and dismay there was nothing like that. There is no business plan there. . . . If the company is lucky and succeeds in getting new orders, it will only put things off a year.[43]

Subcommittees stopped meeting; the full committee never met again.

The company continued its attack on the union and also utilized the politicians in a vain quest for more tank orders. Stanklus demanded $6 per hour concessions from the union,[44] arguing that the union's participation on the steering committee meant it had agreed to ADL's recommendation of a wage cut. Aside from an eventual standoff involving a wage freeze and improved seniority language, this attack resulted in nothing other than a diversion of attention away from their continuing failure to tackle the more fundamental problem of conversion.

Senators and congressmen attempted to obtain further tank orders in exchange for lesser "facility termination costs" for the government. These latter efforts had some amusing moments because the company, in its attempt to manipulate the politicians into pressuring the Department of Defense was occasionally exposed in some misrepresentations.[45] These exertions for more tank orders were ultimately unsuccessful, although they almost succeeded.[46]

The plant completed the last armor castings in the late spring and early summer. Final finishing work meant some employment into the early fall. On 28 October the plant was officially closed.

The company had never intended to upgrade the facility and convert to commercial castings. Statements to the press expressing a commitment to carry out the ADL proposals had been intentional deception. The company intended to "milk" the plant as long as the armor order lasted; then the plant would be liquidated.

The Calumet Project, the union, and UCO had charged that this was true, but could not prove it. The company could always claim with at least minimal plausibility that it did intend to convert but needed more "breathing space" (i.e., more tank orders). The politicians who were frantically intervening to obtain more tank orders believed the company on this score.

But in the fall of 1989 an ex-manager confided to me that Robert J. Tomsich, chief executive officer of the new company, told the very top level of local plant management that "from day one" they had only intended to "run the armor work out to the end, and then dump the joint."[47] Tomsich had expected to get two years of armor work; he miscalculated and got only one. It is unlikely that he and his fellow investors lost anything, however. They bought the company for what my informant labeled "peanuts," and got the Department of Defense to pay them for a major share of the unfunded pension liabilities.

Even the pension question was to end on a sour note. In January 1992, the Pension Benefit Guarantee Corporation (PBGC) announced that it was forced to terminate the remaining Blaw-Knox pension plan for hourly employees due to underfunding of $81.6 million. The government-funded PBGC assumed responsibility for basic benefits; supplemental plant closing benefits for those under age 62 were discontinued. Former union president Thomas Patterson was one of those who lost money: $400 a month, one third of his pension. He expressed concern to the press:

> "It's going to take tightening up and making adjustments," said Patterson, who said he will probably have to start dipping into savings and his Individual Retirement Account.[48]

While Patterson and other retirees worried about further possible loss of health and life insurance and the taxpayers through the PBGC assumed pension obligations, the company continued operating at Wheeling, West Virginia.

CONCLUSION

The Blaw-Knox foundry closure illustrates the difficulties facing workers, unions, and local communities in most plant closing situations. Absentee conglomerate owners like White Consolidated make economic decisions based on corporate structures, options and priorities far removed from the local geographic area. White Consolidated had narrowed the local product line to one product, a defense-related item scheduled for extinction. It had also disinvested in major portions of the facility. At the same time WCI had further consolidated its position in its "core" business, home appliances, at the expense of its other divisions. Ex-managers from the East Chicago facility also claim that the Blaw-Knox company method for computing the size of pension payments to its two top officers in Pittsburgh biased them toward closure. Since their retirement pensions were directly related to profitability levels in the final years before their retirement, these men chose to close the plant while milking it for high profits, rather than reinvest and lower short-term profits, according to these allegations.[49] None of these business decisions responded to local East Chicago concerns because structurally and economically the corporate decision makers were never required to.

Corporate secrecy is one source of community weakness. Throughout this case, corporate decision makers utilized the "confidential" nature of their private business affairs to thwart any effective worker or community intervention. Repeated instances of deception, both large and small, surface. Even without intentional deception, the union and community and local government are unable to effectively plan or to counter corporate decisions because they lack the necessary information.

But this case also demonstrates that early warning of a shutdown can be effective and that a "save jobs" campaign of some duration is possible. Despite ultimate defeat, union and community forces were able to contest the shutdown decision and raise fundamental issues of corporate responsibility to affected workers. And through press scrutiny the company was forced to reveal more than it wished to and to respond to community issues.

Political power is a major potential source of leverage. Corporations depend on a supportive political environment for their success. If the good will of senators, congressmen, governors, and mayors can be made to be dependent on the corporation's behaving in a manner beneficial to the local community and workforce, significant pressure can often be brought to bear.

In this case, political pressure was only partially applied. Tied to a "business climate" conception of government-business relations, the political community was more often used and dictated to by the corporate owners than vice versa.[50] The lack of political will power was evident in the unwillingness of local political figures or their economic development allies to push the corporate owners in even minimal ways. They were unwilling to insist that they be allowed to interview potential buyers to ascertain their intentions toward the local plant. Once the foundry was sold, they were afraid to approach the new owner to insist that they be informed of its business plan. Fearful of taking even these milder measures, they were definitely unwilling to consider the use of eminent domain to take possession of the premises. The city's refusal to set up a public development corporation to acquire and broker the plant was yet another example. Despite the limitations in this actual case, political clout could provide considerable leverage to local communities, were it developed.

In this case the union had more collective bargaining power than do many unions facing closure. It represented and bargained for the workers in all Blaw-Knox facilities. It did not have to contend with nonunion plants, different national union affiliations, or lack or coordinated bargaining.

Nevertheless, union power was severely limited. The union was mostly focused on labor relations matters, which is only natural, but this meant that it would and could play only a limited role in the broader struggle to save the plant. It is important to emphasize the degree to which the union did play a positive and important role. The initial memo from the local president was the catalyst for the entire effort. The Steelworkers district director repeatedly took the initiative to call meetings at his office, which forced the Blaw-Knox Steering Committee to account for its actions to the press and the local workforce. It was mainly union pressure that kept the steering committee itself from operating in secret. However, the union did not play an aggressive or initiating role. For example, the union could have chaired steering committee meetings, developed the agendas, and so on, rather than letting this central role fall to a regional economic development official who would defer to company agendas. But this did not happen because the union was still largely reactive, rather than active. Given this lack of forceful initiative, the Blaw-Knox Steering Committee fell under the sway of the company at the end, just at the time the new owners were bent on deception as they milked the dying facility.

This is related to the biggest weakness of the campaign. The union local and the Calumet Project failed to convince local political figures and economic development officials to wholeheartedly adopt their viewpoint, their "definition of the problem." Instead the "good business climate" viewpoint prevailed; the familiar business standard of corporate profitability remained supreme while causal responsibility was deflected from corporate disinvestment to loss of military contracts. These key players were unwilling to adopt a remedial action plan challenging "private" corporate decisions and prerogatives.

This could only have been changed had the union, the Calumet Project, and UCO community activists been able to forge a lasting and sizable coalition around an alternative vision. Such a coalition might have been able to force politicians to play a more aggressive role challenging secret company shutdown plans. But weaknesses in local union leadership, inexperience on all sides, UCO preoccupation with other community issues such as education, and the Calumet Project's lack of its own independent base at the time prevented an effective coalition at the bottom. The "coalition" at the top in the Blaw-Knox Steering Committee therefore refused to challenge company plans. The key to a strong coalition had to be an activated local union leadership and membership, but that was thwarted by union presidents who saw no need for such membership activism.

PUBLIC SUBSIDY ABUSE AT THE COMBUSTION ENGINEERING PLANT

The following case study concerns the 1986 closure of a northwest Indiana plant producing coal pulverizers. It relates a turbulent labor relations history closely tied to the parent company's internal structure and national bargaining posture, and it demonstrates the influence of the parent company's internal financial accounting system and its overall corporate strategy on the closure decision.

Early warning signs, product market conditions, and the possible effect of alternative or additional product market lines are analyzed. Corporate abuse of public subsidies and local government fear of calling the company to account for it due to fear of harming the city's "business climate" are also detailed.

A corporate accountability campaign demanding that pledges be kept and that there be a public return for a public investment in the company was mostly unsuccessful. Labor-community forces were not able to prevail with their definition of the problem or their remedial action plan. Alliance formation and mobilization of forces were also fairly minimal for reasons given in the text.

The following sections relate the plant's historical background, the parent corporation's economic and strategic orientation, the state of the plant in 1986, and the campaign for corporate accountability. The final section analyzes the case on several key dimensions.

PLANT BACKGROUND

The Combustion Engineering plant in East Chicago, Indiana, began in 1910 as the Locomotive Superheater Company, which produced superheaters for railroad locomotives.[1] Until 1913 the company licensed others to produce the actual superheaters, but by the end of that year it began its own production. Later the company also produced economizers and superheaters for stationary boilers and changed its name several times. By April 1953 the firm was known as Combustion Engineering, Inc.

In the 1950s the East Chicago facility was producing a wide variety of products: steam generators, pump parts, throttle valves, camshafts, cover plates, exhaust steam injectors, and so on. But most production was devoted to making coal pulverizers for electric power plants. The East Chicago plant also contained locomotive engineering, industrial engineering, and research and development departments. By 1951 it was the second-largest plant in the Combustion Engineering chain.

In 1964 research and design activities were transferred to the company's Windsor, Connecticut, facility. The same year superheater manufacturing and fabrication work was transferred to a Chattanooga, Tennessee, plant.[2] By the end of the 1960s East Chicago primarily produced the coal pulverizer (also known as the "Bowl Mill"). In the mid-1960s the plant employed approximately five hundred people, most of them skilled machinists. Corporate headquarters were located in Stamford, Connecticut.

The 1960s were good years for the plant. Approximately 40 percent of all coal pulverizers sold in the United States were made by Combustion Engineering, and virtually all of those were made in East Chicago. In 1966–67 the company spent over $1 million upgrading the plant to produce thirty-ton pulverizers twenty-eight feet in diameter, the largest in the world. In 1968 a tape-controlled vertical turret lathe was added.[3]

The United Steelworkers of America represented plant workers. Labor relations had been peaceful: prior to 1969, only one 2-week strike in 1952 by USWA Local 1386 had occurred over contract negotiations. The Steelworkers also represented Combustion's Monongahela, Pennsylvania, facility; the two bargained jointly for new contracts.

In 1969 Combustion Engineering provoked a strike by the 265 East Chicago union members and their Pennsylvania counterparts by attempting to break the two plants away from basic steel contract patterns, which had governed previous negotiations. But the strike lasted only one day—a Sunday—and did not affect production. The union succeeded in keeping basic steel provisions.[4]

In the 1970s labor relations worsened perceptibly. Every single contract expiration—1972, 1975, and 1978—provoked a strike by Local 1386. The dispute always centered around company demands for a contract inferior to basic steel industry contracts and the union's staunch defense of a comparable settlement.

On 26 May 1972 the 264 steelworkers in East Chicago and the 444 steelworkers in Monongahela, Pennsylvania, went out on strike.[5] Combustion had three objectives in the 1972 negotiations: (1) wages and benefits inferior to those in basic steel, (2) different expiration dates for the two plants, and (3) expiration dates that would precede those in basic steel. In the end the company was to be unsuccessful on all three issues.

Negotiations stalemated for over a month after the strike began. In mid-July the company offered an economic settlement similar to "big steel" wages and benefits but lacking a cost-of-living adjustment (COLA) clause to keep wages current with inflation. On 16 July the East Chicago local accepted this economic package by a vote of 122–86, but the Monongahela local voted to hold out for the COLA clause. The East Chicago local negotiated over "local" issues (e.g., job descriptions, safety matters) while the Pennsylvania plant negotiated over both local issues and the COLA clause. At the month's end Local 1386 threatened to rescind its previous approval of the economic package. The company then capitulated on contract expiration dates and other issues. The union was victorious. Local 1386 President Harvey Mobley called the settlement of the 10-week-old strike "one of the best contracts we've ever had."

The years between the 1972 and 1975 were good to the plant.[6] The energy crisis of the early 1970s created a continual backlog of orders. Plant manager Harry Keightley told the press during these years that his number one problem was a shortage of skilled workers to do all the work. In early 1975 the company announced a $6-million addition to the plant, later scaled back to $5 million.[7]

On 2 June 1975, USWA Local 1386 again struck the company. Once again the issue was parity with "big steel" fringe benefits. Key sticking points were a COLA clause and a "basic steel" dental package. Three hundred twenty strikers manned the picket lines for approximately five weeks. On Thursday, 3 July the local ratified a contract and went back to work.[8] Although they failed to get a dental package or the COLA clause, the workers felt victorious because they improved holiday, hospitalization, and pay rates. Combustion Engineering "corporate policy" forbade a dental plan or a COLA clause, but the workers felt that they had parity overall with basic steelworkers. For the first time the company achieved its goal of different expiration dates with the East Chicago plant contract expiring one month earlier than the Monongahela plant contract. The members of Steelworkers Local 1386 were not concerned about this, but it would have an effect in 1978.

On 31 May 1978 the union struck for the third time in the 1970s. Three hundred sixty-five workers walked the picket line over familiar issues: a COLA clause and a dental plan. Once again, the union membership demanded parity with "big steel" contracts, and once again the company cited "corporate policy" as the basis for refusal of any dental plan or COLA clause.

The bargaining committee and an International Steelworkers staff representative had unanimously recommended an initial settlement without either a COLA clause or dental plan, but local members voted down the proposed contract by a 200 to 61 vote.[9] Given the intransigence on both sides, everyone settled down for a long strike during the month of June.

The lack of a common contract expiration date at the two plants now came back to haunt the Local 1386 workers. As a local with 365 members, 1386 exerted relatively little power over giant Combustion Engineering, which employed tens of thousands of workers at the time. The Steelworkers coordinated bargaining at three plants over the course of the summer, but Local 1386 was forced into a very long strike in the interim. On 30 June, 500 Monongahela USWA workers joined the strike. On 1 September 1,100 USWA members at Combustion Engineering's Tulsa, Oklahoma, plant went on strike.[10] Meanwhile Local 1386 members were locked into a long waiting game with the company, which Steelworkers staff representative John Bierman called a "test of wills."[11]

In July all the industrial unions that bargained with Combustion Engineering met to attempt to coordinate their collective bargaining activities. Yet the practical coordination was minimal because contract expiration dates were widely dispersed through many years; different international unions represented extremely varied bargaining units in numerous product lines; only 25 percent of Combustion Engineering's workforce was unionized; and the unions had not had a past history of close cooperation. The meeting accomplished only an exchange of contracts and information.

In the short run, the real coordination happened within the Steelworkers Union. The strategy was to wait the company out while increasing the number on strike: 365 by 1 June, 865 by 1 July, and 1,965 by 1 September. A steelworker explained:

> We'll have to see if we can hold out that long. . . . But the men seem pretty determined, and if we make it to September we'll be in a pretty strong position.[12]

The ranks of the strikers held solid for over three months. In late August the strikers voted 240 to 10 to stay out—a larger margin than the original 200 to 61 strike vote. On 11 September the company finally returned to the bargaining table. On 13 September a tentative agreement was negotiated, and on 18 September it was ratified by a 223–62 margin. It contained a COLA clause in the second and third years but no dental plan;

however, an eye-care benefit led the union to claim partial victory in this area also.[13]

Once again the union claimed victory: the basic steel pattern had been generally approximated after a sixteen-week strike. In all three strikes during the 1970s, the union fought for basic steel standards while the company, citing "corporate policy" unsuccessfully attempted to lower standards. The company's bargaining was conducted by personnel from corporate headquarters. Relations between the company and the union were peaceful during all three strikes, and no attempt was made to undertake major production during the stoppages.[14]

The East Chicago facility thus ended the 1970s with a legacy of labor turbulence: strikes of ten weeks, five weeks, and sixteen weeks occurred with every contract expiration. All strikes had been provoked by "corporate policy," not by bad relations inside the plant. Ex-workers and ex-managers insist that local plant labor relations were respectful and professional throughout the 1970s and into the 1980s.[15]

The plant entered the 1980s with many back orders. Employment grew to 560 by February 1981, a 47 percent increase since 1973. In 1980 and 1981 the facility received $3 million and $2.4 million in new computerized state-of-the art equipment.[16] General manager Duffeld predicted that the plant would manufacture approximately 150 coal pulverizers and roller mills in 1981, a very heavy work schedule.

When the union contract expired on 31 July 1981, corporate headquarters allowed local industrial relations manager Jack Bixeman to conduct the negotiations, subject to guidelines.[17] In contrast to the previous decade's bargaining experiences, there was no strike. Modest wage increases of approximately $1/hour over three years for the 430 union workers, retention of COLA, and a dental plan in the third year were features. The settlement was less costly to both parties than the 1978 one had been because the company's more flexible bargaining stance meant no strike.

The 1973–74 oil shortage and energy crisis had created an enormous backlog of orders in the late 1970s. By the early to mid-1980s, however, this backlog began to drop because energy conservation measures caused energy consumption to flatten out; utility industry orders dropped. The plant in 1983 faced its first layoffs since 1964 when twenty workers were laid off.

There was also rapid turnover and instability in management ranks. In 1980 long-time general manager Harry Keightley retired, to be replaced by William Duffeld. On 1 January 1983 Duffeld was suddenly replaced by Richard Sikorski, who had previously managed a Combustion Engineering plant in Cleveland that had just shut down. In January 1984 twenty-eight salaried people, including eight top managers, resigned or retired after being offered ultimatums and inducements to do so.[18] Further management shuffles, to be related later, were to occur in the next and final 2½ years of the plant's life.

Contract negotiations in 1984 were again handled by industrial relations manager Jack Bixeman. By this time the basic steel contracts that Local 1386 relied upon for reference were full of union concessions. The negotiations were begun and settled early.

The union claimed that the new contract was not concessionary, but it granted the company work rule changes allowing greater flexibility and dropped the previous incentive plan. Over forty-five months, a maximum total of 10 percent wage increase (including cost of living adjustment) was possible, although most workers would get less. Average pay was approximately $11.50 per hour. The contract maintained all current fringe benefits, including one or two minor items that had been lost in the previous year's basic steel agreements. Local 1386 vice president John Dyke expressed satisfaction: "We don't consider this concessions. We consider this giving them the chance to get us more work."[19]

Pressures other than comparable basic steel contracts were pushing the union local to compromise. By 1984 the plant was eating up its back log of new orders rapidly. To keep operating at full capacity, it needed to capture a larger share of the replacement parts market, but this was dominated by small local (often nonunion) machine shops with low fixed costs. Although unable to produce the original product, they could underbid the East Chicago plant on easier-to-produce spare parts. The new contract was intended to help the plant capture more of this spare parts market.

When Industrial Relations manager Jack Bixeman, a thirty-seven-year employee, retired in July 1985, he felt a great sense of accomplishment.[20] Unlike previous negotiations handled by national management officers, he had successfully and peacefully negotiated contracts in both 1981 and 1984. The plant had achieved greater flexibility, higher efficiency, and cost containment. Although authorized to grant up to $.50 per hour wage increase in the first year of the 1984 contract, he had held it to $.10. Relations with the union local were respectful but firm. Productivity and quality were high; the skilled workforce at East Chicago was unmatched anywhere in the corporation.

Bixeman's one concern was the plant's prospects within the corporate structure. Twice before there had been plans to shut down the East Chicago facility.[21] In 1964 the company had considered consolidating the Monongahela and East Chicago operations into a new facility to be built in Birdsboro, Pennsylvania (near Reading). A consulting firm evaluating the plan concluded that East Chicago operations were too productive to close. It recommended instead closing the Monongahela plant and moving only its operations to Birdsboro. The company did neither, and left both Monongahela and East Chicago running.

In 1972 Combustion Engineering planned to transfer all East Chicago operations to the Chattanooga, Tennessee, plant, but they discovered that the shutdown liabilities were prohibitive. Pension and other costs led them to shelve shutdown plans.

Given this history, Bixeman worried that the local plant management did not advocate enough for the plant at the national corporate level. When the St. Louis plant had been shut down a few years prior, local management refused to seek any of its work. They felt that business was booming for East Chicago's lone product, coal pulverizers, so why bother?

This lack of advocacy was even more disturbing because East Chicago was treated within the corporation as a *cost center,* not a *profit center.* Both fixed and labor costs at East Chicago were relatively high compared to many other facilities, causing corporate officials to complain. In Bixeman's view, this overlooked the high value added by the work done at East Chicago. Although costly to maintain, the facility was producing such high-value equipment that this more than made up for any cost differentials. By any calculation, East Chicago was a profitable plant, but this was obscured by the corporation's internal accounting system, which cast the local plant in a more unfavorable light. Nevertheless, the plant seemed to be in good shape at the time Bixeman retired, although back orders were dropping rapidly. The plant's future seemed to hinge on its continuing performance.

To boost that performance, the company introduced, with great fanfare, a "new era" of labor relations at the plant. In January 1985 the company called a meeting of all employees where all were paid for attending. Donald Lyons, president of the East Chicago plant's corporate division, told the local press:

> We need to convince employees that their contribution makes a difference. . . . American companies have a tendency not to share information to show the employee where the company is going and where he fits in.[22]

Plant manager Richard Sikorski stated:

> These meetings reflect Combustion Engineering's new management style, keynoted by openness in the sharing of information at all levels and more participation in decision making by all employees.[23]

The reaction of the workers was somewhat different. Local union president Bill Shelton was disappointed that there was virtually no time for questions after the prepared script had been run through. He was even more disappointed that there was no discussion of the local plant or its operations: "We have to find solutions to the problems we have here," he stated.[24]

Years later union grievance representative Dave Brebner recalled that there were no follow-up meetings, no changes in basic management style, and no attempts made to actually communicate with or listen to workers. His conclusion:

> It was a "dog-and-pony show" that they brought to us. I think the purpose of it was to impress stockholders. . . . There was not a local person involved in this at all; it was all corporate people. . . . They didn't address one issue out of our local problems in the plant.[25]

If the "new era" of management didn't materialize locally, a second hopeful sign occurred in approximately the same time period. On 5 November 1984 Combustion Engineering requested from the East Chicago Economic Development Commission (EDC) an industrial revenue bond (IRB) to help finance the acquisition of a numerically controlled gantry drill press, a very "high tech" piece of equipment. The IRB program allowed local governments and their related economic development arms to float tax-free bonds to raise money for low interest loans to businesses for economic development purposes. Through this program, taxpayers indirectly subsidized corporations because of lost tax revenues.

In their application and subsequent testimony at meetings and a public hearing, Combustion Engineering promised that the purchase would save eighteen jobs that would otherwise disappear. They requested financing for $1 million of the possible $1.4 million cost. Following meetings and a public hearing, the $1 million IRB was granted and issued on 27 March 1985.[26]

The workers in the plant saw this as a positive sign that the plant was secure. Combustion Engineering was investing in the plant's future. The company predicted that the machine would be in operation by the first quarter of 1986.

Thus the East Chicago Combustion Engineering plant entered 1986 amidst mixed signals. The rapidly dropping backlog of orders and the beginning of layoffs looked bad. But the company had committed to further investment in the plant and had promised to cooperate more with the workforce to solve pressing problems. In the end, 1986 was to be a momentous year for the plant.

THE PARENT CORPORATION

The East Chicago facility was affected by corporate decisions well beyond its control. Although they had not closed down the entire plant in 1964 as planned, the parent corporation had narrowed the product line to one product by moving research and development work to Connecticut and superheater work to Tennessee. Later corporate strategies would also have an impact on the plant.

By the 1970s Combustion Engineering was a large and growing multinational company employing over 40,000 workers. Net sales more than doubled between 1969 and 1976; from 1976 to 1981 they grew an additional 64 percent (from $1.6 billion to $2.6 billion). However from 1981 to 1986 sales dropped about 1.5 percent to $2.55 billion.[27] Net income similarly grew 225 percent from 1976 to 1982 (from $56 million to $183 million). Yet the company lost money over the 1983–85 period and barely turned a profit for the entire 1983–86 period.[28]

How did the company fare so poorly? The answer lies in the internal structure of the corporation. Its operations were divided into four business segments: (1) steam generating systems for the electric utility industry; (2) design, engineering, and construction, primarily for the chemical, petrochemical, and petroleum industries; (3) industrial equipment, and (4) industrial products and services. In 1977 the company's $2 billion in sales was dominated by the steam generating and industrial equipment divisions. Table 3.1 gives sales and profit percentages of each business segment for that year.

The East Chicago plant belonged to the Steam Generating Systems division, the largest in terms of sales at the time. But a 1978–82 boom in oil field exploration led to rapid growth of oil and gas equipment orders. Combustion Engineering invested heavily in its industrial group, both through internal expansion and external acquisition. Capital expenditures between 1977 and 1983 went heavily into the industrial equipment and industrial products and services divisions, while the Steam Generating Systems division got next to nothing. Table 3.2 shows net capital expenditures (capital additions minus depreciation and amortization) during those years for each of the four divisions.

Corporate leaders considered this a wise strategy because electric power industry orders were stagnant despite substantial back orders. The

Table 3.1. Percentage of total sales and operating profit by business segment, Combustion Engineering, 1977.

Business Segment	Sales	Profit
Steam generating systems	37	34
Design, engineering, and construction	15	18
Industrial equipment	29	38
Industrial products and services	19	10

Source: Combustion Engineering *Annual Report*, 1978.

compound growth rate in the value of U.S. shipments of conventional and nuclear power boilers from 1977 to 1982 was -0.8 percent.[29] Therefore it made sense to "starve" this sector and invest in expanding oil and gas markets.

Unfortunately for the company, the energy glut and the recession in the early 1980s combined to knock the bottom out of the company's industrial equipment market. Combustion Engineering's industrial equipment division lost $5.3 million, $27 million, and $43 million in 1983, 1984, and 1985.[30] The company was forced in 1983 to sell off businesses, consolidate facilities, cut its workforce by 30 percent, and take a $190 million pre-tax write-off to escape unprofitable businesses.[31] In 1985 the company wrote off an additional $108 million in offshore oil-drilling equipment businesses and attempted to sell another $435 million of oil-field assets. When the highest bid was less than $100 million, the company faced the prospect of yet another write-off that could exceed more than one half its $664 million total net worth. Only a highly creative and questionable deal with Hughes Tool Co. involving disguised "loans" by Combustion Engineering to itself prevented a massive hit to the balance sheet.[32] In the end, the company would be forced to accept a write-off of more than $400 million in oil and industrial businesses anyway.[33]

The less favored Steam Generating Systems division was pulling the company through the hard times. In 1983, 1984, and 1985 this business segment earned 143 percent, 111 percent, and 124 percent of the entire company's operating profit.

In 1982 Combustion Engineering hired Charles E. Hugel from AT&T as its chief executive officer. In keeping with his "high tech" background, Hugel saw the future of the company in computer software and other forms of high technology. He referred to Combustion Engineering's traditional businesses as "dirt businesses," and stated that in the future,

Table 3.2. Combustion Engineering net capital additions by business segment, 1977–1983. (in millions of dollars)

Business Segment	Average yearly net capital additions
Steam Generating Systems	0.8
Design, Engineering, & Construction	5.3
Industrial Equipment	33.8
Industrial Products & Services	38.0

Source: Combustion Engineering *Annual Reports*, 1978–1983.

"We're going to be an intellectual property company." Between 1983 and 1987 Combustion Engineering went on a massive shopping spree, spending $545 million for companies selling high-tech and computerized measuring devices, pulp machinery, computer control systems and electrical instruments, software programs, and the like. Although purchased at a steep price, these companies collectively returned only 3.7 percent pretax earnings as of 1987. A building materials "dirt business" was sold for $62 million that was worth nearly four times that a few years later.[34]

Within the East Chicago plant's business segment, the company attempted to take a larger share of the after-sales service market. In 1986 Hugel explained:

> We've shifted our emphasis. Last year, for the first time, service and maintenance contracts with electric utilities exceeded those for new equipment, both fossil-fuel and nuclear.[35]

The company also concentrated on developing the newest technology of fluidized bed combustion and cogeneration plants, which are designed to burn coal cleanly and efficiently.

In 1988 the company lost $245 million, as cost overruns and needed repairs in the new fluid bed combustion systems and waste recovery systems overwhelmed a small operating profit in other areas. High tech became very costly, as unproven technologies developed significant and expensive problems.

But in the mid-1980s these problems were unforeseen. The company was being restructured rapidly through massive manufacturing employment reductions; sale or liquidation of marginal, unprofitable, or nonstrategic businesses; rapid acquisition of high-tech firms; and internal reorganization to correspond to the new direction of the corporation.

THE EAST CHICAGO PLANT — 1986

In 1986 the East Chicago plant's back orders were disappearing. In the first quarter of 1986, the Steam Generating Systems division of the parent company saw a 30 percent decline in net sales compared to a year earlier.[36] The *U.S. Industrial Outlook* described the dismal state of the market that year as follows:

> Shipments of fossil-fuel generating systems dropped in 1986 to about 19 million pounds of steam an hour, the lowest level in more than 15 years. This was less than half the 1985 level of 39 million pounds and less than 12 percent of 158 million pounds, the average from 1972 through 1975. Manufacturers are subsisting on maintenance and repair work and a very few new orders.[37]

For the first time in decades, major layoffs hit the workforce. By the middle of the year, hourly employment was under 200.

The apparent bright spot was a new product. East Chicago was to build a prototype of the so-called "super-mill," an extremely large pulverizer beyond anything previously built. The mill, which workers claimed was worth about $7 million, was built on time and was flawless. Employees believed that a job well done meant further work. Dave Brebner later recalled:

> The people really got behind the super-mill, thinking that it could be our savior if we could produce this thing on time and do it right. We even worked outside the bounds of the contract at times, because it needed to be done to get this thing completed. And we did it.[38]

Company notices on the bulletin board throughout the early months of 1986 congratulated the workers for their efforts and posted them on their progress in being on time.

Despite the implied promises and the praise, the workers in the plant were worried about their future. Large layoffs, few incoming orders, instability in the ranks of management, and the like led them to be concerned about the plant's future. On 10 May 1986 three Local 1386 officers attended an "early warning signs" class conducted by the Calumet Project for Industrial Jobs.[39]

As part of the training, workers learn how to fill out an "early warning scorecard" with numerical scores on different factors that have been associated with shutdowns in previous situations. A high numerical score means a high degree of danger. A copy of the (now outdated) scorecard being used at the time is reproduced in figure 3.1.

Filled out scorecards showed such high overall scores that immediate action was indicated. Additional blank copies of the scorecard were brought back to the plant. Thirteen scorecards filled out by union officers and other strategically placed union members throughout the plant again were high. Composite results are given in table 3.3.

Since the average scores were approaching 60, this was extremely serious: "D-" or "F" in the Calumet Project's scoring system.

At a 28 May meeting of the local's Executive Board with Calumet Project personnel union members related additional reasons for their fear. Two months earlier, yet another plant manager had been hired, marking the fourth manager of the plant in the past six years. Plant rumors had it that Combustion Engineering would abandon manufacturing entirely. Unlike local management's previous yearly budgets, this year's ended with June. Drastic personnel cuts left some departments with a supervisor/worker ratio of 1 to 4. They also alleged there were serious mismanagement problems.[40]

The next day, 29 May, the Combustion Engineering Vice President of Production for Fossil Power Systems wrote a letter to Local 1386 president William Shelton notifying him that the company was seriously considering closing the plant. It also offered to meet with the union to discuss the matter. The company attributed the plant's likely closing to changing technology and a deteriorating market. Combustion Engineering spokesman Ken Pilon said that the market was one fiftieth of what it had been in the 1970s and that sulfur dioxide emissions concerns made utilities favor fluidized bed combustion equipment over the older-style equipment manufactured in East Chicago.[41]

At a 5 June meeting the company told the union that a final decision to close would be made within the week and that no union concessions or other actions could affect the decision. On 12 June the official announcement to close came out. Remaining work for the plant, which had been operating at under 50 percent capacity, would be transferred primarily to Combustion Engineering's Wellsville, New York, plant and secondarily to its Enterprise, Kansas, plant.

Two important facts quickly emerged. First, at an April meeting only six weeks earlier, the company had misled the East Chicago mayor, his business development director, and a leader of the East Chicago Chamber of Commerce at a meeting intended to uncover any signs of potential problems. Asked if they needed anything from the city, Combustion Engineering cited only a minor garbage pickup problem. Either intentionally

Figure 3.1. THE EARLY WARNING SCORECARD

This scorecard should help you and your union members put together what you see in the plant and draw some conclusions about what the future may hold for your job. As with your own health, early warning may give you time to "save the patient."

To fill out the scorecard, circle the points for each question. Base your answer on the best information you can obtain. It will be useful to involve people from a variety of departments who have access to different kinds of information.

PRODUCTION AND LABOR

(1) Has the number of people working declined in the past year or two?
Peak employment: ____ (19__). Main reason(s) for job loss:

Hiring No Change Declined
0   1   2   3   4   5

(2) Has work been contracted out? Explain. (To whom, what kind, how much?)

No   Yes
0   1   2   3   4   5

(3) Has the number of hours worked per week changed?
From ____/wk when ____? To ____/wk now.

No   Yes
0   1   2   3   4   5

(4) Has production gone down? become irregular? From ___ when ___? To ___ now.
What if any product lines have been eliminated? Or transferred to another plant?

No   Yes
0   1   2   3   4   5

(5) Is overall maintenance of the plant worse than a year or two ago?
Explain (Lack of preventive repairs, refusal to spend for good replacement parts??).

No   Yes
0   1   2   3   4   5

(6) Has inspection/quality control been cut back? Explain (decline in the number of inspectors, standards lowered, more defective or bad product shipped, etc.).

No   Yes
0   1   2   3   4   5

(7) Is the building in bad shape? Explain:

No   Yes
0   2   4   6   8   10

(8) Have there been major changes in the levels of inventory of finished product?

No   Yes
0   1   2   3   4   5

MANAGEMENT

(9) Has the plant been bought by a conglomerate or involved in a recent merger?
Give name and circumstances.

No   Yes
0   2   4   6   8   10

(10) Has your company opened a new plant, or installed new equipment, in another location to produce the same or similar product that you make? Explain:

No   Yes
0   1   2   3   4   5

(11) Have managers, skilled labor, or equipment been moved to another plant?

No   Yes
0   1   2   3   4   5

(12) Has local management changed within the past year? Explain (when, who, less competent? refused to move into area?).

No   Yes
0   1   2   3   4   5

(13) Has re-investment in the plant stopped? What investments have been made? When? What was the dollar value? (Use another sheet if necessary.)

No   Yes
0   2   4   6   8   10

(14) Has management been complaining about inventory or property taxes? Explain (also list other complaints).

No   Yes
0   1   2   3   4   5

(15) Has the company cut back on advertising or customer services or sales force? Explain.

No   Yes
0   1   2   3   4   5

(16) Have major customers been lost? Examples? Reasons?

No   Yes
0   2   4   6   8   10

POINT TOTAL: _____

0 – 25	Give your plant an A and let us know when you're hiring.
25 – 35	B keep an eye on things
35 – 45	C keep a sharp eye on things
45 – 60	D begin intervention efforts
Over 60	F start campaign to save plant

NOTE: a 5 or 10-point answer on several of these questions may be cause for concern, even if the total point score is low.

Table 3.3. Results of early warning scorecard rating by 13 officers and members of USWA Local 1386.

Question #	Mean Score	Median Score	Highest Possible Score
1 – Employment decline	4.46	5	5
2 – Work contracted out	2.77	2	5
3 – Work hours	3.77	4	5
4 – Production drops	4.00	4	5
5 – Plant maintenance	4.00	5	5
6 – Quality control	4.46	5	5
7 – Building condition	5.23	4	10
8 – Inventory changes	3.15	3	5
9 – Recently acquired	.62	0	10
10 – New plant opened	1.08	0	5
11 – Resources moved out	1.31	0	5
12 – Management changes	4.54	5	5
13 – Reinvestment	6.00	6	10
14 – Management complaints	3.54	3–4	5
15 – Sales budget cuts	1.77	3	5
16 – Lost customers	7.38	10	10
TOTALS	58.08	59.5	100

or because local management was also in the dark, the imminent closing was hidden.

Second, the company had never used the $1 million from the 1985 industrial revenue bond (IRB) for the promised purpose. They had simply obtained the money at below-market rates, deposited it in the bank, and left it there for over a year.

THE CAMPAIGN FOR ACCOUNTABILITY

Working with the Calumet Project, the union local chose to resist the company's plans. The possibility of saving the plant looked discouraging. The market for conventional coal boilers (and therefore the plant's coal pulverizers) was severely depressed. The only hope for the plant appeared to be to develop an entirely new product line, or to operate the machine shop (approximately 50 percent of employment) as a local "job shop" while waiting for the market for boilers to pick up again, which was considered a possibility by the very late 1980s or early 1990s. Neither was promising for a plant facing liquidation within two to three months with an unwilling seller and no prospective buyer. Local 1386 leaders and Calumet Project staffers therefore decided that attempting a reversal of the closing was not feasible unless a buyer surfaced quickly.

The focus shifted to the issue of company accountability to the community and the workforce. The abuse of the industrial revenue bond and the bad faith with the city during the April visit became the main focus of a public campaign against the company. Subsidiary themes were union busting, since most of the work was being transferred to a nonunion plant in Wellsville, New York, and "mismanagement," which the workers claimed was endemic to the local facility.

On 14 July the local union leadership and Calumet Project staffers met with East Chicago mayor Robert Pastrick and his top economic development aides. Pastrick expressed concern over the IRB issue and promised a further investigation.[42] When this impending investigation became public, Combustion Engineering announced plans to repay the IRB loan as quickly as possible.[43]

On 21 July the mayor called a special meeting of the East Chicago Economic Development Commission (EDC) to investigate the company's breach of trust and possible abuse of the IRB financing. At this hearing Local 1386 president William Shelton questioned the company's good faith and demanded that they be held accountable:

> Combustion Engineering knew about the requirements of this kind of subsidy. But no drill was ever bought. Instead of retaining jobs and payroll, our members have been steadily laid off. Now we are told there will be no jobs at all. . . . If the company intended to act in good faith then why didn't they indicate at the time, or earlier, that there were problems with the purchase of the gantry drill? Why didn't they notify the city at the time of their shutdown announcement that they would pre-pay the bond? Why did they wait until our union and the Calumet Project raised the issue with the city and the public?
>
> We urge this committee, the mayor and the city council to pursue actions against the company for breaching the agreement. They have abused your trust and ours. You can do something about it. You can hold them accountable.[44]

Calumet Project staff person Thomas DuBois testified that the company saved a minimum of $60,000 in interest because of the subsidized interest rate, and that at least $140,000 in interest should have been earned over the sixteen months that the loan was held. Therefore he suggested that the EDC require $200,000 from the company in addition to the payback of the $1 million principal. The $200,000 could then be used for the original purposes of the IRB financing: job retention. DuBois suggested that a tripartite committee of employee/community/city government representatives oversee the use of these funds.[45]

The company countered through the press by claiming that there was no bad faith: the company had intended to buy the drill press, but first a supplier problem and later a downturn in the market had delayed and ultimately killed the purchase. Second, it claimed to have actually lost money on the loan because it was paying 5 percent interest and was only making 4 percent from its investment through the escrow account in which the money was deposited.[46]

The EDC took no action but directed its legal counsel to prepare a report on possible further action. Meanwhile, it refused a company request to allow immediate repayment of the $1 million.

East Chicago was reeling from the impact of the shutdown combined with other closing announcements and the bankruptcy declaration of LTV, the city's second-largest taxpayer. Taxable property in the city dropped 25 percent in one month; LTV was 18 percent of the city's tax base, while Combustion Engineering was 7 percent. This might mean a 25 percent or more tax increase on remaining taxpayers or a drastic reduction in city services including the city's beleaguered school system. A city councilman remarked, "This is drastic. We have a deadline to get the budget out, and this is like a time bomb being dropped on us."[47]

On 4 August East Chicago EDC legal counsel Joseph Costanza issued his report on the IRB issue.[48] After reviewing basic facts, like Combustion Engineering's promise in the loan agreement to "acquire, construct and install" the gantry drill press and the lack of a specified time limit within which they must do so, Costanza reviewed legal theories under which a remedy could be sought. In his view, breach of a promise, lack of specific performance, unjust enrichment at public expense, or similar legal theories were irrelevant. The only issue was: did the company have a fraudulent intent at the time they applied for and received the IRB financing? Since this could not be proved, Costanza recommended no legal action.

Costanza had met frequently with Calumet Project Director Lynn Feekin prior to issuing the report, but he rejected her perspective and discounted evidence she gave on a previous similar case. He was concerned that East Chicago would "chill" the interest of prospective investors if it should undertake legal action. He thought that any such measure would seem "anti-business."[49]

Costanza also viewed with considerable skepticism an example from nearby Chicago of legal action forcing a company to keep faith with the community following the granting of an IRB. In 1980 Playskool, Inc., a subsidiary of Milton Bradley (in turn owned by Hasbro Industries, Inc.) had received $1 million in IRB financing to purchase equipment that they claimed would create four hundred new jobs in the plant. Instead, employment dropped from twelve hundred to seven hundred by September 1984 when the company announced the imminent closure of the plant. Following a public outcry and community mobilization, the city of Chicago filed suit in December 1984 to force Playskool to remain open and to honor the terms of the IRB agreement. By the end of January 1985 the company settled out of court with the city, providing for (1) keeping the plant open for one year with a minimum employment of one hundred, (2) giving its "best effort" to find a buyer committed to using the facility, and (3) setting up relocation and training funds and programs.[50] Costanza felt this was unimportant because Playskool never admitted any liability and the settlement was out of court and thus established no legal precedent.[51]

The East Chicago EDC followed Costanza's recommendation and took no legal action. One of the Playskool attorneys disagreed strongly. In a letter he noted:

> It is clear to me that the City of East Chicago has an excellent case against Combustion Engineering for fraudulent concealment of its failure to use the Economic Development funds for the intended purpose. . . . In my opinion, Combustion Engineering certainly had acquired fraudulent intent when it omitted or concealed from the City of East Chicago its material change of plans. In fact, the action is so shocking that I cannot understand why the City failed to seek redress in the form of punitive damages. I think the City could make a substantial recovery and deter other applicants for loans from such misconduct in the future.[52]

But neither the city nor its economic development commission was willing to risk a step they considered potentially injurious to the local "business climate" for uncertain legal results.

Faced with this setback on the legal front, the Local 1386/Calumet Project forces turned to other avenues for redress. Together with the United Citizens Organization, they sponsored a community meeting to demand "settlement terms" from the company. Democratic congressman Peter Visclosky and East Chicago Director of Community Development John Artis attended, along with approximately 100 workers and community residents. At this meeting a list of proposed settlement terms was ratified. The list included:

- The company fund a feasibility study to see if all or part of the facility can be operated profitably;
- The company seek a purchaser; or donate the plant for restoration of manufacturing jobs;
- The company establish a job placement center as well as provide job training, education, and career counseling;
- The company pay other employers $500 for each ex-Combustion employee hired (to cover retraining expenses);
- The company pay any ex-employee $100 for each new job they find for a co-worker;
- The company provide each employee relocation expenses and assistance up to $500;
- The company establish a $50,000 financial assistance fund to assist ex-employees in personal and family emergencies.[53]

The following day Congressman Visclosky wrote a letter on behalf of himself and mayor Robert Pastrick to Combustion Engineering CEO Charles Hugel presenting the proposed settlement terms and requesting a meeting no later than 5 September.[54] On 29 August Combustion Engineering Vice President of Fossil Manufacturing J. C. Campbell replied to Congressman Visclosky.[55] His letter detailed the declining market for power generation equipment, pointed out that the company had negotiated closing terms with the union local, stated that the company planned job search seminars for displaced workers, and noted that the building would soon be for sale following the scheduled 26 September closing. However, it failed to address any of the proposed settlement terms, and avoided the subject of a meeting.

Under strong pressure from the union and The Calumet Project, Congressman Visclosky was unwilling to accept these evasions. On 9 September his chief aide met with the Washington representative of Combustion Engineering. The company requested examples of other firms doing more for their workers in a shutdown situation. The Calumet Project supplied the Congressman with several examples, which were relayed to the company. On 15 September Campbell flew to East Chicago and participated in a meeting with the Congressman, Local 1386 officials, and

Calumet Project staff. He committed to nothing, but agreed to review the issues at corporate headquarters.

On 17 September Congressman Visclosky wrote Campbell requesting a prompt review of possible corporate actions regarding job retraining, job search training, a feasibility study, environmental integrity of the plant, incentives for reemployment, and an emergency aid fund.[56] On 25 September, one day before the closing of the plant, Campbell's reply agreed to provide $10,000 immediately for retraining purposes, plus an additional $35,000 if government matching funds could be found. (Subsequently, federal double matching funds turned this $35,000 into $105,000 for the approximately two hundred workers, or a little over $500 per worker.) Also, pursuant to an agreement with Local 1386, it would extend its outplacement workshop training to an additional ninety employees who were on layoff at the time of the closing announcement.[57] The company agreed to cooperate with any feasibility study, but declined to fund what they considered a useless exercise. The company also declined to provide a hiring incentive for hiring ex-employees, which it considered an unwise expenditure of limited resources. However, it pledged to widely advertise the availability of skilled employees, both through direct mail and the media. Finally, the company pledged to pursue a program of extensive environmental testing and compliance if necessary, coupled with a careful "moth balling" operation to keep the facility in perfect condition for resale. (This included a security program to protect against vandalism.)[58]

While not everything asked for, this was more than would have been attained prior to the "public accountability" campaign. Congressman Visclosky reacted positively:

> "Today we can claim at least a partial victory for the people who have worked faithfully for Combustion Engineering," he said. "I'm satisfied that the CE management has taken significant steps to see that their employees are more fairly treated."[59]

On September 26 the plant was closed. Throughout the month of October a few workers remained in the plant removing machinery and preparing the plant for resale. The city of East Chicago pledged to monitor future IRBs more closely.

ANALYSIS AND CONCLUSION

Four issues emerge from this case study: (1) reasons for closure; (2) early warning signals and systems; (3) government public policy; and (4) effectiveness of the labor-community intervention. Each will be considered in order.

REASONS FOR THE CLOSING

Conventional wisdom frequently attributes closings to foreign imports, excessive government regulations, or American workers who have "priced themselves out of the market." This case does not easily fit into such superficial explanations. Imports were not a factor at all; neither were government regulations. And no account, including that of the parent company, argued that wage costs were the cause of this closing.

Because of decline in demand for its sole product, the plant would have been viable only if the product line were expanded. However, this did not occur for a variety of reasons. Lack of local management advocacy within the parent corporation, unstable management ranks (including three new plant managers in four years), and possibly local managerial incompetence and thievery[60] complicated chances of a decision to diversify product lines.

Larger strategic corporate decisions also hurt. Disinvestment in the steam generating systems division to finance enormous expenditures in oil and gas exploration equipment was a classic case of "milking" to aid a different business segment. The new investment turned into a $400-million boondoggle, making the company more prone to close marginal enterprises. The reorientation from "dirt businesses" to high-tech ventures also proved both costly and detrimental.

What role did labor relations play? In the July/August 1987 issue of *Industrial Development and Site Selection Handbook,* Combustion Engineering attributed the move to "overcapacity and labor strife." Referring to the Wellsville facility,

> CE officials were also favorably disposed toward the site because the workforce was not unionized, an important element given the union friction in East Chicago (where the closed CE plant was located).[61]

This confirms antiunion motivation as one basis for the decision to close the East Chicago facility, which is technically illegal under the National Labor Relations Act.

Local 1386 officers and members deny that they had obstructed smooth relations in the plant. As evidence they cite peaceful relations in the 1980s, union attempts to help correct operational problems, the meaninglessness of the company's "new era" of labor relations, and extraordinary cooperation on the "super-mill." Local management sources, while not agreeing with all of these sentiments, do agree that *locally* labor-management relations had been good at the East Chicago plant. Strikes in the 1970s are attributed to "corporate policy." It is important to guard against self-serving accounts from those involved, but it is striking that I have been unable to find *any* management or union sources willing to claim bad labor relations at the plant locally prior to the final year. (During that final year demoralization grew within the plant and some aspects of labor-management relations did take a turn for the worse.)

In short, the key reasons for this plant's demise stem from its vulnerability due to a single product line in a declining market, lack of local management advocacy within the corporation for the plant, management instability and perhaps related problems of competency and honesty, antiunion motivation, corporate "milking" to finance more glamorous ventures, and a corporate restructuring toward high-tech and service businesses. The most popular explanations usually given for plant closings either do not apply (e.g., excessive wage rates, too much government regulation, foreign competition) or apply only partially (declining market — clearly an important factor but correctable through new product lines).

Early Warning Signals and Systems. In this case warning signs appeared well before the shutdown. The Calumet Project's early warning scorecard captured many of them. However, the union local got involved in it too late to be really effective.

Even without a formal system, workers can and do recognize early warning signs. Local 1386 leaders were worried even prior to the project's training session. What they lacked was a systematized and coherent way to put the warning signs together and a way to act on the knowledge they did have. The Calumet Project supplied both.[62]

A second lesson is that local management is an unreliable source for early warning. The city's "visit with management" was worse than useless: it falsely lulled the city into believing all was well only six weeks prior to the shutdown announcement. It does not really matter whether this was intentional deception or merely the result of *local* management ignorance. In either case, local plant management is not a trustworthy source of information.

Government Public Policy. This case illustrates the degree to which corporations feel free to utilize public subsidies to aid them in their business planning with no accountability to the community or the local government in return. Combustion Engineering treated the subsidized $1-million loan from the IRB as its private capital, not as a public sector subsidy demanding a commitment to the public sector in exchange. Given the original intent of the loan, the IRB program was abused; yet the company felt no need to inform the city of its change in plans until they were publicly called to account by the union and the Calumet Project. It is highly unlikely that any fraudulent intent existed from the beginning; rather, the company felt no need to be accountable. They saw the $1 million as "their own" rather than a public trust with strings attached.

The city's approach to the IRB program encouraged this view. Firmly wedded to a "business climate" conception of government-corporate relations, the city of East Chicago conceived of its role as aiding the company as much as possible while imposing the least possible restrictions or requirements in return. A completely dependent relationship between government and corporation is assumed; the government prepares the most advantageous environment or "business climate," but the private corporation makes the decisions that determine the fate of the community, free from community obligations. The fact that nearby Chicago had made considerable gains by breaching this customary business climate approach with a lawsuit carried little weight with a city administration feeling itself helpless and dependent in the face of plant closings and a shrinking tax base.

Only Congressman Peter Visclosky was willing to take independent action. He too accepted the conventional "business climate" wisdom but tempered this with a belief that community and worker interests deserved corporate attention also. The concessions won were meager, but were more than would have been obtained without the public campaign and the consequent political pressure on the company.

The company was able to abandon East Chicago at a cost of only minor concessions. At the new site in New York it received nearly $1 million in job training funds, almost $.5 million in preferential fuel rates, $870,000 in tax exemptions, and a 10-year freeze on tax assessments.[63] East Chicago is not the only locality that is governed by the business climate conventional wisdom of public expenditure for private profit.

Effectiveness of the Labor-Community Intervention. The Calumet Project/union intervention was mostly unsuccessful, despite success in extracting minor concessions. The difficulties were due to (1) circumstances making plant preservation almost impossible; (2) the less intense or wide-spread appeal of more realistic goals such as corporate recompense; (3) local officials' uncritical embrace of a "business climate" ideology; and (4) consequently, less than overwhelming formation of alliances or mobilization of forces.

The steep market drop for conventional boilers made it unrealistic to demand the plant be kept open. With little time, entirely new product lines also appeared impossible. So the Calumet Project and the union shifted focus to corporate abuse and betrayal of public trust. But this formulation of the problem, while having some appeal, could not galvanize anywhere near the effort or passion a realistic plant-saving effort would have.

The remedial action plan, even if acted upon, would have only returned some money to the city, not the vastly more important jobs being lost. Furthermore, corporate accountability and recompense would require a breach of the "business climate" viewpoint universally held by local public officials.

Battling these odds, the labor-community coalition was able to wrest limited concessions from the company, but there was no sustained or mass movement. Settlement terms were improved, largely through extraordinary efforts by the local Congressman, who was being pressured by workers and community residents. A limited alliance with limited objectives, this constellation of forces did at least improve the lives of some displaced workers. Perhaps equally important, the corporate accountability issue was publicly and forcefully raised; once in the open public arena it would remain there for future battles.

SUCCESSORSHIP AND MANAGERIAL COMPETENCE AT THE STRATOJAC PLANT

This case study concerns a northwest Indiana family-owned producer of men's overcoats that was sold to a group of investors in 1984. New management took public subsidies from a state program, mismanaged the business, closed the plant with no warning to the employees, moved to Amsterdam, New York, and eventually drove the firm into bankruptcy after taking millions of dollars in public subsidies at the new location.

This particular case demonstrates few early warning signals beyond very general ones. Mismanagement is often easier to hide than other signals. Labor-management relations were not an issue, but both the company structure (aging single owner) and strategy after the sale played a major role. Economic conditions in the product market also had some importance.

The case demonstrates the vulnerability of a low wage, mostly female workforce in an intensely competitive industry. Neither an abortive attempt to create an employee-owned company (ESOP) nor other attempts to define and build support for an alternative were successful because circumstances were overwhelmingly unfavorable. Employees locked into such an unfavorable labor market segment have little protection and few avenues to power.

In the following section, I outline the historical background of this company, followed by accounts of its sale and the closure of the Hammond, Indiana, plant under new ownership. Additional sections relate the fortunes of the company at its new location in Amsterdam, New York, and ill-fated attempts by Hammond workers to reopen the Indiana plant. An evaluation of the case concludes.

BACKGROUND

In 1904 Meyer Winer opened a work clothes factory just south of Gary, Indiana, in the town of Crown Point. This began a family dynasty of garment manufacturing in northwest Indiana. Sons Arthur Winer and Louis Winer later founded men's pants and overcoat operations.

Louis Winer operated in Hammond, Indiana. A key product line was labeled "Stratojac," named after a type of lining, and his company became known as the Stratojac Corporation.

Stratojac was typical of clothing manufacturers in the post-World War II years. It was run like a family business, with Louis Winer personally running the plant on a daily basis. Employees found him autocratic but generally a reasonable and fair person to deal with. Phyllis Jordan, president of the production workers' union for eighteen of her twenty-two years with the company, characterized Winer as "a good employer to work for."[1]

Employees were represented by the United Garment Workers of America Local 256. Employment remained a relatively steady two hundred from the 1960s into the 1980s. Seasonal layoffs would occur, but workers were always called back when the cycle picked up again. Employees were overwhelmingly female; only a few males in the cutting room remained by the 1980s.[2]

Wage scales were low but average or even slightly above average for this competitive, low-wage industry. The 1 January 1984 three-year union contract guaranteed all employees $3.574 per hour after an initial break-in period.[3] Piecework bonuses raised sewing machine operators' pay to about $5 per hour; very fast experienced operators could make up to $7 per hour. Other workers earned between $4.25 and $7.50 per hour, depending on skill and speed, with most closer to the bottom than the top.

Plant equipment was old; some sewing machines predated World War II. More of the equipment was 1960s vintage; there was also modern "fusing" machinery to attach inner linings and related parts. But generally the equipment was not modern and consequently was less productive than the equipment that some competitors used. But this industry is not noted for technological innovation, and many of Stratojac's competitors used equally old equipment.

The plant produced a very high quality product. Stratojac overcoats were sold at high quality stores like Macy's, not Kmart. Ex-employees and ex-managers considered the product top-of-the-line, calling it "Even better than London Fog."

SUCCESSORSHIP QUESTION

Approaching his mid-seventies, Louis Winer became concerned in the late 1970s about a successor. He hired Edward Lieser as executive vice president on a ten-year contract with a salary "in the six figures."[4] Winer's estimation of Lieser dropped dramatically when it became apparent he was not capable of running the company. Lieser's only contribution was a supplementary sideline to Stratojac's main business through the importation and resale of leather jackets and cheaper cloth jackets. Winer gave up the idea of grooming him as a successor.

The company prospered throughout the late 1970s and into the 1980s. Following industry trends, imports gradually became a larger share of the total company volume, but domestic production remained the main business.

Profitability was squeezed because New York sales were increasingly dominated by a few large volume customers such as Macy's (often averaging over $1 million with Macy's alone). Smaller men's retail stores continued to shrink in importance.

Large buyers forced a change in Stratojac's strict policy that "return privileges" (rights to return unsold goods for credit) be limited to 5 percent of the order. Returns grew to almost 10 percent, and money officially considered an "advertising allowance" was really being used as "markdown money" (discounts used to induce the retail merchandiser to keep the product rather than return it, or used to sell the returned product to other retailers at below-market rates). This cut profitability, but Stratojac turned a profit every year Winer owned the company; in some of those years a very good profit.

In the early 1980s Winer decided to sell the company and retire. Some investors were interested but required a business manager before they would make an offer. Winer placed an ad in trade journals in early 1983 seeking applicants for the position of "assistant to the president."

Three finalists were selected. Steve Sakin, a man with executive experience in the apparel industry, was eliminated because he demanded too high a salary. An accountant was eliminated because of his lack of broader management experience. Israel "Izzy" Strauss, with a background in the industry but currently selling roll shutters, was hired at a salary "in the high five figures" with a contract of some years duration.

Winer wished to sell the business as *a going concern.* He had been insulted by an offer of $.5 million for only the Stratojac label by Edward Lieser and the Stratojac sales manager Frank Feingold in late 1982. By mid-1983, with Izzy Strauss in place as the man ready to run the business, Winer proceeded to market the company. Mesirow Finance, a Chicago holding company, was interested, but rejected Izzy Strauss as the manager of operations because they considered him incapable of running the company. Winer suggested that Mesirow contact Steve Sakin, the candidate he had rejected a year earlier as too expensive.

NEW OWNERSHIP

On 1 January 1984 Mesirow bought the company and hired Steve Sakin as president. Sakin brought Alan Franklin into the company as executive vice president, secretary, and treasurer. Reportedly Sakin earned $125,000 per year; Franklin $50,000.

Winer was to be paid $3 million for the company. The equipment was on a lease/purchase agreement, whereby the rental payments for eight years would buy the equipment. The building was leased, not bought. Winer was to leave $1 million of the $3 million in the company for a limited time for operating purposes. Of the remaining $2 million, Winer would later forgive $.5 million of it for obsolete inventory, refurbishing returns, and waived final sales value. Thus, he received $1.5 million and was owed the final $1 million at a later date.

Steve Sakin invested $50,000 in the company, as did Alan Franklin. The Corporation for Innovation Development (CID), an Indiana venture capital group created by state government action and which gives a 30 percent state income tax credit to its investors, invested $500,000. Mesirow financed or arranged financing for the rest through other arms of the Mesirow grouping of companies.

The board of directors of the new company consisted of Sakin, Franklin, CID representative Donald Taylor, and Mesirow representatives Lester Morris and James Tyree. The board gave Sakin and Franklin free reign in running the company.

By all accounts Steve Sakin cut an impressive figure.[5] He spoke and acted in a most convincing manner, quickly gaining people's confidence. He also claimed a most impressive background: former medical officer in the U.S. Army, ex-law student, former vice president of several major apparel firms, and presently a senior vice president of a hosiery company. Sakin convinced Winer that he would relocate from New York to northwest Indiana, and that he would continue running the company "as a family." Shortly after the sale, Winer remarked to an employee, "I have definitely found the right man to run the company."

In February 1984 Sakin's wife and Franklin's wife toured the plant and informed workers that they would be relocating from New York to northwest Indiana in the near future. One month later word came back that the two had decided against moving because they did not like the location. Subsequently Sakin commuted by airline from New York and never did move to the region.

Sakin lived an expensive and flashy lifestyle, driving a Jaguar and exhibiting expensive items. Franklin appeared the same to the workforce; it is said he drove a Porsche. All who met Sakin were convinced that all was well with the company.

However, beneath the surface problems existed. Apparently Winer had never checked Sakin's references; the talk of being a past "medical officer" was nothing more than having driven a medical supply truck for the U.S. Army, according to the rumors that eventually followed him. The "law school" credential has never been verified. While he claimed to be employed as an executive vice president at the time he was hired by Mesirow, some of my informants claim he was actually unemployed but using the trappings of an employed business executive.

Sakin fired Izzy Strauss shortly after taking over the company. Strauss promptly sued for breach of contract and won a settlement that is reputed to be in the vicinity of a couple hundred thousand dollars. Sakin also vowed to "wake up this sleepy company" by increasing production a good 10,000 coats beyond the 80,000 produced the previous year. He vastly overproduced coats which he was unable to sell at normal prices. Consequently he was forced to discount so drastically that he was selling below cost. This happened not once, but twice. Winer typically had an inventory of 10,000 coats at year's end; Sakin had 50,000 at the end of his first year.

Sakin also alienated Frank Feingold, the company's New York sales manager. Feeling harassed, Feingold quit the company and went to work for a competitor in late 1984. Since New York represented 60 to 65 percent of the company's market, this was a serious setback. A replacement was found, but damage had been done to the company's marketing operations.

The company claimed a profit of $100,000 on $10.8-million sales for 1984, but this was largely the result of a manipulation of the books. In reality the company had lost $400,000 that was turned into a $100,000 profit by getting Winer to agree to a $500,000 credit on inventory and returns.

Due to the seasonal nature of the business, bank credit is necessary to continue operations. Approximately half of the revenues for the year are collected in November and December. By late fall Winer typically owed millions, but he never had a problem obtaining the needed credit. Sakin was on a much shorter leash: daily reports on all changes in accounts receivable had to be forwarded to the Irving Trust Bank in New York, his prime lender.

In 1985 a $.5 million order for imported leather jackets was obtained from Abraham & Straus in New York. Sakin was providing Irving Trust with invoices that showed Stratojac being paid well over cost. In reality, there was a 50 percent discount being given to Abraham & Straus, which was not reflected on these invoices to the bank. With the 50 percent discount, the jackets were being sold well below cost, losing money on each sale.

Eventually auditors working for Irving Trust discovered the deception that was being practiced on the bank. When Irving Trust attempted to contact Sakin, he was vacationing with his family in Europe and was unreachable. Eventually he was contacted, and in September Irving Trust cut off the credit and called in its debts.

The company now faced bankruptcy; loss of key sales personnel, continuing losses on discounted merchandise, high overhead, and loss of credit spelled doom. From September to November plans were hastily worked out to salvage the company, while all appeared well on the surface.

In November layoffs began. The workers interpreted this as the usual seasonal layoff that always occurred around Thanksgiving. However, the layoffs were slightly earlier than usual, and management was taking unusual care to see that all inventory was thoroughly packed. All workers were laid off.

THE PLANT CLOSING

In early December Local 256 President Marge Luzader was picking up her paycheck at the plant when she encountered Louis Winer shouting and acting very agitated. "Cash your paycheck quick!" He's leaving town!" Winer was yelling. The workers were thus notified that the plant had been closed behind their backs.

Winer had cause to be upset. First, Sakin was forcing him to forgive $.5 million of the final $1 million owed from the sale; if Winer refused, Sakin threatened bankruptcy and *no* repayment. Second, Winer was left with a building and a broken lease. Third, Sakin had closed down his "family" firm. A close acquaintance told the media, "He's very upset about the whole thing. He spent his life building the firm. It's just like a family."[6] Out of anger Winer forced Sakin out by the end of December, faster than Sakin had planned to vacate.

On 18 December employees were officially informed of the closing. Sakin stated that he was moving operations to a New York plant because Indiana lacked the necessary aid and programs to keep businesses open, unlike New York.[7]

Indiana had actually subsidized Sakin's initial purchase of the company through its 30 percent tax credit to the investors who invested

$500,000 in the company through the Corporation for Innovation Development (CID). CID's sole purpose was to subsidize venture capital for investments in businesses operating *in Indiana*. Stratojac's abandonment of the state was embarrassing CID. CID Vice President Don Taylor expressed unhappiness:

"We're not real happy about it," he said. "But the business reasons to move were very compelling."[8]

Taylor later told the media that the CID investment had been a mistake:

"Our crystal ball was not perfect," said CID Director Donald Taylor. "We would never had made the investment if we thought they would leave the state. . . ."
"The alternative was that if they didn't improve their business they probably wouldn't have a business," Taylor said. "Is it better for a company to leave and stay in business and our investment has a chance to be returned, or to have them stay and the company would have shut down and we would lose everything?
"We intended that the investments would be in companies that would stay in Indiana."[9]

THE NEW LOCATION

Management and marketing problems, not tax and other state incentives, caused Stratojac's problems. However, public incentives were financing the move to New York. The New York state Urban Development Corporation (UDC) agreed in late January to buy the Casualcraft (Mohawk Sportswear) facility in Amsterdam, New York, for $1.575 million, pending investigation and approval of the project. The UDC would then rent the plant to Stratojac at a rental fee that would pay off the purchase price at 5 percent interest in twenty years, when ownership would transfer to Stratojac. An additional $400,000 for leased equipment brought UDC's total investment to $1.975 million. Sakin also requested a $300,000 loan from Amsterdam Industrial Development Agency (AIDA), a city entity.[10]

Sakin further requested a descending property tax abatement on annual taxes of $44,000 over ten years. Stratojac would pay only half of normal taxes the first year, 55 percent the second year, 60 percent the third year, and so on, until 100 percent payment was reached in the tenth year.[11] The city council promptly granted this abatement amid positive press statements from city aldermen about the jobs boon to the city and the need to compete.[12] Amsterdam community organization We the People spoke out against the abatement to no avail.

But the city agency AIDA was having second thoughts. Tough questions about Sakin's past behavior and intentions arose. At a January 1986 public hearing on the UDC $1.975 million loan, Amalgamated Clothing and Textile Workers Union (ACTWU) representative William Towne related Sakin's use of $.5 million of Indiana state-subsidized money to help purchase Stratojac, only to abandon the state two years later. Towne asked for guarantees that Sakin would not also abandon New York after receiving the public subsidies. He was told that there were "no guarantees."[13]

Sakin defended himself by appealing to American patriotism and scapegoating the union workers back in Hammond. He labeled his firm a "domestic manufacturer fighting an import surge," and noted that they "have enough guts to stay in this country and produce in this country." He said another reason for leaving Indiana was "a high rate of absenteeism among union workers there."[14] No Indiana source validates his absenteeism claims.[15]

AIDA backed away from the $300,000 loan. Publicly they claimed they did not have the money; privately, a local newspaper reporter told Indiana contacts that the real reason was suspicion of Sakin's past behavior and present intent.[16]

Loss of the AIDA loan was a serious blow, because the state UDC normally requires local city government aid as a condition for its assistance. To fulfill the "local participation" requirement, UDC asked the city to apply for money from the federal Housing and Urban Development (HUD) agency under the Small Cities Grant Program. The Amsterdam Urban Renewal Agency applied for and received $300,000, which was subsequently loaned to Stratojac in 1987 to pay for inventory and training costs.[17]

Sakin painted a glowing picture of the firm's operations and its future. Advantages such as more space, state-of-the-art equipment, combined Casualcraft and Stratojac markets, and a new vice president for finance meant projected sales of $17 million for 1986 and $25 million for 1990. (Stratojac had approximately $11 million in sales in 1985; Casualcraft approximately $7 million).[18]

Despite favorable press accounts, questions continued to surface. In late February the Amsterdam daily newspaper carried a story about Sakin's closing of the Hammond plant with no notice and his use of Indiana CID money ostensibly to retain employment but actually to abandon the state. Calumet Project Director Lynn Feekin was quoted. Her conclusion:

> The more I uncover, the more I think this looks like a smelly oper-
> ation. . . . It would be good if Amsterdam took a second look at this. . . .
> I think it's absolutely unethical.[19]

Sakin responded that the union in Hammond was "very satisfied" by
how the plant was closed, claiming that virtually all of the displaced
workers had already found new jobs.[20] The next day he called Feekin and
threatened to sue her for libel.[21]

Despite questions, on 30 April the New York UDC finalized the
$1.975 million-assistance package. UDC Chairman Vincent Tese said:

> I'm proud to say we've moved very fast on this project. Five months
> after our initial approval, the company is up and running in its new
> home and providing 125 jobs.[22]

Employment estimates were exaggerated. Two weeks earlier Sakin had told
the press that employment was now two hundred, up from one hundred.[23]
Managers who had moved with the plant to Amsterdam told Indiana
contacts that only forty were employed.

In October 1986 Steve Sakin resigned as president of Stratojac,
which was subsequently run by an executive committee of four.[24] Press
accounts do not state the reason, but former company managers say he
was forced out by his major stockholder, Mesirow Finance, disgusted with
his mismanagement.

ATTEMPT TO REOPEN AT HAMMOND

The former workers in Hammond had not accepted the closing passive-
ly. United Garment Workers Local 256 officials contacted the Calumet Project to jointly plan ways to reopen the plant.

Contacts were made with Hammond economic development officials, former management personnel, the union regional representative, and
a New York City business analyst who specialized in employee-buyout feasibility issues. Two possible alternatives were explored: finding a buyer or
employee ownership.

Ex-management personnel had a mixed prognosis for the Hammond
plant.[25] On the positive side, many managers would return to the Hammond plant if it reopened. The cutting room and sewing room foremen,
the two key sales managers in Chicago, the western region salesman, the

vice president and coordinator of facility operations, and possibly the controller were interested.

The plant's reputation for quality meant buyers would likely be receptive despite loss of the trademark. Furthermore, the trademark could be obtained if Sakin failed in Amsterdam, as all were certain he would.

Other positive trends were a slight decline of imports in the quality woolen men's overcoat market niche. Although imports were flooding the apparel industry market in general, they were not affecting the high quality end as much because fashion turn-around time, quality control, and up-front payment at government warehouses made imports less attractive.

Negatives were also pervasive: the building was old and most ex-managers favored a move to a nearby plant. Much equipment was also old; Sakin had taken the computer to Amsterdam; the phone system needed to be completely replaced (at $15,000); the roof needed repair (costing $150,000); the air conditioning system needed either repair or replacement.

Competent management was also needed. Management personnel who had moved to Amsterdam recommended Bob Cornell, manager at the Amsterdam site, for plant manager if he was interested. Many believed that the Hammond operation had been top-heavy with nonproductive management, including a six-figure vice president living in Florida and a financial advisor few ever saw. One ex-management official estimated that a reopened plant could cut $400,000 a year from excess managerial payroll costs at the plant.

Even if these claims and estimates are exaggerated, excess and incompetent management had been a problem, which a reopened plant would have to overcome, along with "start-up" cost, marketing, and name recognition problems. Louis Winer, now eighty-five, was refusing to lease the plant or to meet with or to help those attempting to reopen the plant because he felt he had been "burned" in his previous deal with Sakin. The national United Garment Workers Union felt that employee ownership was guaranteed to fail, and they did not know of any other potential buyers.[26]

Obtaining the necessary working capital was a further enormous obstacle. Due to the seasonal nature of the business, debts could reach $5-6 million before payments came in. Either the new owner would have to have "deep pockets" or a large credit line — a difficult prospect.

In early March the union's executive board met with staff from the Calumet Project and decided to proceed cautiously despite the obstacles. A survey determined how many ex-workers had found employment. A 16 March general membership meeting was attended by 140 of the 180 in the former bargaining unit.

Survey results revealed that only ten of the 135 contacted had found reemployment, more than three months after the shutdown. A Calumet Project analysis showed that close to $3 million had been lost in buying power due to the shutdown; government costs would rise almost $2 million because of additional unemployment compensation, township relief, and food stamp outlays.[27]

Ex-employees elected representatives to a steering committee composed of former management, production, shipping, and clerical employees. The committee was to examine the potential viability of an employee-owned garment operation at the Hammond site. A "prefeasibility" study would be commissioned if needed. Local union president Marion Lawrence told the press, "Although the effort appears to be a long shot, there are enough possibilities here to make it important to pursue the effort further."[28]

In late March and early April efforts were made to develop a rudimentary business plan. The Calumet Project contacted the Industrial Cooperative Association (ICA) in Massachusetts for assistance. ICA is one of the premier employee ownership research and consulting firms in the country. ICA brought in New York-based business analyst Roland Cline.

In early April it became apparent that the "long shot" of employee ownership was out of the question. Lack of a capable manager, the near impossibility of raising the necessary working capital, loss of the label, uncertainty about marketing and a sales force, and the like presented too many obstacles. On 3 April Cline recommended abandonment of the employees ownership idea; his recommendation was accepted.

The union local then tried to pressure the city to find a suitable buyer. On 18 April Local 256 President Marion Lawrence wrote Hammond Mayor Thomas McDermott a letter requesting aid.

On 1 May and 15 May local union leaders, Calumet Project staffers and Hammond clergy met with Mayor McDermott and Hammond Economic Development Director Ed Krusa. McDermott expressed interest, and convinced the union leadership that employee ownership may yet be feasible.[29] However, nothing came of it. Potentially interested buyers who wanted to produce tote bags and bowling shirts briefly surfaced, but neither remained interested for long.

In June the union turned to pressuring the mayor to assist in reemployment efforts. Responding to pressure, the mayor claimed to put all displaced workers in the city's job bank computer file.[30] Subsequently, ex-union leaders were not aware of anybody who obtained a job through this computerized service.[31]

Throughout July the city kept promising elusive "leads" that may provide funding, but nothing materialized. On 5 August the union exec-

utive board met and disbanded the union. A letter informed all members
of this decision and of trade adjustment assistance benefits information.[32]

The union local wrote a letter to Calumet Project staffers Tom DuBois
and Lynn Feekin thanking them for the assistance in the joint effort. In a
surprise move they also presented Calumet Project Director Lynn Feekin
a check for $500, saying "we know it's not much but it's all we have."[33]

In December the U.S. Department of Labor ruled that the displaced
Stratojac workers were eligible for trade adjustment assistance under the
1974 law. Displaced workers were now entitled to extended benefits and
some retraining money.

END OF STRATOJAC IN AMSTERDAM, NEW YORK

Stratojac continued to experience difficulties. In November 1988 the regional press reported that it was $7 million in debt. It was six months
behind in its payments on the $300,000 1987 loan from the Amsterdam
Urban Renewal Agency. The state UDC also was not receiving timely
payments on the $1.97 million they were owed.

James Tyree, president of Mesirow Financial Holdings, which was
the major creditor and investor in the company, told the press that his company had sunk over $5 million into Stratojac. In addition to the initial $2
million to help Sakin take over, Mesirow had put $1 million into the
move to Amsterdam and another $2 million into day-to-day operations.
Without mentioning Sakin, Tyree blamed previous mismanagement:

> "It's a touchy subject, because the problem was the previous man-
> agement," Tyree explained. That, combined with a two-year slump in the
> apparel industry, is what he said has knocked Stratojac into a financial
> tailspin.[34]

Despite the problems, Tyree believed that the underlying company could
be viable in the long run:

> Despite the grim industry outlook, though, Tyree said he is con-
> vinced Stratojac can turn a profit if given the time. He said the private
> company has had sales in the $12 million to $15 million range in years
> past, and is confident it can do the same this year.[35]

In December 1988, Fred Slamin, associated with a Chicago crisis
management firm, was brought in as Stratojac president. Shortly thereafter

creditors pulled the plug on the company. In mid-March 1989 three creditors which were owed slightly over $1 million filed a chapter 7 involuntary liquidation petition.[36]

The company quickly closed down manufacturing operations. In late April Stratojac petitioned the bankruptcy court to switch from chapter 7 liquidation status to chapter 11 bankruptcy status, which would allow the company to try to reorganize.[37] In May this request was granted.[38] But the company was unable to attract the financing necessary to reorganization.

In June, Alliance Importing of New York City offered $150,000 for the Stratojac and Casualcraft labels.[39] Competition forced Alliance to raise its bid to $225,000, which secured the trademarks on 6 July 1989.[40] Alliance Importing President Norman Weisfeld made it clear that he was only buying the trademark because of a long history and reputation, not recent events:

> "We didn't buy (the names) for anything (Stratojac) has done recently," Alliance Importing's Weisfeld said. "We're buying it for the goodwill."
>
> He said the Stratojac name goes back ninety-five years and is known in the industry, as is Casualcraft. . . . His hope is that the names themselves will be enough to resurrect the consumer confidence that they once enjoyed.[41]

In late 1982 Louis Winer had been insulted by a $.5 million offer for the Stratojac trademark. By mid-1989, the *combined* trademarks of Stratojac and Casualcraft could not command one-half that.

In October Stratojac machinery was auctioned, bringing in $113,800.[42] The New York State UDC claimed the proceeds, but Stratojac disputed this by claiming that UDC's purchase and leasing of the plant had really only been a cover for UDC financing for Stratojac, which actually owned the equipment and was entitled to the proceeds.[43] The dispute would be settled in the courts.

EVALUATION AND CONCLUSIONS

This case raises issues that fall into three categories: (1) reasons for closure; (2) public policy; and (3) effectiveness of the intervention measures. Each will be considered separately.

Table 4.1. Percentage changes in domestic wool coat production,
1981 to 1989*

1982	1983	1984	1985	1986	1987	1988	1989
+12	-4	-10	+4	-12	-23	-39	-41

*In 1981, 326,000 dozen wool coats were produced domestically; percentage
figures indicate the change from this base.

Source: Author's computations, derived from figures supplied by the Office of Textiles and Apparel,
U.S. Department of Commerce.

Reasons for the Closure

Was the plant closing inevitable, or was it due to mismanagement? Both
cases can be argued, but mismanagement deserves most of the blame. By
all accounts the plant was badly (and perhaps unethically) managed after
new owners took over.

While mismanagement is undisputable, it might still be argued that this
was ultimately irrelevant to the closing of the Hammond and Amsterdam plants. In the 1980s imports captured ever-increasing shares of the
U.S. apparel industry market. Wasn't it perhaps inevitable that the plant
would close, given the intense competition from foreign producers?

According to the U.S. Department of Commerce Office of Textiles and
Apparel,[44] domestic wool coat production in the 1980s held relatively
steady until 1985, but from 1986 on it declined along with a general
slump in the market. Using 1981 as a base year, 1982–85 production
fluctuated between +12 percent and -10 percent above or below 1981
figures. However, 1986–89 shows a steady decline: from -12 percent to
-41 percent compared to 1981 levels. Figures are given in table 4.1.

Imports also took an ever larger share of the market from 1981
through 1986. Domestic production dropped from 92 percent to 61 percent of the total market. Table 4.2 gives the domestic production market
share of the total U.S. market for 1981 through 1989.

Thus the overall market situation for domestic manufacturers was
poor in the mid- and late 1980s. Perhaps the decline was less of a problem for Stratojac's high-end, high-priced market niche because import
penetration was lower. However, England supplied the largest number
of imported wool coats; Italy the fourth most, and Canada the sixth most.
All supplied high-quality products.

Table 4.2. Percentage of the total U.S. market for wool overcoats supplied by domestic producers, 1981–1989

1981	1982	1983	1984	1985	1986	1987	1988	1989
92	91	84	71	67	61	61	61	64

Source: Author's computations from figures supplied by the Office of Textiles and Apparel, U.S. Department of Commerce.

Therefore the Stratojac Corporation faced a stagnant and then declining market in the 1980s. Would it have survived under competent management? Probably, but there was a continuing shakeout in the industry that had been occurring for some time. Production employment in the Men/Boys' Suits/Coats industry (SIC code 2311) had declined at an annual rate of -5 percent from 1972 to 1986; 1981–86 figures show an identical -5 percent annual change.[45]

Firms with a greater disadvantage in name recognition, efficiency, cost structure, marketing, and so on, were eliminated in the competitive struggle. Stratojac had both advantages and disadvantages in this struggle. On the plus side, it had very positive name recognition among retailers and consumers because of its long history and consistent record of high quality. Prior to the loss of Frank Feingold as sales manager, the company also had an excellent sales and marketing apparatus. The company in Hammond had been less favorably situated in terms of cost structure: expensive and unproductive excess management, somewhat dated equipment, a relatively costly-to-maintain building, and possibly inefficiencies in the production process were disadvantages.

The company earned a profit every year Louis Winer owned it, and competent management may have been able to trim management overhead, upgrade the building or move to a more modern site, upgrade equipment, or possibly adjust piecework incentive rates and/or the work process, and find a stable financial base to withstand possible losses for 2–3 years if all of the other adjustments failed to achieve immediate results.

Even with the best of management, employment at a Hammond Stratojac facility may well have declined in the late 1980s. Yet there is no question that the workforce would have fared better under an ethical and competent management. Under the very worst of circumstances a plant closing would have been carried out more humanely and at a much later date. Under the best of circumstances, the plant would have maintained or even augmented market share, requiring few or no sacrifices from the workforce. More likely than either of the above, sacrifices and a diminished but viable future would have faced the workforce.

Public Policy Issues

This case is one more instance of public subsidies extended to a company with little or no requirement for accountability in return. The Indiana legislation creating the Corporation for Innovation Development did not require that firms receiving CID investment remain in the state. Thus, the supposed reason for taxpayer subsidy — the creation or retention of jobs in the state — is not required. Programs like this easily turn into nothing more than a tax shelter for wealthy investors and a cheap pool of capital for companies to use as they wish. In this instance Indiana taxpayers helped subsidize a runaway plant to New York, the exact opposite of the intended consequence.

In New York, the Urban Development Corporation likewise demanded no "guarantees" in exchange for its almost $2 million in subsidies. The Amsterdam city council also granted tax abatements with no strings attached. The local Urban Renewal Agency extended a $300,000 loan for operating expenses. Following customary practice in economic development circles, public officials saw their role as extending maximum aid with minimum intrusion into the private domain of the corporation. Any demand for guarantees or close questions regarding financial position or past performance may cause a "chilling" of the warm "business climate" that Amsterdam hoped to create for incoming businesses.

Such a conventional "business climate" approach to economic development is risky. The link between the means — public subsidy—and the desired end — creation and/or retention of stable well paying jobs — is by no means assured.

Successorship and the public interest in good management are also issues. This privately held company lacked a viable successor to an aging owner. Entering his eighties, Louis Winer had no family member to run his "family" business, and he was unable to find an outside person to run the business despite repeated and expensive attempts to do so.

This inability to find managerial expertise to run the company was apparently not unique to Winer. James Tyree of Mesirow Finance was later unable to find suitable management for the firm in Amsterdam. One of the reasons employee ownership was untenable was that the necessary top management was missing. In North Carolina, the Center for Community Self-Help (CCSH) has found the same problem in its work on successorship problems: lack of competent management often is a more significant hurdle to succession than is lack of capital.[46]

If public policy is to address successorship problems for family firms, the initiatives will have to go well beyond identification of aging owners and arranging for buyers and/or financing. At least that is the implication of this case, supplemented by additional evidence. Identification or development of a pool of potential managers may be necessary to successful transition.

To the extent this case can be generalized, public policy also needs to address managerial competence issues if effective plant closing intervention measures are to be formulated. Mild measures, such as development of public technical assistance measures or governmental identification of pools of managerial talent, may be useful. However, in most cases, the current management is unlikely to seek out or accept technical assistance from public sector interveners when mismanagement is destroying the company. And publicly identified pools of managerial talent are likely to be transient, difficult to create, and largely unused by a private sector that resents "government intrusion."

Stronger public intervention into mismanagement situations could include governmental requirements of managerial changes as a condition of public assistance, threat and use of "eminent domain" (forced sale of the facility to government "for the public good") where this is necessary to preserve the jobs, and the like. Such actions are generally considered unthinkable by economic development and government officials because they violate the dependent "business climate" relationship between government and business they believe proper and inevitable. Until this changes, public policy may be unable to address mismanagement as an issue.

Effectiveness of the Intervention Measures

Intervention measures were ineffective: jobs were not saved and a labor-community coalition of any size was not forged. From a broader perspective important issues were publicly raised and public awareness of corporate public subsidy abuse grew, but immediate objectives were not attained.

The reasons are multiple. The Calumet Project/union definition of the problem was persuasive, and causal responsibility lay with mismanagement, but all circumstances made a realistic remedial action plan impossible. The company had already left and was immune to local influence. The most valuable assets — the trademark, the computer, much of the sales force, and the "deep pockets" financier (Mesirow Finance) — had been stripped from the plant. Remaining assets — a workforce, antiquated equipment, outmoded building, some supervisors — were inadequate for an employee-owned start-up or for an attractive sales candidate.

Consequently an attractive plan of action never materialized. Lacking a realistic plan, no major alliances were attempted and no major mobilizations outside the union's ranks were accomplished. Local political figures, therefore, felt minimal pressure and produced nothing beyond token gestures.

An overwhelmingly female workforce with eleven years average seniority and forty-seven years average age, the workers were particularly vulnerable and powerless. Many could not speak English or spoke English poorly; virtually all were trapped in the segment of the labor market characterized by few skills, low wages, and economic insecurity. Reemployment prospects were difficult.

The problems in this case were closely interconnected. Management talent was scarce, probably because a declining industry like this is unable to attract the brightest fresh talent available. Capital also becomes scarce when the market drops and management competence declines. Technological innovation necessary to competitiveness either fails to happen or is confined to the largest domestic and foreign competitors, further driving out mid-sized manufacturers such as Stratojac. The workers who end up in declining low-wage industries like the apparel industry are virtually always trapped there by labor market dynamics that make them especially vulnerable to the negative consequences of job loss. Thus a vicious circle of market decline, managerial quality decline, inadequate technological innovation, undercapitalization, and workforce vulnerability combine to continually deteriorate the job security, stability, and living standards of the industry's workforce. And case-by-case interventions in such an industry are virtually certain to fail.

STRUGGLE TO REOPEN THE
HAMMOND LTV STEEL BAR MILL

This case study concerns the closing of a steel bar mill in Hammond, Indiana, in 1986 and a subsequent struggle to reopen the plant. The case contains some early warning signs that were not recognized by the local union. A history of contentious labor relations may have been a factor in the company's choice to close this mill rather than a neighboring one in Gary.

LTV's corporate structure and strategy were central to the closing. Depressed economic conditions in the product market provide a backdrop but cannot explain the shutdown of this efficient mill.

Local government's role and battles over problem definition are central to this case. Extraordinarily adept alliance formation and mobilization of forces allowed the Calumet Project and the union workers to wage a two-year battle that won the public relations contest but failed to reopen the mill in the short run.

This plant closing campaign succeeded in forcing local government officials to militantly confront the company, partially breaking the usual "business climate" taboo. The dynamics of effective leadership, alliance formation, and mobilization that allowed this to happen are analyzed in the following pages.

The following section details the historical background to the case, followed by a section on the campaign to reopen the facility. The concluding section analyzes the case in terms of the power dynamics at play.

THE BACKGROUND

In the 1940s a newly opened steel facility in Hammond, Indiana was used by two companies.[1] Monarch Steel produced steel coils there and Holiday Steel used it as a service center. In 1956 Jones & Laughlin (J&L) Steel Company bought the plant; in 1965–66 they expanded it.

In the mid-1970s the conglomerate corporation LTV purchased J&L. In northwest Indiana, this meant that LTV owned J&L's flagship basic steel plant on the Lake Michigan Indiana Harbor as well as the smaller Hammond bar mill.

In 1984 LTV merged with Republic Steel, adding yet another bar mill in Gary, Indiana, to its steel facilities in the region. After the merger, LTV owned fourteen bar-making facilities (two hot-rolled plus twelve cold-drawn mills), giving it considerable overcapacity in a chronically stagnant market. The company quickly closed a number of its bar mills but spared both the Hammond and Gary mills. By 1986, only two hot-rolled and six cold-drawn facilities remained.

The Gary mill was older and slightly less productive, but it had a broader product range. In 1984–85 the Gary mill was idled for seven months (while the Hammond mill was running) as the company sought to force major wage cuts and working conditions concessions on the union. The Gary local then agreed to large-scale concessions and the plant was reopened. Working in the more modern and productive mill, the Hammond workers had rejected concessions and maintained a contract comparable to those in the large integrated basic steel mills.

The two plants had negotiated a joint contract in the past, so the Hammond local and the national union considered Gary's separate concessionary contract unenforceable and illegitimate. The two locals split: the Hammond local (USWA Local 6518) accused the Gary local (USWA Local 3069) of "selling out" while the Gary local believed their Hammond counterparts were unconcerned about saving Gary jobs.

The company tried to intimidate the Hammond local into accepting the Gary concessionary package. At captive audience meetings on company time, workers were threatened with closure if they did not cave in. Managers claimed that a shutdown was happening, but another vote to accept concessions might avert it.

Under tremendous pressure, the workers voted to accept the concessions. The district director of the United Steelworkers declared the second vote invalid because there were no contract provisions to re-conduct votes, especially by only a portion (the Hammond portion) of the bargaining unit workforce. A negotiated compromise allowed the Gary local to reopen under the concessionary agreement while the Hammond plant would operate under the old, nonconcessionary agreement. Shortly thereafter, a joint contract was negotiated for both plants with identical contract language. By mid-1986 both plants were operating under the same conditions, but the company was displeased with the Hammond local (USWA 6518) for resisting concessions.

In the summer of 1986 the Hammond plant employed approximately 150 workers. Their wages averaged $10.21 per hour; 94 percent had 10 years or more seniority; 56 percent lived in Hammond with the rest coming from nearby communities. In 1980–81 the plant had employed 285 peo-

Table 5.1. Man-hours per ton of product, LTV cold-drawn bar mills, 1986.

	January	February	March	April	May	June	6-month average
Beaver Falls, Pa.	3.98	4.23	4.76	4.66	5.50	5.09	4.70
Gary, Ind.	3.86	3.83	3.94	3.67	4.20	4.90	4.07
Hammond, Ind.	3.35	4.20	3.79	3.48	2.98	4.50	3.72
Mahoning, Pa.	3.57	4.39	4.58	4.61	4.45	4.56	4.36
Massillon, Ohio	7.17	6.63	6.63	7.57	7.82	6.54	7.06
Willimantic, Conn.[1]	2.38	2.37	2.09	2.95	3.06	2.93	2.63

[1] Primarily a warehousing operation.

Source: Internal LTV company data given to the United Steelworkers of America.

ple; in the 1970s employment had peaked at 310. In April 1986 the company considered hiring additional workers because the plant was running at full capacity.

But LTV declared Chapter 11 bankruptcy in July 1986. The Hammond bar mill was shut down and put on "indefinite idle," meaning there was no final decision that the closing was permanent. Under the union contract LTV was not liable for severance and pension obligations until the earlier of two years or permanent closure.

Union representatives considered the idling a ploy to force the militant local to accept concessions, much as the Gary workers had been frightened into concession two years previously. By September, twelve workers remained in the plant.

Union confidence came from the plant's relatively modern equipment and the skills of the workforce. Modern draw benches had been added to the plant in 1965–66, particularly the #3 draw bench that accounted for over half of the plant's output. The union claimed this equipment was the best in the nation. Figures for the entire industry are not available but data the union obtained from the company substantiates this claim for the company's six facilities. Except for a facility used mostly for warehousing, the Hammond plant was most productive. Figures on man-hours per ton of product for LTV's six cold-drawn bar mills in the first half of 1986 are given in table 5.1.

These figures should be interpreted with caution because the plant variations in product mix are ignored. Some product lines are more labor intensive by their very nature, making plants that produce them seem less efficient. For example, the Massillon, Ohio, plant may be such a plant, accounting for its high numbers.

Nevertheless, the Hammond plant appears more productive than its counterparts. Compared to Hammond, the Gary plant took 9 percent more labor time to produce a ton; Mahoning, 17 percent more; Beaver Falls, 26 percent more; and Massillon, 90 percent more.

The Hammond plant was not an inefficient operation, but the industry market situation was not favorable. Imports had climbed from 9.2 percent of market share in 1980 to 25.1 percent in 1985.[2] In 1986 imports declined both absolutely and percentage wise but not by that much. Also, the total market was stagnant throughout the 1980s; 1984 shipments were 6 percent below 1980 shipments and 1985 shipments were down an additional 15 percent. In 1986 shipments increased but not enough to return to 1980 levels.

Industry overcapacity was shown by an estimated capacity utilization of about 50 percent. LTV, in particular, needed to consolidate operations. The merger with Republic and the bankruptcy declaration added further pressure to scale back.

Why did LTV close the Hammond plant rather than another one? For geographic dispersal reasons they may have determined that either the Gary or Hammond plant would be closed. The Hammond plant was more productive, but the Gary plant had a broader product range and had three heat-treat furnaces compared to Hammond's one. USWA Local 6518 leadership was convinced that the real reason was the company's desire to "get" the union local for its past stance against concessions. It is impossible to verify or refute this belief.

THE CAMPAIGN TO REOPEN THE PLANT

On 3 November the company announced that the idling would be a permanent closure. During November and December local union members and officers met with staff persons from the Calumet Project to decide what to do. As a result USWA Local 6518 formed the Alternative Ownership Committee (AOC) in January to push for a reopened facility under different ownership.

A preliminary goal was to obtain a "quick look" feasibility study on the viability of a reopened plant. On 20 February 1987 Local 6518 President Chester Smithers wrote the United Steelworkers District 31 Director Jack Parton requesting the district's support "both organizationally and financially" for a feasibility study.[3] The local requested that Locker and

Associates, a union-friendly consulting firm specializing in steel, be brought in for a "quick look."

Smithers also filed a grievance alleging that LTV had broken a verbal commitment during negotiations to keep the plant open. As a settlement the union requested that management retain present equipment and either reopen the plant or sell it. The grievance was summarily denied; there were no grounds for it under the union contract, which contained a "management rights" clause ceding to management the right to make all decisions concerning investment, production, and the like.

However, the request for a feasibility study was acted upon promptly. Steelworkers District 31 hired Locker and Associates to provide a preliminary analysis, which began in early March.

Meanwhile other issues needed attention if the plant was to be saved. First, the company intended to move the #3 draw bench to its Massillon, Ohio, facility. This would mean the Hammond site would lose over 50 percent of its capacity and its most prized piece of equipment. The local requested the national union's legal department to file in bankruptcy court to get the creditors to prevent LTV from moving the equipment.[4] The basis for the lawsuit would be that LTV was wasting resources and costing them money by the move. The union's legal department replied that this was hopeless: such "ordinary business" was not legally subject to creditor approval; furthermore, the creditors were unlikely to find the #3 draw bench of more value in a closed facility than in a functioning facility at Massillon.[5]

Second, the political community was mobilized to support the effort to preserve jobs. Hammond mayor Thomas McDermott accepted an invitation to attend the March union meeting, where he was pressured into a commitment to contact LTV to learn their plans for the plant. He also agreed to see if the city could join the bankruptcy court legal case and to look for well-paying jobs for displaced workers. A relatively conservative Republican, McDermott was not inclined toward such an activist role, but he was pushed into it by the many displaced workers who lived in Hammond. The only immediate result was a letter from McDermott to LTV President David Hoag asking for the price and sale conditions for the building. His letter did not ask about LTV's intentions or press LTV to sell the facility intact.[6]

Local Democratic Congressman Peter Visclosky, on a first-name basis with LTV President Hoag due to his active role in the Congressional Steel Caucus, provided more effective political intervention. On 29 April he called Hoag, requesting that LTV either resume production in Hammond or sell to someone who would. A letter the next day pressed the central issue:

I cannot overemphasize the importance I attach to getting this facility back into production and in the employment of as many severed LTV workers as possible. Should LTV decide not to re-open the plant, I urge you to properly maintain all important equipment, while aggressively marketing the facility to potential buyers interested in similar manufacturing.

I am delighted from your comments that you "understand the employment component" in this situation and "want to cooperate" in investigating every option for the plant.

Dave, I intend to follow these upcoming discussions closely. I remain ready to help in any appropriate manner to get the Hammond facility back into production.[7]

Unlike McDermott's letter, this was real pressure on the corporation. Visclosky also wrote to displaced workers informing them of the efforts to reopen the plant.

In April, the AOC surveyed former workers to determine their employment status and attitudes. Results showed that over two thirds were still unemployed; over half with new jobs had lost substantial wages; and over 92 percent would return if the facility were reopened.[8] The need for action was clear.

On 8 May Locker and Associates released their much anticipated results.[9] Based on discussions with senior LTV executives, Locker and Associates found that:

1. LTV planned to remain in the bar business but to trim its hot-rolled capacity to one plant (Canton, Ohio) and its cold-rolled to three (Massillon, Ohio; Beaver Falls, Pennsylvania; and Gary). The Massillon plant would be the main cold-rolled facility because it is close to Canton.

2. LTV intended to move the #3 draw bench to Massillon. Because the #3 draw bench was one of the most versatile and efficient in the industry, this would greatly improve the company's main cold-drawn facility. This move was already budgeted and would not require creditor approval.

3. LTV planned to keep the Gary plant open; this was the main way it would maintain a presence in the Chicago area.

4. LTV did not want to sell the Hammond plant, *with or without the #3 draw bench,* because it feared that competition from Hammond under new ownership would cut into Gary (and perhaps Massillon) markets. The Gary plant may be jeopardized by a reopened Hammond plant.

Given these facts, Locker and Associates analyst John Lichtenstein was pessimistic about reopening the Hammond mill. *With the #3 draw bench,* the mill would be quite viable; without it, much less so. And even without it, LTV was unwilling to sell. Therefore, the chances for reopening were extremely slim.

The leadership of the union local's Alternative Ownership Committee (AOC) rejected such pessimism. The AOC operated with the official blessings of the local's executive board, but its leadership was different. Jerry Brown, a seventeen-year veteran of the mill who had served on the local's negotiating committee for the last two contracts, led the AOC. In addition to a long history in the plant, Brown had wider contacts. He had attended classes in the Labor Studies program at a nearby university, and he had previous contact with the Calumet Project.

Brown refused to accept LTV's goals as unalterable; energetic leadership and a close partnership with the Calumet Project helped him convince much of the local's membership to participate in a struggle to reopen the plant despite LTV's determination to keep it closed. Throughout the two-year campaign to reopen the plant, consistent turnouts of 40–100 people at union meetings called by the AOC testified to the strength of that vision within the membership. Many workers were active in the campaign.

In May 1987 the task looked hopeless: a small union local of under 150 members aiming to reverse the plans of a conglomerate company. Nevertheless, the AOC and the Calumet Project proceeded by developing a three-pronged strategy. First, LTV had to be persuaded or forced to not move equipment from the facility. Second, a suitable owner had to be found. Third, LTV must be convinced or pressured to sell the plant.

Finding a Buyer

Progress was fastest on the second goal, finding a suitable buyer. A couple of long shots were complemented by solid interest from an established company. One long shot was Woodruff Imberman, claiming to represent a group of Chicago investors interested in the mill. Imberman, who headed the Chicago-based management consultant firm of Imberman and De-Forest, wrote USWA District 31 Director Jack Parton in August 1986 indicating that he had written LTV about an interest in buying the Hammond plant.[10] LTV replied by phone that the plant was not for sale; Imberman wanted Director Parton to use his "clout" to convince LTV to sell.

On 6 July 1987 Imberman confirmed his interest by telephone and letter to Lynn Feekin of the Calumet Project.[11] On 3 September AOC and Calumet Project personnel, accompanied by a business analyst, met with

Imberman. Imberman was positive in attitude, grandiose in rhetoric about employee involvement and corporate commitment to employee welfare, and vague and secretive about actual investors or acquisition conditions and plans.

Imberman was an unlikely and unreliable ally for a union-based effort. He was notorious within the labor movement as a "union buster" who conducted management seminars on how to remain union-free. The AFL-CIO included him on their national list of notable "union busters." "Imberman and DeForest" was a front for a one-person operation: "DeForest" was fictitious and had never existed. Imberman wrote numerous antiunion articles for industry and management publications under pseudonyms like "Mathew Goodfellow." He never produced either a serious offer or genuine investors with an interest.

A second long shot was employee ownership. On 14 July the AOC wrote LTV that they were interested in considering an Employee Stock Ownership Plan (ESOP).[12] The AOC was mostly interested in using this option to obtain financial information from LTV on the plant. With this information, they hoped to broker a deal involving minority employee ownership together with substantial investment from whatever private party they could find. LTV said they were willing to meet, but they never followed through. An initial verbal agreement to provide financial data was quickly withdrawn.[13] Throughout the summer and early fall, LTV's position was that (1) they would not deal through a broker, only with principals; and (2) AOC was not a serious bidder.[14]

A third potential buyer was both serious and credible. A salaried individual in the front office slipped the name of an interested Canadian steel firm to the AOC.[15] Union Drawn Steel, Canada's largest cold-drawn finisher, was interested in entering the Chicago area–U.S. market. On 30 July they wrote to the Calumet Project expressing interest in the plant, pledging to give preference in hiring to former employees, agreeing to recognize the United Steelworkers, and indicating a willingness to allow partial employee ownership as long as majority ownership remained with the company.[16] As of the summer of 1987, it looked like the AOC and the Calumet Project had found the perfect buyer.

Persuading LTV to Sell

The two remaining goals were convincing LTV to sell and convincing them not to move out equipment. To meet the main objection to selling, the Calumet Project developed a possible way to avoid direct competition with the LTV Gary mill. Working with a retired local steel executive who claimed to have markets in China, they hoped to assure LTV there was no competitive threat, so they should sell. Unfortunately, this executive never produced anything concrete. Further efforts at persuasion would be needed.

Pressuring LTV to Not Move Equipment

The planned removal of the #3 draw bench would also seriously detract from the viability or value of the mill. On 16 June the local requested from the Steelworkers District Director that the union's legal department prepare to file a court injunction preventing removal of equipment pending settlement of a filed grievance.[17] As before, the union's legal department argued that such action was fruitless.[18]

The AOC refused to accept this pessimistic assessment. In September they hired a sympathetic lawyer at reduced rates who filed as a party-in-interest in bankruptcy court. The legal brief argued that LTV should be required to sell the plant intact because it was worth more to creditors that way. However, all legal challenges were ultimately abandoned when the weak legal basis for them became apparent and the AOC found itself unable to afford them, even at reduced rates. Ultimately, the law provided no help to the campaign.

The Turn Toward Public and Political Pressure

Finding legal actions, foreign markets, and the more conventional methods ineffective, the AOC and the Calumet Project turned toward public pressure tactics. An open public meeting on September 24, 1987 was attended by 150 union members, community residents, and political figures from the area. The campaign was publicized. Widespread press coverage was different than the AOC had hoped. A reporter focused on loose talk by the local's president and one member about "blood in the streets" if LTV should attempt removal of the #3 draw bench, rather than the broader message of LTV's refusal to market the plant intact.[19]

The following Monday ex-employees packed the city council chambers as the council debated a resolution of support for the AOC/Calumet Project effort. By unanimous vote the city council passed a resolution that:

> 1. Gave full support to the AOC in efforts to find a buyer;
> 2. Requested LTV to not remove equipment until the AOC could secure an offer, and to provide full financial information to the AOC;

3. Called upon the Hammond mayor and city departments to convert a $90,000 tax delinquency into a legal lien putting a claim in the property (including the #3 draw bench); and

4. Directed the city's department of economic development to explore use of eminent domain (involuntary sale to the city at a "fair" price "for the public good") if necessary.[20]

The city council also set up a committee to work with the AOC in taking any further action toward sale and reopening of the plant.

The AOC and the Calumet Project were accumulating resources and momentum in their campaign. However, LTV refused to deal with them seriously, using "semantics" to avoid any direct talks with the AOC and to avoid giving out financial information.[21]

To increase credibility and pressure, the Calumet Project and the AOC undertook a number of actions during October 1987. Both Union Drawn Steel and Woodruff Imberman were requested to write letters to the Calumet Project indicating an interest in the mill. Union Drawn promptly did so, but Imberman never did. A plant tour for Union Drawn President R. F. Hawkins was arranged for 8 October, but before it could occur, LTV wrote him:

> While we are prepared to discuss sale of the property with you, I would like to make it clear that the large #3 draw bench line and both size 2 Schumag lines will be excluded from the transaction. This equipment will be removed and transferred to our operating mills prior to the closing on any Hammond sale.[22]

This meant that 60–70 percent of the plant's capacity would be gutted. Hawkins asked for a postponement of the plant tour.

The campaign also progressed on the legal, political, and community support levels. Legally, the city of Hammond was induced to join the suit to prevent transfer of the #3 draw bench. This might give the suit greater credibility.

Politically, the Calumet Project and the AOC convinced Congressman Visclosky to write another letter to LTV President David Hoag. The 6 October letter stated, "I still feel that you would like LTV to be perceived as a responsible neighbor in the community" and urged LTV to:

> 1. Provide pertinent financial data in a timely manner to allow the AOC and other potential investors an opportunity to put together a serious offer;

2. Permit the Committee access to the facility;

3. Consider legitimate purchase proposals *which include the plant's key equipment* [emphasis added]; and

4. Pledge not to move any of the plant's vital equipment until a purchase proposal can be tendered.[23]

Hoag's 6 November reply assured the congressman that LTV was willing to sell the facility and to grant access to any interested potential buyer. However, on the key issues of providing financial information and pledging not to remove equipment, he declined to commit:

> With respect to requests for financial information about the plant, because the plant was a component of a larger division, financial data was not maintained for Hammond on a "stand alone" basis. In any event, those financials would be irrelevant to the next operator who would have to establish his own supply contracts, labor agreements and credit arrangements.
>
> The relocation of the Number 3 Drawbench to our Massillon, Ohio, facility has stirred some controversy. . . . Removal of this machine will not, however, render the Hammond plant inoperable. Also, similar pieces of equipment are readily available . . . and . . . could be purchased. . . .

Noting the court suit, Hoag concluded that "It appears that now the ultimate resolution of these issues must be guided by the decision of the Court."[24]

Broad public support for the campaign was solicited by an 2 October letter from the AOC to community and union leaders relating the campaign's progress to date and requesting that supporters be prepared for a plant gate rally if needed to stop equipment removal. An 23 October press release, which received national press exposure,[25] charged LTV with breaking promises. Agreements to provide financial information and to market the plant were reneged upon. AOC member Ron Chorba was quoted in the release:

> LTV is discriminating against us and failing to treat us as serious buyers. They did not withhold financial information from the workers at LTV/Republic Storage or LTV/Republic Container when those companies were sold via ESOPs in 1986. ". . . We demand that LTV treat us like any other buyers."

AOC spokesperson Jerry Brown accused LTV of duplicity:

LTV is being two-faced. On the one hand, they appear to be cooperating with us by giving us the plant tour, but on the other hand, they
are torpedoing any real chance for a sale by keeping all the best equipment for themselves.[26]

The combination of Congressional intervention, threat of a lien on the
property, talk of eminent domain proceedings, unfavorable press publicity, and legal intervention finally forced LTV to deal with the AOC and
the Calumet Project face to face. A 12 November meeting in Chicago focused primarily on AOC/Calumet Project proposals for the plant, especially
the option of producing for export. Calumet Project Director Lynn Feekin
told the press:

"We felt we had a hearing on our proposals," said Feekin. "Prior
to this, LTV had not been willing to meet with us or had not met with
us. They came, they listened, and said they would get back to us."[27]

Earlier the same day the AOC/Calumet Project had met at the Steelworkers district office with representatives from the Indiana Department
of Commerce, the state's two senators, the Hammond mayor, regional economic development officials, and the president of the business-based economic development organization, the Northwest Indiana Forum. All had
pledged support of various types for the effort to reopen the mill.[28]

A mid-November phone call to Union Drawn indicated that the company was still interested in acquiring the facility intact, but only if this were
possible without incurring LTV's enmity. As a smaller company, Union
Drawn needed a "compatible" relationship with LTV and was not "going
to the mat with LTV, with or without you" (i.e., with or without the
Calumet Project and the AOC). Union Drawn was waiting to see what
developed.[29]

LTV was making final plans to move the #3 draw bench. On Monday, 23 November the issue came to a head when an Ohio contractor
sent to remove the equipment met an early morning picket line and rally
of approximately 120 people at the plant gate. The rally was addressed by
the Hammond mayor, the district director of the United Steelworkers,
local clergy, AOC spokespersons, and others. The contractor refused to
cross the picket line; LTV dispatched executive personnel to the site.

LTV was now unhappy with recent events. Responding to threats of
a legal lien, company lawyers were trying to settle the $90,000 back prop-
erty tax debt. LTV exasperation was evident in a press interview:

We have permanently closed the Hammond bar plant. . . . We have dealt with all of the contractual obligations with the work force. That plant is officially, permanently shut down. We own the property and we're going to deal with that property in the way that appears the most sensible and benefits the company.[30]

The picket line forced LTV into a marathon morning-to-evening negotiating session with the AOC, the Calumet Project, Hammond mayor Thomas McDermott, and the United Steelworkers district representatives. The bargaining position of the two sides reveals their respective strengths and weaknesses. LTV had the stronger position strategically, despite tactical vulnerabilities. It had ownership of the mill, with all the legal rights to dispose of the property as it saw fit that accompany that ownership. Bankruptcy court imposed no serious legal barriers. "Business as usual" relations with the media, local public officials, the union local, or the local community would not pose any threat to its plans.

On the other hand, the AOC/Calumet Project campaign had disrupted business as usual. The threat of a legal lien and discussion of eminent domain proceedings meant that local public officials were at least verbally contemplating strong measures against the company. The publicity generated by the campaign had perhaps damaged the company. The congressman from the district was urging the company to sell the plant intact. The ex-workers, backed by their union and the most visible elements of the community, were picketing to prevent equipment removal.

But LTV's adversaries had limited power. Each source of leverage over the company had real limitations. A lien and eminent domain proceedings were threatened, but there was little chance of either. Hammond mayor McDermott was a business-oriented Republican who admired Jack Kemp; he was extremely unlikely to resort to "extreme" measures contrary to his ideology. Although Congressman Visclosky was more attuned to worker interests, he too would not undertake punitive action against the company over this one issue, and it was unclear what that action would be even if he were so inclined. Bad publicity could be contained. Most negative press coverage would be local, where it would matter the least. Also, the company had considerable press expertise and media contacts, if needed.

This left the picket line as a potentially serious impediment to LTV's plans. This was important, but it too had limitations. First, it would be very difficult to maintain on a twenty-four-hour-a-day basis, seven days a week, over the long run. Second, LTV could simply hire another contractor who would be willing to cross a picket line, perhaps late at night or with a large contingent of individuals. In the event of a showdown, the Hammond police would likely support the company and arrest the workers, as they had done only weeks before in a strikebreaking picket line crossing at another Hammond facility.

By the evening of 23 November, a compromise agreement was concluded. LTV was allowed to move the #3 draw bench and associated equipment, but it had to return the building to original conditions in all other respects. It also committed in writing to (1) actively seek plant buyers; (2) retain a qualified appraiser and advise the union of the appraisal results; (3) cooperate with the AOC and the city in efforts to sell the plant; (4) attempt to sell *as a steel processing unit;* (5) encourage any buyer to rehire the former employees; (6) retain all remaining equipment until 31 March 1988 (later changed to 30 April); and (7) allow the AOC to inspect the plant to ensure compliance.[31]

The agreement was a victory for LTV, because it achieved its primary goal: moving the #3 draw bench. It also represented a qualified success for the AOC/Calumet Project forces, because LTV was compelled to commit itself to their #1 goal: sale and reopening as a steel facility. Calumet Project director Lynn Feekin told the press:

> It's a win, might-win situation, and we're on the end that might win. . . . It's a first step. It's a victory, but there aren't any jobs there yet. It's a first step that might lead us to the ultimate victory. What this means is that they're not going to slowly pull things out of there. That may mean that the plant's viable with a small investment.[32]

As of December 1987, success for the campaign to reopen the mill depended heavily on two things: a qualified buyer and holding LTV to its commitments. The most promising potential buyer was Union Drawn Steel, so it was a major blow when Union Drawn withdrew from active pursuit of the site. Union Drawn President R. F. Hawkins told the Calumet Project by phone that they were "backing away with some regret."[33] The company told the press that removal of equipment had lowered their interest.[34]

The AOC and the Calumet Project were convinced that LTV had intimidated Union Drawn into withdrawal, because private phone explanations did not match public press explanations. The real motivation of Union Drawn officials is unknown, but the result was the same in any case: the only credible potential buyer had backed out.

LTV's sincerity also became a major issue. In mid-December AOC Chairman Jerry Brown asked Mayor McDermott by letter to pressure

LTV into providing promised lists of remaining equipment, appraisal information, and the like. McDermott did so a week later.[35] LTV chose not to respond until 12 January, approximately seven weeks after the 23 November agreement. On that date they mailed an equipment list and appraisal results to the Calumet Project.

But their delay in complying with previous commitments brought charges of bad faith. Even the letter's timing became evidence of bad faith, since it coincided with a public meeting to which LTV had been invited. At that 12 January public meeting AOC members reported that more equipment had been removed than specified in the agreement. Mayor McDermott stated,

> I'm looking at maybe a class action suit on behalf of the alternative ownership committee and the city for violation of the agreement. . . . I'm willing to go out and hold a (picket) sign at one of their sites.

Democratic Hammond city councilman Edward Repay also expressed strong support: "I'm willing to go to the wall; I'm willing to go through the wall."[36]

LTV defended itself by claiming good faith, timeliness, and ongoing efforts with at least three interested but unidentified buyers. LTV spokesperson Mark Tomasch stated, "It has been our intention all along to deal in good faith with the alternative ownership committee."[37] Ten days later the LTV General Asset Manager wrote a letter to McDermott stating that "LTV Steel intends to meet the commitments which it has made and is concerned when the impression is given by public officials that LTV Steel has not complied with its agreements."[38]

Whether LTV did attempt to actively market the plant is difficult to assess. It appears they put the plant up for sale through a realtor but made no effort beyond that. From February to April LTV claimed two interested buyers to the press, but refused to reveal to anyone — press, mayor, AOC — their names, and there is no evidence that any serious negotiations occurred. The local real estate agent did show the building to twelve to fifteen inquirers, about half of them claiming an interest in setting up some type of manufacturing.

The AOC and the Calumet Project, distrusting LTV and impatient as time ran out, attempted a limited marketing effort of their own. Calls were made to members of the Cold Finished Steel Bar Institute, but no interested buyer was located.

Despite lack of a buyer, the remainder of the campaign took off. During the months of February-May 1988 the former workers undertook a massive effort at community outreach. Close to 5,000 flyers were distributed in residential areas of Hammond. Letters to the editor of both major local daily newspapers appeared once or twice a week for close to two months. Lynn Feekin of the Calumet Project produced a fifteen-minute video that was shown at meetings of community organizations, union meetings, on local cable TV. Community awareness and support were high.

But, in the end, no buyer surfaced. The 30 April deadline passed, but the AOC/Calumet Project continued their efforts through May and June. But by mid-July, LTV announced that they had sold the remaining equipment, thus killing remaining hopes.[39]

But the AOC kept monitoring the site and discovered in the fall that a Minneapolis-based steel tubing company was interested in the mill. Metal-Matic, Inc., planned to employ approximately 90 to 100 workers. Metal-Matic expressed a willingness to rehire former LTV employees and indicated that they would not oppose unionization. According to AOC spokespersons, Metal-Matic was so sure of final purchase that they moved forty truckloads of equipment into the vacant plant for storage.[40]

The AOC/Calumet Project now believed that victory was within their grasp. But in early November LTV announced that the property was contaminated with polychlorinated biphenyls (PCBs).[41] Metal-Matic awaited more tests to determine the extent of the problem, but it stated that "any deal is contingent on LTV cleaning up PCB contamination at the site."[42]

In late November the Hammond city council passed a resolution calling for collection of back taxes, a lien on the property, investigation of the possible use of Community Development Block Grant funds for retraining, and immediate steps to clean up the property.[43] But this resolution was of little practical value to the AOC. Hopes now rested with the slim possibility that further environmental tests would reveal that contamination was limited to one area of the property. Metal-Matic might lease and operate the clean portion pending final clean-up of the rest of the property. Hopes were dashed on 11 January 1989, when LTV revealed serious contamination everywhere. Metal-Matic vice president Robert Van Krevelen indicated his company was leaving:

> At this point it is taken off the list of possibilities. . . . We can't wait for a clean-up that is scheduled for some indefinite time in the future. . . . We're investigating several other sites.[44]

The AOC, the Calumet Project, and Hammond-based Interfaith Citizens Organization (ICO) held a 12 January meeting with environmentalists to demand that LTV release all known environmental information, test the health of all ex-employees, perform in-depth ground water and soil tests on-site and in the neighborhood, and provide jobs or equivalent compensation to all ex-employees.

Bitterness at LTV was evident. In December LTV had held private "briefing sessions" with the editorial boards of the area's two major daily newspapers and had succeeded in getting one of them to write an editorial favorable to the company. Quoting the editorial that "LTV deserves praise for being a good neighbor," the coalition released reasons to be thankful:

- Thank you, LTV, for shutting this plant down and putting over 150 people out of a job.
- Thank you, LTV, for costing the city of Hammond and surrounding communities over $4 million in lost purchasing power.
- Thank you, LTV, for removing the draw bench equipment, eliminating the possibility of another bar operation locating there.
- Thank you, LTV, for refusing to pay nearly $200,000 in delinquent property taxes.
- Thank you, LTV, for waiting over two years after the closing to test the environment.
- Thank you, LTV, for effectively eliminating the possibility of jobs at that site for years to come.[45]

But bitterness was all that the coalition had left at this point. The battle for jobs was lost, killed by site contamination. Environmentalists, some community residents, and the AOC turned the campaign into an effort to ensure a cleanup of the toxic waste dump. In early March LTV announced that cleanup would take many more months and hundreds of thousands of dollars.[46]

The Calumet Project then left the campaign, since the jobs issue was moot. A visible and confrontational campaign for cleanup continued for the next year and a half.

By early 1991 LTV had cleaned up the property. A newly incorporated company, Alpha Steel, won approval from the bankruptcy court on 8 May 1991 for a $1.5 million-bid on the property. Alpha planned to do steel fabrication and storage on the site, eventually hiring as many as 120 people. It approached the city of Hammond for tax abatements and aid in securing an industrial revenue bond (IRB). Both the city council and the city's economic development department contacted AOC leader Jerry Brown to get the AOC's approval for proceeding. A recent AOC poll of ex-workers revealed that eighty-five would return to work under comparable wages and working conditions, so the AOC requested rehiring of interested former employees as a condition of public aid. Alpha officials agreed to do this.[47] The mayor had earlier assured Brown that any disposition of the property would fully involve the AOC.[48] Alpha Steel eventually started up and employed approximately a dozen ex-LTV workers wanting to return.

ANALYSIS AND CONCLUSIONS

This case illustrates both the power and the limitations of local labor-community coalitions. Both institutional factors and subjective factors played a large role in the successes and failure of the AOC/Calumet Project campaign.

Factors Favoring the Campaign

One element that gave enormous strength to the campaign was its unusually dedicated and able leadership. One individual within the union initiated the contact with the Calumet Project and provided leadership within the AOC thereafter. Jerry Brown became *de facto* leader of the workers after the closing; he inspired his fellow workers to continue in a struggle that lasted for years against enormous odds. The AOC also developed a secondary core of leaders who exhibited persistence and resilience over the long haul.

The Calumet Project was also invaluable. Brown has stated repeatedly that without the Calumet Project there would have been no campaign. Calumet Project Director Lynn Feekin provided strategic and tactical expertise. The Calumet Project also provided contact with a wider network of supportive structures: a Chicago business analyst, sympathetic lawyers in Chicago, local community support networks and organizations, and the like. The accumulated wisdom of past job retention struggles was put at the service of this campaign through the project's offices.

The number of ex-LTV workers involved in the fight to get their former jobs back was unusual. This should not be overstated: most ex-LTV workers played a somewhat passive role. Nevertheless, a "core" of around 8–10 people in the AOC were able to mobilize 40–100 people consistently to attend meetings, attend rallies, distribute flyers, write letters to the editor, call their public officials, and so on. This was from a local of only 150, only 90 of whom were still working when the plant was idled.

Most efforts to mobilize unemployed workers or victims of plant closings are less successful.[49] Jerry Brown realized this:

> When the plant goes down, people have to survive. They have to
> spend time looking for jobs, trying to support their families. It's hard to
> organize under those conditions.[50]

But he also realized the extraordinary nature of his — and the entire campaign's — accomplishment:

> You have to remember, this membership — this was totally out of
> their experience. We had never had any problems anywhere near this size,
> where we had to go to the community. We had never attended city coun-
> cil meetings. . . .
> As a local union we were much like other locals: really apathetic, even
> in attending union meetings. . . . So, this local did some amazing things.[51]

A second factor favorable to the campaign was a viable plant, at least
prior to the removal of the #3 draw bench. This was not a plant that had
been "milked," or that was uncompetitive in the existing market. Millions were not required to make this plant run well. A chronic problem for
labor/community groups in plant closing struggles — lack of access to
capital needed to modernize — was absent here. *If* the coalition could
find an interested buyer, all the ingredients for a successful operation
were present. When a suitable buyer appeared, the only obstacle was
LTV's willingness to sell.

Other favorable factors included a political community somewhat
responsive to worker interests. Northwest Indiana is a heavily industrialized
area with a large labor movement. The Republican mayor of Hammond
was not ideologically inclined toward workers' issues, but he had to respond to their interests when pressured. The overwhelmingly Democratic (8–1) city council was somewhat more inclined toward worker interests
(one councilman was James Balanoff, past district director for the United Steelworkers). But even here, aside from Balanoff, most councilpersons were more interested in posturing and attempts to embarrass the
mayor than in giving effective aid to the coalition. Democratic Congressman Peter Visclosky demonstrated a moderate pro-labor attitude.

Despite these qualifications, public officials would respond. The coalition therefore adopted a "push the politicians to push LTV" strategy.
Responsiveness had its limits: no politician, not even Congressman Visclosky, would jeopardize friendly relations with LTV for the sake of the
workers or the community. Temporary lapses in this direction occurred
when politicians under pressure employed heated rhetoric against the cor-

poration. But this was not a serious long-term stance: a lien was never attached to the property, eminent domain was never seriously investigated, much less invoked, and a favorable legislative attitude was only partially used as a bargaining chip to induce the company to sell intact. A "favorable business climate" outweighed a commitment to the struggles of a labor-community coalition. Nevertheless, the political context was more favorable than many efforts face.

Another positive factor was extensive press coverage. LTV had to respond publicly to the coalition after initially trying to ignore it. LTV's "good image" was constantly battered, forcing it to respond defensively in the press. Through the press the AOC/Calumet Project defined the overriding issue for the public: corporate responsibility to communities abandoned through plant closure. Had LTV been able to define the overriding issue, it undoubtedly would have been the right of a private owner to dispose of their property as they see fit, free of external restraint or coercion.

Factors Unfavorable to the Campaign

One unfavorable factor was the enormous imbalance in resources. A small union local, aided by a nonprofit organization with fewer than five employees, was taking on a multimillion dollar conglomerate corporation.

Second, the timing was bad. It was initiated *after* the plant was closed. Organizing the workforce is easier when everybody is still working, and the normal union structures are still functioning. A transfer to new ownership is also generally more feasible than is a start-up from a closed plant. This is why "early warning" is so important.

Third, the law was of no use. The U.S. legal system in general protects the rights of private property holders, and the AOC/Calumet Project found the bankruptcy court no more helpful. Jerry Brown later commented:

> The law is not the friend of the working man. . . . Everything is geared to protect the company. In hindsight, I feel we probably wasted a lot of time with legal attempts to stop them. Our best strength is people, as it always is.[52]

The most unfavorable factor was LTV's unwillingness to sell. Although eventually forced to pretend otherwise, LTV had no interest in selling the facility *as a bar mill*. It could only lose from a sale: one more competitor for its Gary facility. The coalition ultimately lacked a strong enough inducement to, or sanction over, the corporation to get it to retain the #3 draw bench and sell the facility intact. The coalition's levers of power over the company were inadequate.

Jerry Brown now believes that the settlement allowing LTV to remove the draw bench was a mistake. If he had it to do over again, he would try to maintain the picket line at the plant gate.[53] But he also admits that this would be difficult over the long haul. It is not clear that this tactic would have worked: if it lacked the manpower or was forcibly dispersed, this might have been a more demoralizing defeat than the actual outcome.

The relatively weak product market also worked against the coalition. Finding a buyer who must also purchase additional major equipment (to replace the #3 draw bench) was insurmountable in a weak market; it may have happened with a stronger market.

Gains and Losses

Even though the mill was not reopened for five years, every member of the AOC I have spoken to thinks the effort was worth it. They claim they would have been victorious but for the unrelated fact of site contamination. They argue that LTV was forced to pay its back tax debt at ninety cents on the dollar (an extremely high ratio) only because of the campaign. They also believe LTV would not have cleaned up the property rapidly or completely without the later stages of the campaign. They feel they pioneered the way for others in a similar situation, and that the corporate community in northwest Indiana has been "put on notice" concerning their responsibilities in shutdown situations.

Whether all these beliefs are correct is a matter of judgment. It does appear that this prolonged and highly visible struggle had three important impacts. First, it transformed some of the people involved. Due to heightened awareness, ex-LTV bar mill workers were to play a leading role in a later struggle.[54]

Second, it began to change the terms of the public debate over rights and responsibilities in the region's economy. After this campaign public officials became more responsive to worker and community demands. A small dent has been made in the "business climate" viewpoint that the locality has no claims against, only duties toward and favors owed to, the business community. To that extent the campaign left a legacy to the region. Finally, a few displaced workers did get their jobs in the plant back five years later.

PREVENTING A DEPARTMENT RELOCATION AT THE LASALLE STEEL PLANT

This case concerns an attempt by a specialty steel manufacturer to relocate a key department from a unionized Hammond, Indiana, site to a nonunion site in a small town about one hundred miles away. The union learned of the plan and initiated a successful joint campaign with the Calumet Project to protect the affected jobs and possibly the entire plant.

Product market conditions were peripheral to the issues in contention, but labor relations played a larger role. The company tried to win wage concessions; failing that and stymied in its relocation attempt, the company later turned toward cooperative relations with its union and was more successful in reaching its operating goals.

The owner's corporate structure had a probable influence on the initial decision to explore relocation, and it also made the plant manager vulnerable to pressures from the campaign. In contrast to earlier cases, local government took prompt action. This chapter analyzes the reasons for the change.

The Calumet Project and the union were victorious because they won the struggle over problem definition and successfully formed alliances and mobilized their forces. The key to success lay in strong leadership, shrewd tactical judgment, specific vulnerabilities of the company, a somewhat changed political and public opinion climate, and proactive intervention. The LaSalle case illustrates the potential power of labor-community coalition efforts. The postcampaign relations between company and union also raise a new set of issues with implications for labor-community coalition efforts.

The following section details the historical background to the case. Following that, I relate the events of the campaign to save the department. The final two sections concern the Calumet Project/union victory and the dynamics of the case.

BACKGROUND

LaSalle Steel Company had a humble beginning as a steel warehouse in Chicago in 1912.[1] In 1920 operations were moved to Hammond, Indiana, for space reasons. Over the years LaSalle grew and prospered. The company underwent large scale expansions in the 1930s, the 1940s, late 1950s, late 1960s, and mid-1970s. During the 1930s depression years the company avoided layoffs by operating a two- to three-day work week. It also distributed food baskets and provided garden plots and seeds to workers.

This paternalistic relationship with its workforce reflected the company management's overall philosophy, which stressed positive employee relations and close customer relations. The company was unionized in 1937 by an independent union confined to this one plant, the Progressive Steelworkers of Hammond. Labor relations were generally harmonious, as evidenced by few strikes. Over time, the union and the company negotiated contracts closely modeled on the patterns set by the United Steelworkers of America and the steel industry.

By the late 1970s LaSalle was one of the largest independent cold-finished steel bar producers in the country, with a history of successful innovations and many patents on an array of products. On 30 December 1981 it was acquired by Houston-based Quanex Corporation for $52 million.[2] Quanex, which had grown from Michigan Seamless Tube Company through acquisitions and expansion, was a specialty steel producer that manufactured hot-rolled and cold-finished steel bars, seamless and welded steel tubing, and some specialized alloy forgings.

The company's long string of successes was challenged in the 1980s. By 1982, capacity utilization in the domestic industry as a whole dropped below 50 percent; profits plunged and companies demanded (and won) major concessions from their union locals. In February 1984 LaSalle's concession demands drove the union to a three-day strike. The company obtained some concessions, but less than those won by the major basic steel companies.

LaSalle fared better than most steel companies during the 1980s, but both it and parent company Quanex encountered problems. Quanex lost money during 1982, 1983, and 1986, although other years were profitable. Table 6.1 shows net income and return on common stockholders' equity for relevant years.

The profitable years 1984–85 and 1987–88 were not sufficient to offset major losses in 1982 and 1986. Quanex's problems in the mid-1980s stemmed from a new hot-finished bar mill in Arkansas. Subsidiary LaSalle consistently made money throughout the decade, although prof-

Table 6.1. Quanex Corporation net income and return (%) on common stockholders' equity, 1982–1988.

	1982	1983	1984	1985	1986	1987	1988
Net income (in millions)	-$34.5	-$3.5	$2.0	$10.1	-$19.9	$5.2	$18.5
Return on equity (in %)	-31.6	-4.0	2.3	10.2	-19.8	5.6	17.5

Source: Quanex Corporation 1992 *Annual Report*, pp. 18–19.

it margins were squeezed. Union sources claim that LaSalle's market share in cold-finished bars dropped from 15 percent to 6 percent by 1985, as nonunion minimills and excess capacity created tough competition.[3] By late 1985 employment was down to 180–200, less than half of 1979 employment of over four hundred.

LaSalle management responded by increasing emphasis on quality and productivity gains. In 1987 Quanex reported that "LaSalle has continued major improvements in productivity showing a 19.3 percent gain over the past two years, due principally to work method changes at the Hammond mill."[4]

Quanex also terminated the LaSalle hourly employee pension plan and replaced it with a purchased annuity to cover existing pension obligations plus a new plan with the same payout scale. In the process they pocketed approximately $12 million in "excess" money beyond existing payout obligations from the old pension plan. Thus a two-tier pension system was created; old pension payouts were frozen, and any improvement negotiated in the 1987 contract negotiations would apply only to the new plan covering years of service after 1986. Pension plan terminations of this nature enabled Quanex to turn an operating loss into a small overall profit for 1987.

The 1987 contract negotiations resulted in a three-year wage freeze. The union granted a temporary two-tier wage structure: new hires began at $3 per hour below standard scale, which was regained after three years.

The Progressive Steelworkers had participated in the Calumet Project's Early Warning System. Both completed early warning scorecards and analysis of corporate financial data and strategy indicated that there was little likelihood of Quanex selling LaSalle or of "milking" it for profits while disinvesting in the facility. LaSalle's business segment, the steel bar group, was the core of Quanex's business (about 40 percent of all assets and

80 percent of all profits in 1989, according to published data). LaSalle fit well with other Quanex businesses, such as the MacSteel hot-rolled bar producer; it was consistently profitable; and it fit into specialized metal product markets (a "strategic goal" of Quanex). Consequently, neither the union nor the Calumet Project feared an imminent sale or complete shutdown of the mill in the late 1980s.

One other feature of Quanex's structure helps explain the later behavior of the LaSalle plant general manager, who was also a Quanex vice president. Quanex operates on a decentralized basis, allowing business unit managers to make their own decisions and rewarding them according to profit performance. In its own words,

> Quanex is lean, market-driven, and focused on customer needs. Decentralized decisions and prudent risk-taking support an entrepreneurial culture that keeps Quanex close to its markets. Superior performance is rewarded with incentives, which are a large proportion of total employee compensation, based on each business unit's return on net assets.[5]

Management incentive bonuses were large: in 1989 the top seven corporate officers received bonuses of 79 percent of their regular salary.[6] Therefore a manager had a direct material incentive to cut costs and increase profits in his facility.

The 1990 contract negotiations resulted in a thirty-two-day strike from 15 February to 19 March. An agreed-upon $1.90 per hour pay increase over the four years of the proposed contract — the first pay increase in six years — was not the stumbling block. Three issues separated the two sides: (1) pension fund increases for *all* years, to eliminate the new two-tier structure; (2) improvement in the cost-of-living (COLA) formula; and (3) elimination of the two-tier pay structure.[7]

The company wanted to increase pension payments under the "old" pension plan by $3 per year of service, while years covered under the new plan would go up $6. The union wanted uniform provisions of $35 per year of service under both plans, giving a thirty-year employee a pension of $1,050 per month. On the COLA issue, the company wanted no cost-of-living hikes unless inflation exceeded 4 percent in a quarter; the union wanted no such restriction although it was willing to put a cap on total COLA payments. The union wanted to eliminate the two-tier scale, and the company wanted to retain it.

Company and union versions of the negotiations were quite different. Quanex Vice President and LaSalle General Manager Richard W. Treder told the press:

We are really at a loss to see how a well-funded pension plan that provides improvements . . . is anything but an excellent plan.

We believe that we have made our employees a very generous proposal. Their wage and benefit package is already the highest in this country's cold-finished bar industry. The increases we have proposed will make it even better.[8]

Referring to the $12 million the company took from the workers' pension plan in 1986, union lawyer Bernard Mamet commented, "They (Quanex) raped these people, one does not have to be an Internal Revenue auditor to see that."[9] Union secretary Alan Pearson stated to the press:

I feel they're just in business for the profits and they don't care about us. They don't care about what happens when we retire. They're just looking out for themselves.[10]

Two hundred eighty of the 317 union members voted on the company's final offer. They rejected it 277 to 3. A long strike began. The company used supervisors to continue production. Workers later claimed all work had to be redone because supervisors were unable to properly run the machinery.[11]

On 12 March, twenty-six days into the strike, the union again rejected a revised company offer, 254 to 39. The company had agreed to treat pension benefits for all years of service equivalently, but their $28 per year of service offer represented no new money, only a reshuffling of benefits under the old offer.[12]

Yet the union accepted a contract offer that was only slightly different six days later. On 19 March the union voted 183 to 90 to end the strike. The agreement provided for two pension formulas. One was a flat $28 a month per year of service; the other provided $25 per year of service up to $196, with increasing amounts after that. One formula favored older workers, the other younger ones. Individual workers would get whichever formula paid the higher amount. A worker with thirty years of service would get $1,040 a month, very close to the union's initial goal of $1,050. The company, however, prevented elimination of the two-tier pay scheme. The COLA was very slightly improved. Neither side claimed victory.[13]

In the 1984 and 1987 negotiations, the LaSalle workers had conceded less than comparable steelworkers in other cold-finished bar mills. Their compensation was above industry norms. Apparently this independent union had taken a harder stance against concessions than had the

United Steelworkers in comparable plants, and the single-facility nature of the company's cold-finished bar production, combined with the company's technological and quality edge over competitors, enabled the workers to protect their compensation and conditions better than other union workers.

But General Manager Richard Treder was not happy. Rumors circulated through the plant that he was considering relocating the turning and grinding department out of the Hammond facility. Since this department is a high "value added" part of the mill, the union was concerned. Although only about fifty jobs were directly at stake, workers were afraid that if the "heart of the mill" were removed, the rest of the mill might follow. Approximately 350 union members were working by the fall, when the rumors spread.

CAMPAIGN TO SAVE THE DEPARTMENT

On 27 October four LaSalle workers attended an early warning training session for area unionists. Overall scores on the early warning scorecard indicated little danger, but the threatened departmental relocation was discussed.

Shortly thereafter Calumet Project Director Lynn Feekin spoke to the union's executive board meeting about options to deal with the possible relocation. The union decided to join the Calumet Project and to launch a campaign to save the grinding department.

From the beginning the union's executive board worked closely with the Calumet Project to develop a strategic approach to its work. Goals, tasks, and timelines were determined by mid-November. The union set up three special committees to carry out the work.

The Corporate Research Committee researched the parent and local company, the network of suppliers, customers and competitors, corporate strategy, regulatory agencies and environmental issues, market conditions, and the like. This committee was to provide information on company strategies and possible vulnerabilities.

The Workplace Committee was to map out the work flow in the plant, product line information, employment according to category and department, and so on. This committee was to provide information needed to deal with quality, efficiency, and work-flow issues.

The Workforce Analysis Committee undertook a survey of the membership to determine demographic statistics for public relations efforts and to collect data on the members' community and religious affiliations for community outreach efforts. It was also responsible for building solidarity within the local and developing a common membership understanding of union strategy. All three functioned well, especially the Corporate Research Committee.

On 16 November LaSalle General Manager Richard Treder wrote newly elected union president Zed Rixie about rumors concerning possible relocation, calling them "premature" and "unfounded comments." But it did admit that relocation was being considered:

> First, while the Company is considering the possible transfer of our grinding operations in connection with the establishment of a new Turning Center, no decisions have been made. Currently, we are only studying the possibility of such a move.[14]

Treder assured Rixie that the company would notify the union prior to making the final decision, for discussion. But the letter requested the workers to cease further activity until the company had completed its analysis and made a decision.

On 26 November Rixie wrote thanking Treder for providing information, and added:

> I believe the union has information, expertise and opinions which would be of value to the company in making this decision. We would like to take this opportunity to request union participation in the meetings and consultations which will lead to this decision. . . .
>
> We hope you respond to our request in the spirit it's made — full cooperation in an effort to make LaSalle Steel the best it can be.
>
> Please let me know at your earliest convenience whether and how the union can be involved in this process.[15]

On 30 November Treder responded that a meeting with the union was probably premature under the union contract language (which called for consultation thirty days before final decision), but the company "probably would benefit from the Union's input." Therefore, "in the spirit of cooperation mentioned in your letter," the company would meet with the union. Since the union had requested an early meeting, the present letter should be considered "notification of proposed closure called for under Article XIII, Section 8 of our labor agreement."[16] Under contract terms this meant that a final decision would have to be made in thirty days.

At this time three union representatives in the turning and grinding department wrote to Quanex Chief Executive Officer Carl Pfeiffer. Knowing Treder had prepared a pro-relocation report for the Quanex Board of Directors (obtained "accidentally" from the company Xerox machine), they countered claims of bad department product quality and a high customer return rate. Most returned defective product had been subcontracted out to a competitor but was being charged to the grinding department, creating bogus statistics to discredit the department. The letter stated:

> We are quality minded workers. . . . Unfortunately, our quality in this department has been misrepresented by the returned goods statistic. Such a statistic may play a big role in deciding whether to move P.S.D. (the grinding department — BN) or not. . . . As you know, we have had an unusually high percentage of returned goods in our department, mainly due to a high volume of our grinding stock being subcontracted out to our competitors. These competitors have a much lower standard of quality than at LaSalle. . . . These competitors ship this poor quality out to our customers. The customer returns the product to P.S.D. . . . This is an unfair reflection of our work, and we feel we are being blamed for poor quality in a LaSalle management plan to move our division to another location.[17]

On 3 December Pfeiffer's reply assured them that all facts would be considered before reaching a decision. He referred them to Richard Treder for a meeting if they wished further input. The letter made no mention of the specific issues raised in the workers' letter.[18]

Despite the lack of substantive response, the exchange did accomplish some of the union's purposes. First, the union had insisted on being part of the decision. Second, they circumvented Treder in communications to the top whenever Treder went against their wishes. Both features — insistence on inclusion in the basic decisions and circumvention of Treder when necessary — were to characterize the entire campaign to save the department.

A third feature soon surfaced: heavy publicity. A 6 December press conference alerted the public to the possible relocation and called for a public meeting on the issue. Union leadership expressed concern that the entire facility was endangered:

> Special products, such as those made in the grinding department, "are the life blood of this plant" said Rod Fields, union treasurer. "If they start spinning these departments off, it's death (to the plant)."[19]

Treder angrily responded to the press that the union was "sensationalizing the situation by going public before a meeting between the company and the union could be arranged."[20] "I'm a little disappointed they've gone public with this," he stated.[21]

At a meeting with union leaders the next day, Treder denounced the union for publicizing the situation. But he did state that the search for a site for the grinding department had been narrowed to two locations: Hammond, or Frankfort, Indiana, approximately 120 miles to the south. He refused to share any studies on the relative merits of different sites. Because a new $2.08-million turning machine was on order to arrive by August, he indicated that a decision on its (and the department's) destination would have to be made by 1 March. But he withdrew the thirty-day closing notice, claiming more time was now needed.[22] The final decision would be based on three factors: (1) space (material flow) considerations, (2) efficiency, and (3) cost effectiveness. He declined to give the union any information on the company's figures or calculations about any of these.

On Monday, 10 December the union and the Calumet Project hosted a public meeting of over eighty people. A "fact sheet" drawn from the Workforce Analysis Committee's survey was distributed, showing that LaSalle employed 356 production and maintenance workers with an average age of forty-four (62 percent over age forty). They averaged 15.9 years of service, with an average wage of $12.68 per hour. Total annual income of these workers was $11 million. The grinding department employed forty-three, with an annual income of $1.48 million. The community impact would be substantial if the department were relocated and even more devastating if the entire plant closed.

Union and Calumet Project spokespersons explained the worker and community stake in preserving the jobs in Hammond. Three city councilmen, the mayor, a state senator, and a representative from Congressman Peter Visclosky's office all attended. City Councilman Ed Repay pledged council support for any program the union put forth to save jobs. Mayor Thomas McDermott also pledged support, volunteering to put together a tax incentive package to "outbid" any Frankfort might offer. State Senator Frank Mrvan, a Hammond resident, promised to contact Lieutenant Governor Frank O'Bannon to ensure that state programs and incentives were not used to lure jobs from Hammond to Frankfort. Thomas Brown, aide to Congressman Visclosky, stated that Visclosky would meet with Indiana governor Evan Bayh to ensure that all state actions were geared toward retaining the jobs in Hammond and against "whipsawing" of one Indiana community against another. All present pledged to aid the campaign to save jobs and volunteers signed up for a task force to carry on the work throughout the community.[23]

Despite the unanimous support, there were differences of approach. Mayor McDermott was offering to engage in a "bidding war" with Frankfort, while other public officials were attempting to prevent such a bidding war. The next day the union wrote McDermott thanking him for support but expressing the union/Calumet Project position against a public subsidy competition with Frankfort:

> We appreciate your willingness to offer assistance to the company, in the form of tax abatements or other subsidies, in order to induce them to expand here, rather than relocate the work elsewhere. If that effort was successful, we would be very grateful. However, we do want to be clear that *the union does not want to get into a bidding war with another community.*[24]

Attached to the letter were conditions the union felt should be honored if the company were to receive assistance:

> 1. No public assistance is to be given without company commitment to retain grinding department in Hammond.
> 2. If jobs are relocated in the near future or at a later date, any subsidies which are given can be revoked and the lost revenue recaptured.
> 3. No public subsidies are to be given if total local payroll shrinks (dependent on maintenance of current payroll dollars).

On 18 December the Hammond City Council's Economic Development Committee met and decided to contact Quanex management regarding the company's intentions toward the Hammond plant. On 20 December committee chair Charles Pettersen wrote to Quanex CEO Carl Pfeiffer expressing "concern regarding your company's Hammond Plant" and offering to immediately meet with the company about saving jobs.[25]

In a 4 January letter of reply, Pfeiffer thanked the committee for its interest, but noted that the relocation decision would be reached principally by LaSalle management in Hammond. He suggested contacting Richard Treder for further communication.[26]

The union was attempting to meet with Treder, but he was unavailable until early January. The Calumet Project urged the union to maintain the initiative by adopting some holiday tactic that would involve the members and/or maintain a public presence. One idea was member involvement in a "Christmas card to Treder with a message" campaign. The union would collect Christmas cards for Treder from the workers. In addition to the card's usual season's greetings, each worker would add a message such as "My Christmas would be even happier if my job was secure" or "It's a merry Christmas if the grinding department is staying in Hammond."

The executive board of the union was divided on the wisdom of further public or membership pressure. Some felt that it would be "going too far" to do something like this. Others were all in favor. But the executive board as a whole decided to take no further action at this time.

Although the Calumet Project felt that losing the initiative at this point was a mistake, the union had the final say. The Calumet Project never attempts to go it alone without the union. The roles of the two organizations have to be clear: the *union* is the representative of the workers, the Calumet Project a coalition partner and co-strategist. The union has a veto over all actions.

In early and mid-January Treder kept avoiding meetings with the union. However, other events occupied the union's attention for a brief period. The owner of a local trucking company informed the union that he was planning to purchase LaSalle. He claimed he had almost bought the plant four years earlier but something had come up, preventing the sale. He offered the union 10 percent equity in the firm plus a seat on the board of directors, at no cost. He also vowed a strong commitment to retaining jobs in Hammond, promised not to relocate the grinding department if he purchased the plant, offered a "full partnership" to the union, and asserted that he would buy the company, with our without the union's help. But parts of his story were suspect: he had not made an offer, had not informed Quanex that he was interested in buying, and planned to finance the purchase entirely through the sale of bonds. Even more implausibly, he had no evidence — only a conviction — that Quanex wanted to sell the LaSalle subsidiary.[27]

The union paid some attention for a brief time, but this potential "buyer" was not to be taken seriously. He disappeared quickly. There is no evidence that Quanex had any interest in selling LaSalle, which was strategically positioned within the parent firm and profitable.

On 25 January 1991 Treder ended the union's inactive period by officially notifying them of a tentative decision to close the grinding department *and* the "short cut" line.[28] The addition of the short cut line was even more serious: a half dozen additional jobs would be lost, and the short cuts product line was a new and expanding one serving the automotive strut market. A final decision was to be made within thirty working days.

The union immediately took action. On 29 January the union and the Calumet Project held plantwide educational sessions for all three shifts at the union hall. Over one hundred members attended. At the programs, members learned of the company's plans, its rationale for those plans as the union understood it, and the union's counter-proposal to retain the department in Hammond. Many workers signed up to work on an outreach plan with the union's message.

A minor controversy over the publicity for these programs illustrates the inner tensions within the union over the best way to proceed. The Calumet Project had prepared the flyer advertising the educational sessions. Titled, "What's the Union Doing to Save Jobs at LaSalle?" the flyer contained a brief explanation of the times and purpose of the sessions. A cartoon showed an individual, labeled "LaSalle Mgmt." kicking another, labeled "Grinding Department" through a door, while proclaiming, "Sure I believe in workers' rights . . . 'right' out the door!!" Union president Zed Rixie came under considerable criticism from the company over this — they considered it a harmful criticism that could only damage company-workforce relations. Rixie felt that the flyer had been too anticompany, but others among the leadership and activist core felt that it was appropriate.

At this time the union attempted to involve the United Steelworkers of America in the campaign. The United Steelworkers represented the seventeen workers at LaSalle's Fluid Power Division plant in nearby Griffith, Indiana (only a few miles from the Hammond plant). Since the Fluid Power plant received its product raw material from the grinding department, it seemed to be endangered if the grinding department were moved 120 miles away. The Progressive Steelworkers proposed to the United Steelworkers a joint campaign to save jobs at both plants. The United Steelworkers district director turned it over to the staff representative who serviced the Fluid Power local, but the staff representative never responded, and no joint cooperation materialized. Maybe old union rivalries, belief that Fluid Power jobs were not really endangered, or other reasons explain this failure to develop a joint campaign.

By mid-February the union and the Calumet Project had mailed to local public officials, community leaders, and the press a detailed document on the three criteria determining the grinding department's fate (work flow, efficiency, and cost effectiveness).[29] The document demonstrated how each of these factors could be addressed by remaining in Hammond. It questioned the efficiency or cost effectiveness of shipping product 120 miles away simply for final finishing, then shipping most of it back 120 miles to LaSalle Fluid Power and/or to steel service centers in the Chicago/Hammond area. It also showed that necessary building expansion in Hammond was spatially possible and cheaper than construction or acquisition of a new building in Frankfort.

Table 6.2. Estimated comparative number of jobs, hourly labor costs, total labor costs, and annual labor savings at different sites for the LaSalle grinding department.

	Hammond before	Hammond w/ new equip.	Frankfort	Gary	Griffith
Total # of jobs	54	47	43	46	44
Hourly labor cost (wages & benefits)	$21.68	$21.68	$12.00	$17.50	$17.50
Total labor cost (millions)	$2.341	$2.038	$1.032	$1.610	$1.540
Annual labor savings (thousands)	—	$303.52	$1,309.44	$731.44	$801.44

Source: Computations given to the union by the company.

The document called for an objective third party study of ways to keep jobs in Hammond. A feasibility study could examine work-flow issues, cost estimates, and financing and ownership options, including a possible employee stock ownership plan. However, "for a feasibility study to be effective, the company should agree to cooperate with the consultants conducting the study and hold any final decision until completion and review of the study's findings."[30] A cover letter asked community leaders and public officials to endorse the union/Calumet Project plan.

At a 12 February meeting with the union leadership Richard Treder shared the company's comparative analysis of costs of locating the grinding department in four different locations (Hammond, Frankfort, and Gary, Indiana, and the Griffith Fluid Power facility). Table 6.2 shows company estimates of comparative jobs, hourly labor costs, total labor costs, and annual labor savings at the various sites.

All locations would employ fewer workers than the fifty-four now working at Hammond. Hammond with the new equipment needed forty-seven; Frankfort, Gary, and Griffith would all need one less utility person, for unexplained reasons. Griffith would save two additional packaging jobs (by using existing employees to do the work); and Frankfort would save three additional jobs *by providing no vacation coverage.*

The company also planned to save approximately $4.18 per hour in either Gary or Griffith, presumably with a union contract paying that much less in wages and benefits. Frankfort workers were expected to cost $9.18 per hour less, presumably because they would be nonunion work-

Table 6.3. Estimated building construction costs for siting the LaSalle grinding department (in thousands of dollars).

	Hammond	Griffith	Frankfort
Land	—	—	$125
Site preparation	$100	$750	$600
Building cost	$960	$1,890	$1,765
Cranes / runways	$50	$200	$200
Contingency (x15%)	$165	$425	$400
TOTAL	$1,275	$3,265	$3,090

Source: Computations given to the union by the company.

ers working at 30–45 percent below industry standards. Since total labor costs were planned at $12 per hour, these workers would either receive no benefits with a $12 per hour wage, or they would receive normal benefits with $7–8 per hour ($7.44 if their wage/benefit ratio was identical to that for LaSalle's present workers), or perhaps $8–9 per hour with an extremely skimpy benefits package. These workers' jobs would be among the most skilled in the industry.

On the basis of this data, Treder claimed that Frankfort would bring labor savings of $1.3 million, far superior to any alternative. However, building construction and freight costs also were relevant. Table 6.3 shows the company's estimate of comparative building construction costs (Gary is left off because it would be a rented building, not a new one).

From this table, it is clear that Hammond had a large cost advantage over the other two in building costs. It also had a yearly freight cost savings of $240,000 over Griffith, $296,000 over Gary, and $694,000 over Frankfort.

Consolidating this but ignoring building construction cost differentials, Treder presented a summary to the union, which is given in table 6.4.

On the basis of these figures, Treder claimed over $600,000 per year savings from a move to Frankfort. It was widely reported in the local press that $600,000–$700,000 would be saved by the move.[31] Treder told the union that it was up to them to make up the difference. The union interpreted this as a call for massive concessions, which they rejected.

Yet the $615,000 figure was highly misleading. First, unless the company planned to deny Frankfort workers any vacations forever, Frankfort

Table 6.4. Savings from locating the LaSalle grinding department, by site.

	New Hammond	Griffith	Gary	Frankfort
Labor savings	$303,520	$801,440	$731,440	$1,309,440
Additional freight	—	$240,000	$296,000	$694,000
Net savings	$303,520	$561,440	$435,440	$615,440

Source: Computations given to the union by the company.

too would soon need vacation replacement workers, eliminating three of the four job "advantages" of the Frankfort site over Hammond. Second, it ignored the $303,520 savings even if the department were retained in Hammond. The appropriate figure would be $615,440 minus $303,520, or $311,920 if a comparison were sought. Third, it ignored almost $1.8 million in additional capital costs needed for a new site in Frankfort. Fourth, it ignored likely bottleneck and handling inefficiencies from long distance transport finishing. Fifth, it ignored additional administrative and overhead costs from operating an entirely new facility in another city. And finally, perhaps most important, it relied on wage levels in Frankfort that seem totally unrealistic, given the extremely high quality, "close spec" nature of the product market niche served by the grinding department. One of LaSalle's competitive advantages was its reputation for error-free production. Whether workers earning approximately 60 percent of industry norms, would continue that high quality, high value-added production without a hitch, was problematic.

The union and the Calumet Project noted these problems. They did so as a part of a six-point strategy:

1. Reject all concessions;
2. Expose inadequacies in Treder's analysis and figures;
3. Develop a counter-analysis, given available information;
4. Call for a neutral third party to do a feasibility study of how jobs could be economically saved in Hammond;
5. Persuade or induce LaSalle to cooperate with the feasibility study and to postpone any final decision until it was completed and considered; and
6. Keep pressure on Treder to cooperate.

The first four parts of this strategy have already been discussed; parts 5 and 6 were also undertaken immediately.

Momentum grew for the position of the union/Calumet Project. On 14 February the daily newspaper the *Hammond Times* issued an editorial backing the union/Calumet Project proposals. Titled, "Big pay cuts aren't the best way," the editorial stated:

> The company has told the Progressive Steelworkers Union the company could save $600,000 to $700,000 a year by moving its grinding operation, which employs 54 people when operating at full capacity, to Frankfort, in central Indiana.
> LaSalle said it will keep the grinding operation in Hammond only if union concessions make up the money the move would save.
> Union members fear if the grinding operation is moved, the rest of the Hammond plant's operations may follow suit. Then about 340 jobs, not 50, would be at stake.
> LaSalle apparently has forgotten loyalty is a two-way street.
> The employees have been loyal to the company, but the company is ready to run off to Frankfort and leave its Hammond workers in the dust. . . .
> The company should consider a feasibility study for expanding operations at the Hammond plant. The Calumet Project for Industrial Jobs, a grass-roots labor group, and the union want a third party to examine ways to keep jobs at LaSalle's Hammond plant. . . .
> LaSalle should be loyal to the workers who have worked hard and been loyal to the company. LaSalle should be eager to help its workers by agreeing to further study of how its goals can be achieved.[32]

The next day the Calumet Project revealed through the media that LaSalle had received $97,500 tax abatement in 1989 for the very same "short cut" line it was now planning to move out of Hammond. In the tax abatement application the company had promised to retain its present employment plus six additional workers. A Calumet Project spokesperson called the company's plan to move those jobs "a clear betrayal of public trust":

> They took tax abatement money for installing equipment and now they're threatening to pull it out. This is not a show of good faith to the community. . . . They promised to retain jobs and these are the very same jobs they're moving.[33]

At this point Treder was so angry at the continuing press coverage of the union/Calumet Project campaign that he refused to speak to reporters.
The city now sided with the union/Calumet Project position that any public subsidies should have strings attached. Mark McLaughlin,

Hammond's economic development director, announced that the city had met with LaSalle about incentives but only in exchange for company commitments:

> "The next step is theirs," he said. "Right now, our position is the city will provide whatever incentives we can in exchange for LaSalle's commitment that no divisions will be moved out of the city."[34]

On 20 February the union and the Calumet Project sent a letter and document of its position to public officials that requested a meeting to discuss the situation. The same day Treder wrote to "employees, retirees, and other friends of LaSalle Steel Company" where he attempted to counter-attack on all the major issues involved in the campaign to save the department. He argued that the company's first duty was to *all* employees, suppliers, customers, and stockholders; the grinding department was losing money and had to be made profitable or all would lose out as it dragged down the company; relocation would actually benefit everybody because higher efficiency and profitability at the new location would make existing Hammond jobs more secure; contrary to fears, there were no plans to shut down the entire plant; LaSalle had not asked for "concessions" from its workers, only "savings"; the company would like to retain the department in Hammond if it could be done economically.[35] A similar letter from Treder appeared in the *Hammond Times*.[36]

Due to Treder's refusal to speak with the press, the *Hammond Times* business writer was forced to call Quanex headquarters for reactions. Quanex president and chief operating officer Robert Snyder stated that the relocation decision had only been made "to stimulate discussion. Our desire would be to keep it (the grinding operation) in Hammond."[37] But he also added that profitability came first. He did not favor a third party feasibility study; he wanted the union and the company to work it out privately. He denied that the company was asking for concessions; rather, they wanted employees' input on ways to make the department more efficient: "'We're strong believers in employee involvement,' Snyder said."[38] Top Quanex officials now appeared to be involved in the decision.

The following week the company's relocation plans received another blow. On 25 February Hammond City Council Chairman Robert Markovich wrote two letters. One was to Richard Treder endorsing the union/Calumet Project proposal for an independent feasibility study and asking for the company's cooperation.[39] The other was to the Frankfort City Council. It requested that "no public subsidies would be offered from Frankfort to LaSalle in an attempt to lure jobs from one Indiana community to another," adding, "We are sure you realize that any sort of 'bidding war' between our two communities would not be fruitful."[40]

The next day Hammond Mayor Thomas McDermott wrote Treder requesting the company to cooperate with the union to preserve jobs. McDermott, a conservative business-oriented Republican, indicated the degree to which the union/Calumet Project campaign had affected his thinking by stating:

> Over the years I have had the opportunity to meet and work with many employee units that work for companies within the city of Hammond. On many occasions I have found the bargaining units to be both difficult and disruptive. This just is not the case in my meeting with representatives from LaSalle's Grinding Department.
>
> In meeting with the representatives I had hoped to bring them into line with my thinking that there had to be concessions. After meeting with them I find myself agreeing with their position.[41]

McDermott also wrote to Frankfort Mayor Don Snyder, asking that no subsidies be given LaSalle and requesting that Frankfort not engage in a "bidding war" over the company. Mayor Snyder stated that he "sympathized with Hammond officials":

> "We're certainly not going to keep anybody out that wants to come here," he said. "But I can't see us offering incentives for them to come here because I wouldn't want that to happen to any of our companies.[42]

Hammond's economic development director began echoing the union's (and the Calumet Project's) positions. He warned the Hammond city council that departmental relocation may foreshadow a full-scale shutdown despite company denials[43] and argued in favor of an independent feasibility study because private company internal ones could not be trusted as necessarily accurate.[44] This independent and critical stance toward the company was a major reversal from his usual "good business climate" attitude.

Quanex CEO Carl Pfeiffer received copies of all press clips, letters from public officials, and so on. A cover letter requested the parent company to join with the union and virtually all interested parties in northwest Indiana in convincing local LaSalle management to agree to the union/Calumet Project proposals.

The original plan to relocate the grinding department now faced enormous obstacles. In addition to original uncertainties about availability and quality of a labor force, land acquisition and building construction, logistical work flow problems inherent in road transportation, and likely initial cost overruns, new obstacles arose:

- The Hammond union was strongly opposed, creating possible labor relations and worker morale problems.
- Concerned public officials at all levels of government opposed the plan. Political good will hung in the balance.
- Extensive publicity had been unfavorable to the company and its plan. Public image was hurt; public definition of the issue was against the company. Further negative publicity was likely.
- Spearheaded by the Calumet Project, all public expressions of community will opposed the company's plan.
- Even Frankfort, the intended recipient site, probably would not extend public subsidies to the corporation because of doubts about company motives.
- Within the company, Richard Treder was repeatedly circumvented by communiques (and eventually reporter's queries) to higher officials.

As he faced the situation, Richard Treder must have seen a united wall of opposition to his earlier plan.

VICTORY FOR THE UNION

On 5 March 1991 Treder released a written statement reversing the earlier plan. He refused to speak to the press; reporters could get no explanation. The statement claimed all plans were on hold due to a weak economy:

> While the new turning equipment we have purchased is scheduled for delivery in August, we are not at present making plans to install it anywhere, because demand for the product has dropped and prices are soft. . . . If the situation improves and the decision is made at some later date to install the new equipment, we would prefer that it be located in Hammond.[45]

The claim that the equipment would not be installed was highly suspect. The equipment had been bought; it would be installed *somewhere*. The "reason" (poor economy) appeared to be nothing more than a face-saving gesture for Treder. A newspaper reporter noted that Treder "did not explain how the company would be saving money by not making a move designed to make it more productive."[46]

Union response to the announced change was positive. Union vice president Ron Kelley stated, "We're pleased with the company's decision at this time. We're back at management and the union working together again." President Zed Rixie added, "In the past we've always had a good working relationship (with the company). It kind of deteriorated, but now it's back up again."[47]

Calumet Project Director Lynn Feekin stated that "the union deserves at least some of the credit" for the reversal of the decision:

> It shows that workers doing outreach to public officials and the community can have an impact. . . . I think the union can be proud they were active in this, instead of passively reacting to whatever happened.[48]

In May Richard Treder quietly retired, replaced by Patrick H. Wannell, LaSalle's former vice president of sales and marketing. Wannell indicated that he wished to establish more positive relations with the union, the media, and the community. In the fall and winter of 1991–92 the new equipment was installed into the Hammond plant, creating an additional fifteen jobs.[49]

The company and the union began developing employee involvement programs in 1991. LaSalle discovered that a cooperative attitude toward its workforce paid off in a way that its earlier relocation threats and confrontational attitude had not. Assured of at least temporary job security, workers helped improve plant efficiency. Quanex's 1991 *Annual Report* claims union-management cost reduction teams worked well, especially in the grinding department, where productivity increased 24 percent.[50]

In 1992 LaSalle reported a 20 percent sales increase, 2 percent additional market share, 22 percent reduction of lost-time injuries, quality performance improvement of 20 percent, 16 percent lowering of net assets through improved inventory management, 5 percent reduction in variable costs, and a close to sevenfold increase in operating earnings over 1991. The company attributed much of its success to employee involvement, under the theme of "Teamwork for Success":

> All employees are being systematically trained in the technologies of teamwork, problem solving and managing people. The long term objective is full "employee empowerment," recognizing the growth and contribution of every individual employee.[51]

In the first quarter ended 31 January 1993, LaSalle reported further increases of 21 percent in sales and 61 percent in operating income over the same period a year earlier.[52]

The company has been successful since it abandoned Treder's plan to relocate a department from Hammond. The union likewise accomplished all of its main goals in the campaign to stop the relocation. Approximately fifty jobs were saved; additional jobs were added; all jobs were made more secure; and the source of the company's earlier antiunion, antiworker behavior, Richard Treder, was replaced. The union could feel victorious in all respects.

ANALYSIS AND CONCLUSIONS

A minority viewpoint within the union held that the company never intended to move the grinding department: it was just a bluff intended to extract concessions. Possibly, but the company had spent enough time and money to make it unlikely the entire exercise was nothing but a charade. Lacking access to confidential company deliberations, definitive proof is impossible. But it seems that serious consideration of relocating jobs was begun and reversed.

What caused the reversal? Did the campaign influence the company? Some within the union are skeptical, but I believe the campaign *did* have a very real and major impact.

The union/Calumet Project campaign altered virtually every factor in the local environment of the company as it was making its decision. All of those changes made the move less appealing; the risks jumped greatly. These have been enumerated earlier: loss of a positive and productive relationship with Hammond employees, loss of political good will in Hammond, prolonged and intense negative publicity, highly unfavorable community attitudes, and the like. Whether these tipped the scale is hard to prove, but the sequence of events make it likely that they did.

If the campaign was very successful, what lessons can be drawn from it? In a written analysis of the victorious campaign, the Calumet Project drew the following lessons:

1. Ongoing shopfloor Early Warning monitoring is essential. The Project's Early Warning Network let us identify and combat the problems *before* it was too late.

2. Previous plant closing struggles have paid off in greater worker awareness. A number of LaSalle workers were veterans of earlier plant

closings and Calumet Project campaigns to preserve or reopen plants. These "new hires" played a key role in this campaign, particularly because of their understanding of the need for early action.

3. Public officials in the region now endorse (sometimes reluctantly) the Calumet Project's approach. In the LaSalle campaign, they acknowledged the need for public intervention, the need to avoid 'bidding wars' for jobs, and the need for strings on public subsidies. Again, this is the fruit of past Calumet Project activism, changing the "public atmosphere" of the region.

4. Community awareness and support are growing. Pastors called to offer support; the local newspaper editorialized in complete support of the Project's actions and recommendations; community people volunteered to work on the campaign; and university students chose the LaSalle campaign as a class project.

One final lesson from this campaign: the involvement and leadership of the union was crucial. The mutual goals and trust between the union and the Calumet Project made possible a common strategy, with workers committed to carrying it to the end. In the end, it was the workers' willingness to carry this fight into the community that made this victory possible.[53]

I would agree with these lessons. Regarding points 2 and 3, the critical earlier Calumet Project plant closing campaign was the LTV Hammond bar mill struggle related in the previous chapter. Approximately a dozen ex-LTV workers were employed at LaSalle. Some of these workers played a pivotal role by pushing for early and decisive union action. The earlier LTV campaign paved the way for the LaSalle one; a cumulative residue of awareness grew. The LTV struggle also prepared local public officials to quickly side with the campaign.

The union and the Calumet Project were also successful because they maintained a sharp strategic focus at all times. Throughout the campaign they adeptly focused on the critical issue at the appropriate time. The union and the Calumet Project defined the central issue of public discussion and debate. The company was reduced to reactive and usually unconvincing rejoinders. As a consequence, at the end of the campaign, *all* active voices were lined up behind the union/Calumet Project position. Without timely and strategic interventions that kept the issue framed in an advantageous manner (for example: "Why not cooperate with a neutral third party investigation?" rather than "It's the company's right to do whatever they want to."), the union/Calumet Project would not have been able to dominate the terms of the debate.

Two favorable circumstances helped. First, this was a struggle over a departmental relocation, not the shutdown of the entire plant. Consequently the union had more leverage. To the degree that the company needed good relations with remaining workers and the community, this leverage could be effective. Second, the company's original plan was not forced upon it by overwhelming market forces. Alleged savings were uncertain and relatively small, and alternative sources of savings were possible.

The cooperative relationship between the company and the union after the campaign raises additional questions. The union was successful with a confrontational campaign when the company was preparing to take action detrimental to the workers. It has also fared well more recently by cooperating with a company taking a cooperative attitude toward union goals. As long as the company continues to increase market share and to make improvements in productivity and quality, it will likely continue its cooperative attitude toward the union. How well the cooperation would survive an adverse economic turn for the company remains to be seen.

Because of its cooperative relationship with the company, the union is reluctant to publicly discuss the campaign, which is a sore spot with the company. The new president of the union declined to be interviewed for my research in writing this chapter, because he feared offending the company needlessly.

This raises the important question of how union locals can successfully maintain an independent position, or maintain community alliances or coalitions such as exemplified in the Calumet Project, if they are cooperating with their employer to increase its efficiency and profitability. Must one or the other be abandoned, or can they be reconciled? This complex question is beyond the scope of this chapter or book, but it remains a critical issue facing the labor movement in the 1990s, an era when employee involvement is spreading rapidly.[54]

COMPARING THE CASES: CRITICAL FACTORS

Each of the case studies in the preceding chapters was written as a self-contained case, and preliminary conclusions were drawn solely on the basis of internal evidence. Nevertheless, we can learn much more from a comparative analysis that highlights similarities and differences in light of the ultimate outcomes.

Chapter 1 presented five factors influencing the dynamics of plant closing situations: (1) Early Warning, (2) Labor-Management Issues, (3) Corporate Strategy and Structure, (4) Economic (Product Market) Factors, and (5) Role of Local Government. The following five sections of this chapter analyze the cases comparatively on each of these factors, drawing conclusions on the basis of the comparisons.

Following that, I argue that these five factors alone are inadequate to explain the outcomes unless they are supplemented by an analysis of the "social movement" dynamics embedded in the cases. Problem definition and alliance formation and mobilization, to be analyzed in chapter 8, are central to an understanding of the successes and failures detailed in earlier chapters.

Nevertheless, much can be learned from these cases about the role and importance of each set of factors. Because of the limited number of cases, and due to the limitations inherent in case study methodology, conclusions must be considered tentative and subject to wider verification.

EARLY WARNING

As noted in chapter 1, early warning of impending closure became a major public policy issue in the United States in the 1980s. Despite the 1988 federal WARN Act, there is usually inadequate forewarning of a plant closure for an effort to save jobs. Therefore the existence of and means of detecting early warning signs become important for job-saving efforts.

. This section addresses the following questions: Were there "early warning" signs that the plant may be closing? Did the workforce or the local government notice? What should the workers and the local government do if they wish to obtain advance notification? What do these cases tell us about early warning signs and how they can best be read?

The cases in this volume contain both early warning signs and lessons concerning their usefulness and importance. In the Blaw-Knox case, clear danger signals were present. The company had invested little in the plant since the 1960s except when the U.S. military paid the bill. Major expenditures by the U.S. Army hid this disinvestment from workers, however. Only selectively was it apparent: in the antiquated machine shop and the roll shop, but not on the M-60 tank production line. Additionally, the facility's product line had been narrowed to virtually one product, in a notoriously unstable military procurement market. U.S. defense plans were open knowledge: the M-60 tank was being phased out and replaced with something the foundry could not produce. And finally, the parent company's longer-term strategy, short-term restructuring activities, and business press speculation all pointed to divestiture and possibly elimination of this facility.

Despite ominous signs it took the Calumet Project almost five months to prod the union local into action. Denial is one of the first and most natural psychological reactions when faced with unexpected unpleasant news. Even with the delay, the union had close to two years before the plant closed.

Combustion Engineering also displayed severe warning signs in the final months before closure. The product line had been narrowed to one item. Other signs included large employment and production declines, lack of maintenance, decline in quality control, management instability, and lost customers. Beyond this, rumors swept the plant and employees discovered that there was no usual budget for the second half of 1986. Unknown to the workforce, the company's previous history of attempted plant shutdown, coupled with lack of local management advocacy for the plant within the corporate structure, would be danger signals if they could be uncovered. The company's recent strategy downplayed businesses like the East Chicago plant. Combustion Engineering employees vaguely knew of these danger signs, but only systematized and acted upon them through the Calumet Project's early warning system. But the union encountered this system too late to make much practical use of it.

The Combustion Engineering case demonstrates the potential shortcomings of local government early warning systems that rely on local plant management. The city of East Chicago's "visit with management" only weeks before the shutdown announcement failed to provide advance notice. In fact it caused complacency just as the company was preparing for shutdown. A clear lesson is that voluntary systems of management self-reporting need to be supplemented by other methods.

The Stratojac case demonstrates less stark early warning signs. Stratojac had an aging owner with no clear successor — one sign. New management's failure to relocate from New York and its leasing of plant and equipment rather than buying indicated lack of commitment to the site. Mismanagement of the company by the new managers may also have been a warning sign, but this may not have been readily apparent to the employees. Rising import penetration is perhaps also a very diffuse signal but hardly a decisive sign.

The lack of an apparent successor to an aging owner was a clear long-term warning sign, but the shorter term warning signals were less compelling. The shutdown was not preplanned but was rather the result of incompetent (and possibly unethical) management. This can be more easily covered up than long-term disinvestment, lack of maintenance, and the like. This union local *could* have uncovered the coming closure, but it would have been harder than it was for the Blaw-Knox or Combustion Engineering employees.

The key early warning sign for the LTV bar mill was the company's overcapacity relative to the product market following its latest merger. Coupled with the financial difficulties that culminated in the July 1986 bankruptcy proceedings, this overcapacity virtually guaranteed that one of the two bar mills in northwest Indiana would be closed. The only question was which one. Beyond that, many of the "typical" early warning signs were missing; this was a modern, competitive facility. Earlier warning would have been useful to the union local, but they managed a prolonged reopening struggle without it.

The LaSalle case contains few of the usual early warning signs. The plant was modern and competitive; business was fine. It is possible that the strike some months earlier was a precursor to the departmental relocation plans, but the labor strife was hardly a definitive warning sign standing alone. In the LaSalle case, the union was able to use informal contacts with various levels of management to "leak" information that the plant manager undoubtedly wished to keep secret. These rumors proved to be the decisive early warning that the union chose to act upon.

These five cases lend support to the argument that early warning signs visible to the workers are almost always present before a shutdown. They also tend to confirm the accuracy and usefulness of the Calumet Project's early warning scorecard in revealing these signs. (A copy of the latest version of the scorecard is contained in figure 7.1.) On the other hand, they contain no examples of successful early warning by local government. Governments need alternative methods or more candid sources if they desire accurate forewarning.

Figure 7.1. EARLY WARNING SCORECARD

Company Name_____City_____Date:_____

Your Name_____Phone_____

Below is a quick "scorecard" of the most commonly observed early warning signs. In filling it out, circle the appropriate points for each question, basing your answer on how severe the change has been or how big a threat you think this development is to your plant. Please give some examples to explain your answer.

1. Ownership Problems: Recent changes? Conglomerate owner? Aging owner without a successor?

   NO   YES
   0 3 6 9 12 15

2. Disinvestment: Building in bad shape? Inadequate maintenance? Outdated machinery? Major pieces shipped out or sold? Little or no reinvestment in the plant? Explain:

   NO   YES
   0 3 6 9 12 15

3. Declining Sales: Lost major customers? Reduced sales staff?

   NO   YES
   0 2 4 6 8 10

4. Mismanagement: Recent changes in labor-management relations? Incompetent supervisors? Failure to develop new products, processes or markets?

   NO   YES
   0 2 4 6 8 10

5. Job Loss: Recent layoffs? Expected to be permanent? Recent sub-contracting? Current employment:_____ Down from_____when?_____

   NO   YES
   0 2 4 6 8 10

6. Production Level: Decline in production? Any product lines eliminated? Work transferred to another plant?

   NO   YES
   0 2 4 6 8 10

7. Cash Crunch: Suppliers require "COD?" Inventories abnormally cut back, hurting production?

   NO   YES
   0 2 4 6 8 10

8. Production Quality: Lower standards? Cutbacks in quality control? Defective product shipped?

   NO   YES
   0 1 2 3 4 5

9. Management Instability: Managers relocated? Recent turnover? "Hatchet man" hired? Does management live outside the region?

   NO   YES
   0 1 2 3 4 5

10. Management Complaints: About utility costs? High taxes? Labor costs?

    NO   YES
    0 1 2 3 4 5

11. Production Capacity: Too much capacity? Another plant making same product? Is that plant non-union?

    NO   YES
    0 1 2 3 4 5

12. Possible Sale of Plant: Unidentified visitors? Cosmetic improvements?

    NO   YES
    0 1 2 3 4 5

Note: These scoring categories are only general guidelines which cannot be strictly interpreted. Any one of these indicators by themselves does not necessarily mean a plant is endangered. On the other hand, some indicators by themselves could indicate substantial danger.

EVALUATING YOUR SCORE

0 to 20	Give your plant an "A" and let us know if they are hiring.
21 to 30 gets a "B"	Keep an eye on things.
31 to 40 is a "C"	Any changes in plant status should be carefully monitored.
41 to 50 is a "D"	Union should begin active research to find causes for high scores and to learn more about company's plans for the plant. Depending on findings, more research or organizing may be needed.
51 or more is "SOS"	Time to launch a Save Our Jobs campaign within the local. Union should seek allies, resources, and decide on strategy for challenging threat of shutdown.

Please return to: Calumet Project for Industrial Jobs
                      4012 Elm St., East Chicago IN 46312

LABOR-MANAGEMENT ISSUES

The influence of labor relations on either a decision to close or to reverse an earlier closure decision is not clearly understood. This section analyzes the cases in this volume to answer the following questions: Did labor-management issues play a role in the closing decision? What role, if any, did labor relations play in determining the ultimate outcome? Can labor-management innovations help prevent plant closures? Can unions through traditional labor relations mechanisms exert an important influence to prevent or reverse shutdown decisions?

Blaw-Knox exhibited a labor relations system typical of many heavy industries in post–World War II United States. A strong industrial union (the United Steelworkers) negotiated pattern contracts with the steel industry segment of the parent company through coordinated bargaining. The pattern was set by the basic steel industry; oligopolized markets allowed generous wage and benefit packages to be absorbed out of monopoly rents. For the East Chicago foundry, military markets meant no competition and even greater labor cost flexibility. Relations between the firm and the union were adversarial but respectful and relatively peaceful.

This system gave the United Steelworkers considerable influence over traditional collective bargaining concerns like wages and benefits, but very little leverage concerning traditional "management rights" or "entrepreneurial" decisions. Consequently the collective bargaining system gave the Blaw-Knox union virtually no influence over either the sale or the shutdown decision. Labor-management relations had no impact on the closing decision, and only by moving out of its normal role through its collaboration with the Calumet Project was the union able to intervene in the events leading to shutdown.

Combustion Engineering was both similar and dissimilar to Blaw-Knox. The United Steelworkers coordinated bargaining for two plants (later three) of the corporation, again modeling contracts on basic steel patterns. However, coordination was more limited than for Blaw-Knox, and the company chose to challenge the basic steel pattern aggressively. Struggles over common contract expiration dates and basic steel contract provisions created a turbulent labor relations history throughout the 1970s. Once the corporation decentralized its bargaining structure to allow local plant bargaining, relations became more cordial and less expensive to both sides. Possibly the turbulent 1970s labor history contributed to the ultimate shutdown decision. Management subsequently cited "labor turbulence" and a unionized workforce as reasons for transferring production to a nonunion site. (This could be accurate or it could be another ex-

ample of management overstating labor issues as causes for shutdowns —
see Howland.[1])

The company's announced "new era of labor relations" involving a
"new management style" and employee involvement had no impact on
events. It was not a serious initiative, and the union was unable to influence the company through traditional union-management negotiating pro-
cedures. Only a collaboration with the Calumet Project and intervention
by the local congressman won additional concessions from the company.

Stratojac had a very different system of labor relations. A relatively
weak union local being serviced by an international union with few plants
in the area represented low-paid, relatively low-skill female workers with
a privately owned company at one plant. Relations were amiable; pay
was average for this low-compensation industry; a personal and somewhat
paternal relationship with the owner-manager had historically characterized the company. Despite the new management's attempt to scape-
goat the union, labor relations had nothing to do with the plant closing.
Likewise, labor relations issues played no significant role in the doomed
effort to reopen.

The LTV Hammond bar mill had the same structural labor relations
features as those of Blaw-Knox. Pattern contracts based on the basic steel
contract delivered high wages and good benefits to the union membership.
A classic attempt by the company to "whipsaw" two union locals into contracts inferior to the pattern had preceded this closing decision. It is impossible to prove or disprove the Hammond local's belief that it was
"punished" for militant opposition to this attempt. It may well have been.
But labor relations at most determined *which* plant would be closed in the
northwest Indiana area, not that a plant would be closed. Beyond this, labor
relations played no apparent role in the shutdown: contract provisions were
of no use in contesting the shutdown, and the union local had no shop floor
leverage over the company after the idling.

LaSalle Steel dealt with an independent union confined to the one facility. Historically the company and the union had relatively friendly relations. Contract settlements followed those of the steel industry, despite
the absence of formal pattern bargaining.

The January 1990 strike over two-tier wage payment and pension
provisions likely was a factor in the decision to seek alternative sites for
the turning and grinding department. The company wanted permanent reductions in labor costs; after failing to obtain these through a two-tier
wage scale, alternative sources of labor were sought. A nonunion high-quality workforce paid 40–45 percent below industry standards might achieve
the company's objective.

The union also had considerable leverage over the company in the conventional labor relations arena because the relocation was only of a department. The company still needed worker and union cooperation for ongoing production. Although an isolated union operating in only one plant (an "enterprise union") is usually weaker than one with broad industry or company representation, it is not necessarily weaker *within* a plant.

Unlike all the other cases, this union was able to use conventional labor relations channels (formal meetings and quasi-bargaining supplemented by informal shop floor pressure tactics) to help achieve its goal. Alone this may not have been enough, but it worked when combined with the other forms of pressure from the Calumet Project/union campaign.

The LaSalle case also demonstrates that a positive relationship with its union can help a company achieve its goals under some circumstances. At least in the short run, cooperation has benefited the company much more than its previous confrontation. The long-run impact of the cooperation program on the union will depend on its ability to maintain a strong independent power base and the company's fortunes in the product market.

These cases provide limited evidence for certain conclusions. To the extent these cases are typical, labor relations in unionized companies are related to plant closing decisions and struggles in the following ways:

1. Traditional collective bargaining provides unions very little influence over "capital" decisions such as where to invest and where and when to close a plant. At best prenotification may be required.

2. Labor relations may play a role in determining *which* of two plants will close (LTV Hammond, possibly Combustion Engineering), but it plays no role in other shutdown decisions (Blaw-Knox, Stratojac). When labor relations are irrelevant, unconventional roles (such as involvement in labor-community alliances) are the only path to influence.

3. In the one case where labor costs appeared to be central to the decision (LaSalle), the union was able to exert the most influence thorough conventional channels. This is not surprising.

4. Labor-management cooperation to address fundamental production problems is not seriously contemplated by many companies facing shutdown options. Three of these five companies made no attempt at initiating a cooperative program, and one set up only a sham "road show" rather than a genuine program. The one genuinely cooperative effort which worked was only attempted after confrontation ended in failure.

5. Weak union locals representing low-skill, low-wage workers (Stratojac) have the least likelihood of successfully formulating
alternatives or of influencing events. Structural labor market and
product market features doomed Stratojac workers and their
union.

In general, these cases support the prevailing wisdom that union locals are relatively impotent in the face of plant closures unless they assume
new roles and move beyond the traditional collective bargaining system.
The partial exception to this is departmental relocations: here union locals still can usefully utilize conventional shop floor power.

Corporate Structure and Strategy

These cases provide additional evidence to previous theoretical and empirical literature exploring the relationship between plant closures and
the corporate structure and strategy of the owner. The following analyses address these questions: How important is corporate structure and
strategy to determining ultimate outcomes? What corporate structures
make a closing more likely? Which corporate structures are more vulnerable to influence by labor/community coalitions? What role do corporate
strategies play?

The Blaw-Knox foundry fits into a familiar corporate structure for large
Midwestern manufacturing facilities: branch plant of an absentee conglomerate owner. Ex-managers of the East Chicago plant claim that pensions of top Blaw-Knox officials grew through milking and short-term
profits, rather than reinvestment and long-term viability. Beyond these
structural features, Blaw-Knox's parent company had a long-term strategy favoring its home appliances division over others. Thus, both structural and strategic factors put the plant at risk. The last minute sale to a
private holding company was a convenient way to avoid the ultimate
trouble and expense of closing the facility.

Combustion Engineering displayed even more institutional and strategic factors that put the plant at risk. Internal bookkeeping practices cast
the plant in an unfavorable light; top management had twice previously
attempted shutdown. Local management was unstable and experiencing
rapid turnover; moreover, local management had not advocated for the
plant internally. In the final ten years before the closing, the East Chicago plant's division was being milked to pay for expansion and acquisitions
in other divisions. The company's new Chief Executive Officer aimed at
high-tech business segments and away from "dirt businesses" like the

East Chicago plant. This combination presents a bleak picture for the facility, even with a stronger product market.

Stratojac's structure differed: private local ownership of the one facility meant that absentee corporate structures and priorities were not at play. Here the institutional features of importance were an aging owner-manager with no apparent successor and a top-heavy unproductive management team acquired through past attempts to curry an "heir apparent." After the sale, an incompetent (and possibly unethical) management attempted to run the company from the East Coast. Company strategy played no important role under the old owner and was relevant with the new one in the sense that overproduction and selling the product below cost is a disastrous "strategy."

The LTV Hammond bar mill was again owned by an absentee conglomerate. LTV's strategy of buying into basic steel led to its acquisition of both Jones and Laughlin and Republic Steel at a time of low demand for steel bar products. The resulting overcapacity, coupled with its not entirely coincidental bankruptcy, set the stage for the closing of one of its two northwest Indiana bar facilities in 1986. Company overcapacity also meant resistance to efforts to reopen the mill under competitive ownership.

LaSalle Steel was also owned by an absentee conglomerate. The plant manager had authority to make location decisions, subject to board approval at the parent company. LaSalle was strategically important to the parent company and was profitable. Nothing in either the parent company's strategy or its structure (beyond its generic conglomerate structure) indicated likely closure of the entire plant. The departmental relocation was not an immediate move to dismantle the entire plant (although its long-run consequences may have been just that), but an attempt to bolster control over the labor process and perhaps profitability.

These five cases support the claims of Bluestone and Harrison and others that corporate institutional and structural features and company strategies are closely related to plant closures. Both corporate strategies (wise or unwise) and corporate structures can increase the likelihood of closure; thus they should be included in community or union strategic planning for employment stability. New structures (e.g., locally based ownership, partial or complete community/worker ownership, etc.) and new strategies may save jobs.

Economic Factors: Product Market and Capital Needs

The role of strictly economic factors in plant closing situations cannot be ignored. The following analysis addresses these questions: How important is the state of the product market? How large of a role do import penetration, production overcapacity, need for massive reinvestment, and similar economic factors play in determining a shutdown? How important are they in thwarting or aiding efforts to avert a closing or to reopen a facility?

I analyze these five cases in terms of four economic factors: (1) market decline (or lack of it); (2) import penetration; (3) overcapacity in the industry; and (4) industry profit rate. If economic conditions make plant closings inevitable, statistics on these factors should indicate that. If, on the other hand, industry conditions are not dire, all attempts to preserve a plant or to save jobs cannot per se be considered hopeless and counterproductive.

BLAW-KNOX

Market Decline. For Blaw-Knox, market decline can be considered absolute *if* the relevant market is confined to only M-1 tank castings. However the relevant market is the one for all steel castings. This market was somewhat troubled but not in disastrous decline. The market for domestic steel castings from 1981–86 showed a compound annual drop of 4.8 percent in the value of shipments, according to government statistics.[2] Changes from 1985 to 1986, were the same: a -4.8 percent drop. This is a serious decline, but the market grew 5 percent from 1986-87, the very time the Blaw-Knox foundry was closed.

Imports. Import penetration might be considered another serious factor in plant closings. However, a well-designed study in the metalworking machinery, electronic components, and motor vehicle industries found no correlation between imports and plant closures.[3] In the steel foundry industry, the U.S. Commerce Department was unable to accurately estimate true import penetration during the 1980s, because much of it would be indirect imports of castings as part of finished products. Figures on direct imports showed little impact, but the Commerce Department estimated that it was increasing in 1986.[4] Quantification seems impossible; however, no one has suggested that a massive increase in steel castings imports was responsible for plant closings or business failures in this particular industry.

Overcapacity. Capacity utilization figures compare actual output to the total capacity, or ability, of the industry to produce. 100 percent capacity utilization would mean that no more could physically be produced,

Table 7.1. Steel foundry median rate of return on sales, assets, and net worth, selected years (in percent).

Year	Return on Sales	Return on Assets	Return on Net Worth
1983	0.7	0.4	0.6
1986	2.7	4.1	5.7
1988	3.7	5.6	18.2

Source: Dun and Bradstreet, *Industry Norms and Key Business Ratios,* relevant years.

under normal conditions, given existing plant and equipment. Fifty percent capacity utilization would mean that existing plant and equipment could produce twice what was actually produced.

Normal capacity utilization is between 80 and 85 percent. In the 1970s, yearly total U.S. industry capacity utilization varied from a low of 74.6 percent to a high of 88.4 percent.[5] An industry whose capacity utilization percentile was down in the 70s could be considered to have a degree of overcapacity; a percentile in the 60s or below would signal a very serious problem. An industry with a percentile in the high 80s or above could be considered booming.

Government figures on capacity utilization are often aggregated. There are no figures for steel foundries, only for the broad categories of "primary metals" and "iron and steel," which had serious overcapacity. Compared to the steel industry overall, foundries probably had a degree of overcapacity as of 1986 but nowhere near as severe as that of the basic steel industry. An educated guess is that there was some overcapacity, but not a great deal.

Profitability. Reliable profitability figures for an entire industry are difficult to obtain. Dun and Bradstreet figures drawn from samples in the industry are the best we have to go by. In the following, I will be using D&B figures, but the reader should be aware that they are only approximations.

In 1986, the steel foundry business was profitable and was becoming more so. Table 7.1 gives the median rate of return on sales, assets, and net worth for steel foundries in 1983, 1986, and 1988. Profit rates were relatively low, but improving, in the steel foundry industry in 1986 when Blaw-Knox closed the East Chicago foundry.

The economic conditions in the steel foundry industry at the time of the closing of the East Chicago foundry can therefore be summarized as follows. The market had been gradually declining for five years but was just beginning to pick up. Imports were insignificant if measured by direct figures but were more important and probably increasing if hidden "indirect" imports were included. Profit rates were low but growing slightly. Overall, conditions were fairly poor but not overwhelmingly bad. The future outlook was for a slight improvement.

COMBUSTION ENGINEERING

Market Decline. Combustion Engineering faced a much worse market situation. Shipments of electric power generating equipment in 1986 dropped to nineteen million pounds of steam per hour, less than half of 1985's 39 million pounds.[6] This was the lowest in fifteen years, and less than 12 percent of 1972–75 averages. In 1987 they again dropped almost by one half to ten million pounds. The decline in the *value* of shipments was not so steep: a 28 percent drop from 1985 to 1986 followed by a 24 percent drop from 1986 to 1987. Nevertheless, this was an industry in steep decline. Combustion Engineering's particular market niche was, if anything, in worse shape than the overall market.

Imports. Imports in the steam turbine generator market had been declining rapidly for some time. On a compound annual rate, they declined 35.6 percent per year during 1979–84.[7] From 1984 to 1985 they declined an additional 44 percent. Following a temporary surge of 59 percent from 1985 to 1986, they declined an additional 28.6 percent from 1986 to 1987. Imports were not really a factor.

Overcapacity. Capacity utilization figures are not available for the steam turbine industry; the closest we can get is the broad category of "nonelectrical machinery," which showed capacity utilization of about 70–75 percent in the mid-1980s and of 69.6 percent in 1986.[8] This indicates overcapacity; the situation was probably worse in the electric power generating equipment market.

Profitability. Industry profit rates in 1986 were not depressed: 27.4 percent on net worth and 8.8 percent on assets.[9] Table 7.2 gives the median rate of return on sales, assets, and net worth for steam engines and turbines for the years 1983, 1986, and 1988. The industry was doing much better in 1986 than it had previously and better than it would subsequently.

Table 7.2. Steam Engine and Turbine median rate of return on sales, assets, and net worth, selected years. (in percent)

Year	Return on Sales	Return on Assets	Return on Net Worth
1983	4.1	4.4	14.1
1986	4.3	8.8	27.4
1988	1.8	2.1	6.8

Source: Dun and Bradstreet, *Industry Norms and Key Business Ratios,* relevant years.

The Combustion Engineering plant faced an economic environment dictating either that the plant must shut down or change its product line. Steep market decline and subsequent overcapacity meant that it could no longer profitably produce its one traditional product.

STRATOJAC

Market Decline. Stratojac faced a stagnant, but slowly growing, market throughout most of the 1980s. The value of shipments in the men's/boy's/suits/coats market grew at a compound annual rate of 1.4 percent from 1981 to 1986.[10] From 1985 to 1986, it declined 2.4 percent, dropped another 11.7 percent from 1986 to 1987, and grew 10.7 percent from 1987 to 1988. Thus the overall market picture was mixed but stagnant.

Imports. Imports have been a constant threat to this industry for some time. The men's/boy's/suits/coats segment is no exception. Imports in this segment grew at a compound annual rate of 13.6 percent from 1981 to 1986; they grew an additional 13.5 percent from 1986 to 1987 and an additional 12.4 percent the following year. Only in 1989 did imports plummet a mammoth 34.6 percent, followed by an additional 12.1 percent drop in 1990. Beginning in 1988 exports began to grow rapidly, just before imports began their rapid decline. Nevertheless, imports were a major threat to domestic producers throughout much of the 1980s. However, Stratojac ultimately shut down (in Amsterdam, New York) in 1989, just as imports faded rapidly. Although imports were part of the larger intensely competitive environment, they cannot be singlehandedly blamed for the demise of Stratojac, which even the owners attributed to poor management.

Table 7.3. Mens/boys/suits/coats industry median rate of return on sales, assets, and net worth, selected years (in percent)

Year	Return on Sales	Return on Assets	Return on Net Worth
1983	2.3	4.7	9.5
1986	1.3	2.3	8.8
1988	1.9	2.1	7.8
1990	2.6	6.8	14.1

Source: Dun and Bradstreet, *Industry Norms and Key Business Ratios,* relevant years.

Overcapacity. The apparel industry did not have an overcapacity problem in the 1980s. It is doubtful that the men's overcoat segment differed from the overall industry in this respect. From 1981 to 1986, capacity utilization ranged between 80.4 percent and 84.8 percent, which is very average for all industry.[11] From 1987 to 1989, the corresponding figure was always between 83 percent and 84 percent.

Profitability. The domestic men's/boy's/suits/coats industry remained profitable throughout the 1980s, albeit at low rates. In 1986 the median return on net worth was 8.8 percent; in 1988 it was 7.8 percent and climbed to 14.1 percent in 1990.[12] Table 7.3 shows the return on sales, assets, and net worth for this industry segment for the years 1983, 1986, 1988, and 1990. The industry was profitable in the 1980s, but only marginally so. Beginning in 1990, it turned a higher rate of profit.

Stratojac faced a steady but stagnant market, growing import competition, no problems with industry overcapacity, and a marginally profitable set of competitors. A firm with reasonably good management, workforce, technology, and marketing would survive.

LTV BAR MILL

Market Decline. The LTV cold-finished bar mill was operating in a shrinking market. Government data cover all steel mill products, not merely the cold-finished segment, but there is no question that the cold-finished segment shared in the general trends of the industry. From 1981 to 1986 the value of steel mill products declined at an annual 8.5 percent compound rate.[13] The worst of this decline was in the early part of the decade; the

1985–86 decline was 6.8 percent, while 1987 began a large upturn. In that year the value of steel mill products shipped increased 15.7 percent over 1986; 1988 registered an additional 24.5 percent increase. Thus at the time of the 1986–89 battle to reopen the Hammond bar mill, the market was growing but only because it was climbing out of a steep and prolonged downturn of the previous six years.

Imports. Imports of steel products during this period were sizable, but they were not growing. In 1985 they were approximately 17.5 percent of the market; in 1986, only 16 percent; in 1987 and 1988, slightly below 15 percent, and for 1989 and 1990, down to 13 percent and below. The compound growth rate of imports in the first half of the decade was negative: minus 4.9 percent. Given these figures, growth in imports cannot be considered a cause of plant closure in the mid-1980s.

Overcapacity. Capacity utilization figures for iron and steel show that the industry had a great deal of overcapacity in the 1982 to 1988 period. Capacity utilization was only 49.5 percent in 1982; it was 57.7 percent in 1983 and remained in the 63–68 percent range during 1984–86.[14] Only in 1987 did it climb to 76.8 percent and subsequently to "boom" rates of 88.9 percent in 1988. Cold finished steel figures would not be identical, but the pattern is probably similar. There was a serious overcapacity problem at the time the LTV Hammond mill was idled, but it diminished over the 3 years of the campaign to reopen.

Profitability. Profit figures for cold-finished steel in the 1980s are considerably better than they are for the steel industry as a whole. At the time of the 1986 idling of the plant, median rate of return on net worth was 11.8 percent.[15] This was more than double 1983's 5.7 percent. Table 7.4 shows the return on sale, assets, and net worth for this industry segment for the years 1983, 1986, and 1988. The industry was profitable but not entirely healthy.

In summary, the LTV bar mill faced a market that was growing fairly rapidly out of a state of extreme depression, considerable industry overcapacity, declining import penetration, and middling profit rates at the time of closure. These were not encouraging conditions but neither were they an impossible economic climate within which to operate.

Table 7.4. Cold-finished steel industry median rate of return on sales, assets, and net worth, selected years. (in percent)

Year	Return on Sales	Return on Assets	Return on Net Worth
1983	1.2	3.6	5.7
1986	3.5	7.4	11.8
1988	2.1	4.7	11.1

Source: Dun and Bradstreet, *Industry Norms and Key Business Ratios,* relevant years.

LASALLE STEEL

Because the LaSalle Steel case concerns a department relocation, not an entire plant shutdown, the overall economic conditions of the industry are less pertinent. The dispute was not over the viability of the entire enterprise, but rather about the profitability or efficiency of alternate production sites. Therefore general industry conditions will not be given here.

There is no consistent pattern of economic conditions in the industries at the time of shutdown. This is in line with other quantitative research that has failed to find a significant correlation between product market growth or decline and plant closures or between import penetration and plant closures.[16] Typically, the industries were troubled but were not in major trouble. Only in the case of Combustion Engineering was market decline so steep that shutdown or a new product line were the only options. High import penetration, industry overcapacity, or low profit rates were not unambiguous causes of shutdown.

Economic factors within the industry *are* important; certainly, they have much to do with the *timing* of a plant shutdown. It is also true that difficult market conditions make it harder to attract the capital, managerial talent, and so on needed to save or reopen an endangered plant. But the picture of economic market forces exerting an iron determinism over closure decisions does not accord with the evidence.

Role of Local Government

Local government officials played an important role in determining the outcomes of these five cases, both by their pre-shutdown behavior and by the role they chose to play once a shutdown was announced. As explained in chapter 1, governments can respond to closure by adopting one of three roles: a "bystander" role, an "offset" role, or a "player" role. In these cases, the Calumet Project and its allies were usually seeking a populist player role from the government. Its successes and failures in these efforts, and the consequences of the governmental action or inaction, will be the focus of the following analysis. I also examine government provision of subsidies.

The Blaw-Knox foundry had received no local tax abatements, but it had received major federal government support through the Department of Defense. The U.S. Army had provided direct investments; it also provided a sheltered noncompetitive market with virtually guaranteed higher payment in the event of cost overruns. The Army also assumed a large proportion of pension and shutdown costs in the event of a termination of the contracts. This facility had thus received a large, but undetermined, public subsidy.

The A. D. Little consulting firm recommended that local government assume a player role by monitoring any sale of the plant and considering acquisition and brokering of the foundry. Local government and economic development officials were unwilling to move in this direction, however. They feared spoiling the local "good business climate," which they perceived as essential to future investment in the area. A "good business climate" was not seen as a respectful but businesslike relationship between government and corporate investors, but as government subservience to a company's dictates regardless of the immediate losses to or consequences to the community. They were only willing to attempt pro-corporate financial offset measures (to secure more defense contracts) or, failing that, a "hands-off" bystander role.

Blaw-Knox officials manipulated politicians to intervene for more Army orders. After the sale, the company consistently misled those politicians courageous enough to ask about its plans. The company line was, "Help us get tank orders to keep us alive while we convert to civilian production." The actual company plan was to milk the plant for all the defense profits it could get and then shut the foundry down. Such manipulation demonstrates the potential for, or even encouragement of, corporate abuse of the political structure that is built into such an utterly dependent conception of government-business relations.

Combustion Engineering likewise treated government largess as a private right rather than a public investment requiring accountability to the public. Its handling of the industrial revenue bond ignored both the public purpose of the bond and promises made at the time of application. The city was afraid to require restitution, primarily because it feared that such a "businesslike" approach would violate the "good business climate" desired as a means to attract future investment.

The company also misled the city regarding its intentions prior to the shutdown by assuring city officials that all was well less than two months before the announcement of closing. Whether intentionally or inadvertently, the local government was not provided with information needed for effective planning to protect its interests. The company felt no obligation to consider the impact upon, or interests of, the local community in its strategic planning.

Congressman Peter Visclosky was an exception. He did intervene forcefully to persuade Combustion Engineering to make a financial contribution to the "labor offset" measures needed in the wake of the shutdown and to dispose of the site in a socially responsible manner.

The Stratojac case also demonstrates private abuse of government measures aimed at job preservation. The new managers of the company used state-subsidized investments (through Indiana's Corporation for Innovation Development) to remove jobs from the state. Indiana had no requirement that recipient companies retain Indiana employment. When the company moved to Amsterdam, New York, it was able to use the city and local economic development agencies in the same way, eventually squandering well over $2 million in public subsidies with no strings attached.

The LTV Hammond case displays a different set of government-corporate relations. Under strong pressure as a result of effective community organizing, the mayor and the city council and the congressman all took strong verbal stances against the company on behalf of the workers and the community at various points. Threats of a tax lien, talk of eminent domain, joining a lawsuit, pointed letters to top LTV officials, and strong press statements all demonstrate a willingness, under pressure, to breach the most subservient conduct of the "good business climate" approach. Public officials edged strongly but erratically in the direction of a populist player role.

The powerful and sustained campaign by the AOC and the Calumet Project explains the difference. It also explains why later public subsidies to a potential buyer were not granted automatically, but were tied into AOC approval and compliance with publicly desired behavior. The organizing had left a legacy of greater oversight over public subsidies.

The LaSalle case likewise shows considerable change from the earliest cases. Public officials — the mayor, councilpersons, the Congressman, and state officials — immediately joined in the campaign to save jobs at Hammond. And they did so against the wishes of the corporation. Partially this was due to the cumulative effect of previous Calumet Project plant closing struggles that had so changed the "definition of the problem" in the public's eye that they were pushed in this direction. (See next section for a discussion of "problem definition.") Partly it was due to excellent organizing by the union, which meant political pressure was overwhelmingly from the union side. The political costs of siding with the union were not that great: even much of the local business community undoubtedly sympathized with the union. Only a relatively mild form of government intervention midway between an offset and a populist player role was demanded; it did not require a highly unorthodox stance from the public officials.

Nevertheless, the difference from the earlier cases is clear. Active intervention by the Hammond city council and the Hammond mayor with their counterparts in Frankfort, Indiana to avoid a bidding war" was definitely a more assertive and independent role than had been previously evident. The uproar over the tax abatement for the "short cuts" line also stands in contrast with public docility in the face of similar public subsidy abuse by Combustion Engineering or Stratojac.

The Calumet Project and its allies were most successful in pressuring government officials into a populist player role in the LTV bar mill and LaSalle cases. Blaw-Knox began in this direction, but lack of pressure and failure of nerve turned it into a much less extensive government effort.

The evidence from these cases suggests that local governments fare better when they break out of the strictly dependent "good business climate" approach to economic development and adopt a more vigilant, businesslike stance toward businesses operating within their borders. Company obligations to the community in return for public subsidies and requirements for "good corporate citizenship" from all companies make sense. Good corporate citizenship includes lengthy prenotification to local government of a closing, full cooperation with efforts to save the plant through a sale, generous outplacement benefits to affected workers and similar provisions for affected communities, attempts to attract replacement industry, and the like.[17]

This is not to argue that local governments can safely cultivate *bad* relationships with the businesses operating within their borders. But local governments do not necessarily damage those relationships (i.e., the "business climate") when they relate to businesses in a more hard nosed "businesslike" way. Admittedly, these cases do not prove this assertion, which depends on wider evidence for its validation. What the cases do unambiguously show is that the conventional wisdom counseling strict subservience to the corporation actually *invites* abuse. If public resources are made available for purely private profit-seeking ends, they will often be used in exactly that way with no consideration for the public welfare. If

Table 7.5. Comparison of the Five Factors

	EARLY WARNING	LABOR-MANAGEMENT PATTERNS
BLAW-KNOX	clear signals present; discovered 2 1/2 years before closure	pattern bargaining with diversified company; no apparent effect on closure decision; no influence for union through this channel
COMBUSTION ENGINEERING	clear signals present; discovered just before closure	pattern bargaining with diversified company; possible effect on closure decision; no influence for union through this channel
STRATOJAC	some signals present but not clear; not discovered prior to closure	single plant bargaining; paternalistic relationship; no effect on closure decision; no influence for union through this channel
LTV	signals present but not clearly pointing to Hammond site; not discovered prior to closure	pattern bargaining with diversified company; possible effect on which plant closed; no influence for union through this channel
LASALLE STEEL	usual signals not present; discovered through rumors and informal contacts with management personnel	single plant bargaining; probable effect on closure decision; considerable influence for union; later more cooperative corporate behavior

Table 7.5. Comparison of the Five Factors *(continued)*

CORPORATE STRUCTURE AND STRATEGY	ECONOMIC FACTORS	GOVERNMENT ROLE
absentee conglomerate structure; corporate strategy disfavored plant	gradual market decline; hidden imports of unclear dimensions; mild overcapacity; low industry profitability	military contracts and subsidies; unwilling to undertake a "player" role; manipulated into attempts to gain more military contracts
absentee conglomerate structure; corporate strategy and internal accounting practices disfavored plant	steep market decline; insignificant imports; capacity utilization unclear; average industry profitability	public subsidies; unwilling to demand accountability (Congressman an exception; forces company to contribute to "labor offset" measures)
private local ownership; one plant; terrible mismanagement with little overall "strategy"	stagnant market; growing import penetration; no overcapacity; marginally profitable industry	public subsidies
absentee conglomerate structure; corporate strategy leads to overcapacity	strong market decline beginning turnaround; declining import penetration; serious overcapacity; fair profitability	populist player role (inconsistently asserted, and after much pressure)
absentee conglomerate structure; plant manager's autonomy and local strategy lead to confrontation	not relevant to relocation decision	public subsidies; mild populist player role

companies are not required to consider the community impact of their behavior, most will not.

Governments in hard-hit economic regions such as the Calumet Region in northwest Indiana cannot afford to adopt a bystander role in major plant closing situations. The choices are between the offset role or the player role, and between the types of offset and player responses. Populist player responses are by far the most unorthodox; they also tend to strengthen the power and influence of workers and community groups like the Calumet Project. But the most frequent response is limited to pro-business offset approaches. Among the many economic actors, capital holds a privileged position within the political economy of the United States. Mobilization of political pressure can alter this temporarily to some degree, but the Calumet Project and like-minded groups need to build *institutional* mechanisms for a populist player response if they wish to make more permanent gains.[18]

The five issues that have been analyzed in this chapter are summarized in table 7.5. Although these issues are important, they do not provide full explanations for success or failure of efforts to save jobs in plant closing situations. Two of the five measures — corporate structure and strategy, and economic conditions — are usually beyond the ability of any local players to influence. They provide *limiting conditions* to local action, but no more.

The remaining three are theoretically subject to influence at a community level. For example, both union locals and communities can engage in early warning activities, and I would argue that they should, based on the evidence from the cases. Likewise, unions can (and should) utilize conventional or unconventional labor relations strategies to prevent plant closings in those relatively unusual cases where this is a factor.

Local government's role is a major factor. But the role of local government is not a "given"; it can be influenced and changed by political activism. Normally the government will not be supportive of proactive measures to save a plant — the populist player role goes against the prevailing norms in mainstream political discourse. Therefore government will not be inclined toward major efforts unless pushed in this direction.

Conventional and market-driven wisdom counsels that economic realities make virtually all closings inevitable. I have argued that this is not necessarily true. Conventional wisdom would also accept the existing corporate strategy and structure and find them to be further insuperable obstacles to any attempt to alter a closing. The case is overstated. The corporate structure and strategy obstacles are large, but successful examples like LaSalle Steel and partial successes like the LTV bar mill struggle show that they are not absolute. Conventional market-oriented thinking also counsels quiescence toward existing government roles or the lack of early warning. The cases in this book point in the opposite direction.

Acceptance of conventional, market-driven wisdom forces communities, unions, and workers to make choices that could be unnecessary. Communities and workers need to rethink their relationship with corporations. The standard "good business climate" understanding requires them to aid corporate objectives of private profitability but to accept a totally dependent stance free of corporate obligations to the community.

Such a rethinking requires redefinition of how the problem is perceived. It also requires political alliance formation and mobilization to give political muscle to a new outlook. These issues are covered in chapter 8.

PROBLEM DEFINITION, ALLIANCE FORMATION, MOBILIZATION, AND THE SIGNIFICANCE OF LABOR-COMMUNITY COALITIONS

The most important lessons to be learned from these case studies concern the potential power and the limitations of labor-community coalitions. The issues can be usefully examined from the perspectives of problem definition and of political coalition-building. In the following section I will analyze the cases in terms of contending definitions of the problem facing the community. I then comparatively examine the construction of alliances and the mobilization of forces by the Calumet Project and its union partners to back up their conceptualization of the problem. Finally, I place the cases within two theoretical contexts and argue for the importance of labor-community coalitions.

Problem Definition

As noted in chapter 1, problem definition is a crucial aspect of a public struggle. Different players push to have their conceptualization of the problem become the commonly accepted one for all to act upon. A political struggle ensues to determine which definition will prevail.

Problem definition entails three dimensions: (1) a standard used to judge if a problem exists; (2) a causal explanation for the problem; and (3) a remedial action plan to correct the problem. In the five cases the Calumet Project and its allies used a standard of *community welfare,* usually translated into the availability of well-paying quality jobs. Causal responsibility for the job loss was attributed to corporate actions (disinvestment and "milking," mismanagement, etc.). The remedial action plan usually called for an interventionist government role and a corporate reorientation away from strict profit seeking to a social cost accounting.

The Calumet Project's adversaries tended to have diametrically opposed definitions of the problem. The standard employed was private company *profitability* or the local area's *good business climate* (which was equated with the community doing whatever is possible to aid private profit making). Causal responsibility was attributed to purely impersonal market forces beyond anyone's control. Remedial action plans tended toward private market mechanisms free from interference.

In each case the standard employed, the responsibility assigned, and the remedy sought were closely correlated on each side. The rest of this section analyzes each case in terms of problem definition offered and the struggle for its acceptance.

In the Blaw-Knox foundry case the Calumet Project applied the community welfare standard to argue against abandonment of the workforce and the community. The company was depicted as responsible for the shutdown through its disinvestment (milking) and narrowing of product line. The remedial action plan called for modernization in accordance with the consultant's recommendations. Failing voluntary compliance, local public officials were responsible for ensuring that this happened, even if this meant intrusive government oversight or more drastic breaches of normal government-corporate etiquette, such as eminent domain proceedings.

The owners of the foundry used the standard of private profitability. Causal responsibility rested with the U.S. Department of Defense, which was withdrawing the market necessary for survival. The remedy: more M-60 tank orders. All should help persuade the U.S. Army to place additional orders.

Neither side completely succeeded in getting its problem definition adopted. The Calumet Project/union perspective was initially dominant: community welfare dictated the commissioning of a feasibility study on saving the plant. Due to organized pressure job preservation was *a* defining standard, if not *the* defining standard, throughout the struggle. The company therefore had to mislead political figures about intentions to convert to civilian production.

The Calumet Project's definition of the problem was boosted by the feasibility study. As acknowledged experts on the foundry business, A. D. Little could command respect for its recommendations in a way no community group could. However, A. D. Little did not accept the Calumet Project's problem definition *carte blanche*. Little refused to criticize past company behavior and adopted a strict market orientation, which was only natural for a feasibility study. The strong "community welfare" standard integrated into their "bottom line" business analysis was more unusual. It grew from union and community pressures on A. D. Little researchers. Market criteria were stringently applied to the problem, but community welfare criteria were also employed. This hybrid analysis was satisfactory to the labor/community forces, because it offered the most realistic framework within which to save jobs and to bolster union and community influence, given the circumstances.

But the Calumet Project was not able to persuade public officials to carry out the activist measures called for in the A. D. Little report. Such a populist player role violated deeply embedded ideological beliefs that identified "community welfare" with private corporate supremacy in all major economic decision making. Faced with a situation where the apparent community welfare clashed with their ideology, public officials opted for the ideological side of the divide. Only more effective organizing could have reversed the orientation of public officials who did nothing as the plant was closed.

The Combustion Engineering case placed management's problem definition in a strong position. The product market was depressed; production levels could not economically support the enterprise. That was the whole story, from the company's viewpoint: profitability standard, market decline cause, and either no role or perhaps a labor offset role (retraining programs for dislocated workers) for the local government.

The market had declined, and one or more entirely new product lines would be needed to save the plant. Given very little time for a remedial action plan, it was unrealistic to define the problem in terms calling for a reversal of the shutdown decision. Instead the Calumet Project and the union redefined the issue toward corporate responsibility to the community, to force corporate contributions to community and labor offset measures. Since this company had misled public officials and had misused a public subsidy (the Industrial Revenue Bond), this redefinition had fairly broad appeal.

But the remedial action plan asked local government to engage in populist anticorporate actions: sue the company over the public subsidy abuse. Once again, such a course of action contravened prevailing ideology. Feeling no strong pressure, East Chicago officials again chose to abide by their longer-term ideological commitments rather than pursue an uncharted course in alliance with community or labor groups.

Congressman Peter Visclosky used the Calumet Project's standard of community welfare to secure some worker benefits and a company pledge to shut down the facility in an environmentally sound manner. Initially reluctant, the company did eventually accept responsibility to contribute to labor offset measures (i.e., worker retraining).

In the Stratojac case the company did not articulate a clear definition of the problem. To the extent one was offered, it relied on a standard of corporate profitability, a constantly shifting set of targets as causally responsible for difficulties (lazy union workers, Indiana officials unwilling to grant large enough subsidies, growing imports, etc.), and no clear action plan beyond more government subsidies.

The Calumet Project and the union had a clearer problem definition: worker and community welfare was the standard and gross corporate mismanagement was causally responsible. But they were much less able to offer a workable plan of action. The company in Amsterdam, New York, was beyond the reach of any Indiana parties. Alternative ownership plans faced huge obstacles. The coalition could obtain nearly universal agreement with its assessment of the problem, but the agreement could not be translated into meaningful supportive actions.

The LTV bar mill case offers clear articulations of sharply opposing definitions of the problem. Utilizing its familiar standard of community welfare, the Calumet Project/AOC coalition found LTV directly responsible for closing an economically viable operation and called for government officials and community forces to persuade or coerce the company to sell to owners who would run the plant. LTV used the standard of company profitability and private property rights, blamed overcapacity in a depressed market for causing of the closing, and planned to remove key equipment to boost company competitiveness.

In this war of definitions LTV was vulnerable because it could not argue that the plant was inefficient or not viable. The company was forced to define its position in terms of its *right* (based on private ownership) to do something that was harmful to the local community: ensure that the plant did not reopen. Private profitability for the company collided with the local community interest in jobs and economic well being. Therefore the company pretended to cooperate with community efforts to reopen the mill. The company also faced extensive and effective political mobilization by the Calumet Project/AOC forces — something they had not expected from such a small, resource-deficient opponent.

Nevertheless, LTV's claim of a private property right to dispose of its holdings any way it sees fit was firmly and deeply embedded in the legal and cultural milieu of the United States and the region. As one astute observer has noted:

> Private business corporations occupy a powerful position in the urban political economy. It bears repeating that capitalism has bestowed upon the business corporation a position of privilege. This position can be challenged or weakened, but it usually remains intact.[1]

LTV's presumptive right to deal with its property any way it sees fit could be challenged only through "radical" measures such as eminent domain proceedings (actual proceedings, not merely loose talk). Or a massive social movement sustaining a picket line in front of the facility indefinitely was another option. Neither the political will for eminent domain proceedings nor the mass social movement was present, although a surprising degree of progress toward both was achieved.

However, companies winning battles in this manner may be aiding their own loss in a larger war. Power thus exposed is power weakened. If the company is forced to assert naked self-interest and private property rights against a clear community interest, it risks weakening public commitment to its prerogatives. LTV won the battle but lost the "image" war on the ideological front. The Calumet Project/AOC coalition effort began reorienting the terms of the public debate. "Corporate responsibility" and "community welfare" become ever more prominent standards within which future debates are framed. LTV's environmental contamination of the site only enlarged this dimension of the issue.

The LaSalle case proved to be a rather uneven competition over problem definition. The Calumet Project/union forces won hands down. Using the familiar broad standard of community welfare, they also used narrower standards of corporate loyalty to the workforce and responsibility to the community in return for a public subsidy (tax abatement). The labor/community coalition held LaSalle official Richard Treder responsible for a socially undesirable and probably inefficient transfer of production. The remedial action plan called for the company to cooperate in devising ways to retain production in Hammond.

In response, Treder relied on a profitability standard. High labor costs at Hammond caused the impending departmental transfer; the action plan was transfer of production to Frankfort, Indiana. Market mechanisms and private economic decisions, free from external meddling, would resolve the problem. Three things undercut Treder's position. First, his standard of profitability, or competitiveness, was accepted but used to circumvent his decision-making authority. Any efficiency consultant would have to be accepted by the union and the Calumet Project. The consultant would be charged with finding a profitable way to retain production in Hammond. Both conditions undercut the company's freedom to make its own decision. Second, Treder had to convince Hammond officials and community residents that transferring jobs out of the community was good for the community. He argued that this would enhance profitability, making remaining Hammond jobs more secure. This argument was not convincing; the chain of causation was too tenuous, the alternative of preserving *all* jobs was far more attractive, and his "facts" were subject to dispute. Third, the Calumet Project/union side took and kept the initiative: the company was constantly responding.

In the end it was a rout. The labor-community coalition dominated the problem definition. It helped that market forces were not overwhelmingly unfavorable to the coalition's plan of action, press coverage was good, and past Calumet Project struggles made political and public reaction more receptive.

The Calumet Project's labor-community alliances succeeded in projecting a broadly accepted problem definition depending on certain factors. First, their problem definitions were hegemonic if opposing definitions were poorly articulated or were patently self-serving. They were also more successful if backed by strong political organizing that gave public officials little opportunity to evade the issue. Success was greater if the remedial action plan appeared workable without extraordinary measures. And finally, they tended to get the most sympathetic ear when they were "legitimized" by the "objective authority" of some institution or individual considered less prone to bias than a union or a community organization.

Conversely, the labor-community coalition's definitions of the problem were less dominant if sharply articulated, seemingly "neutral" opposing definitions were in contention. They also carried less weight if not backed by strong community organizing and political muscle, no matter how persuasive or coherent. Remedial action plans were less attractive if they required measures of a heroic and highly unusual nature. And they were less appealing if no legitimating authority supported them.

On the whole, the Calumet Project and its allies chose their problem definitions carefully and articulated them well. The most problematic aspect of the chosen problem definitions was that they went against prevailing ideologies of "business as usual." Deeply embedded traditions in the region require deference to corporations, reverence for the private market, and a government-corporate relationship of government subservience.

Yet these cases raise questions about such conventional wisdom. In plant closing situations the workforce and the community are asked to make choices that are harmful to their immediate self-interest. The local government is counseled to accept job loss and economic dislocation without protest so it can preserve its attractiveness for further investors. Workers and unions are told to accept loss of employment as inevitable.

But what if a tougher, more businesslike stance toward the corporation that stressed corporate responsibilities as well as subsidies *didn't* result in major or irreparable damage to the local community's ability to attract and retain job-creating investment? What if some plant closing decisions are *not* unalterable inevitabilities, but are corporate decisions potentially alterable through union, worker, and local community action? These possibilities, raised by the case studies in this book, call for a reconsideration.

Conventional wisdom is based on a market paradigm. Yet the marketplace consistently favors those who have capital over those without.[2] Since market decisions aim to further increase and concentrate the capital stock, they do nothing to redress the power imbalance between capital-rich corporations and workers or communities relatively lacking in capital. Inequalities are therefore reinforced, and social goals have no place alongside profit-seeking goals. If the two coincide, it is more a matter of chance than of any necessary connection.

Struggling industrial workers, unions, and communities therefore need to rethink and challenge the exclusively market paradigm, or they will frequently lose out in a competitive struggle to secure their interests.

But the reconsideration will eventually have to extend beyond the alternative problem definitions detailed earlier. Ultimately unions, workers, and industrial communities need to consider fundamental alterations in both established relationships and legal rights.

One promising avenue is the redefinition of those who have a legal or legitimate right to determine the fate of a productive enterprise. The "stakeholders" concept asserts that local communities and employees have a recognized stake or vested right in industrial enterprises because of their long-term relationships of support for the ongoing venture:

> Stakeholder rights arise naturally as an alternative approach when the stakeholders perceive there to be corporate violations of presumed social contracts between the community and its inhabitants on one side and the firm and its managers and owners on the other. These rights rest on perceptions and experiences that the interests of the shareholders are inconsistent with those of the stakeholders and that the latter need (and are entitled to have) independent rights of property to protect their own interests as well as to promote social well-being.[3]

While such a fundamental change in legal rights is nowhere on the horizon today, it does represent the logical remedy for disadvantaged communities and workers finding themselves ill-served by a strict market orientation.

Any changes in problem definition or in the larger ideological conventional wisdom require organization and struggle. They require sharp struggles.

Alliance Formation and Mobilization

As the preceding analysis has emphasized, the formation of alliances and the mobilization of support is crucial to the work of the Calumet Project and its allies. As an "outsider" pushing for populist responses, the Calumet Project must rely on broadly built coalitions. It is attempting to create a social movement.

In the Blaw-Knox case, the Calumet Project and the union tried to develop an alliance between (1) the union, (2) local public and economic development officials, and (3) interested community residents. Each of these may be subdivided for the sake of analysis. The union can be broken down into (a) the displaced workers (the union membership) and (b) the union as an institution, with leadership and structures at local, district, and national levels. Public officials divide into (a) city and local regional officials and (b) officials elected to national office (i.e., the Congressman). Community forces can be analyzed through the involvement (or lack of it) by (a) community organizations or (b) the religious community — both targeted constituencies of the Calumet Project.

The Blaw-Knox alliance began as a union-led effort with wide participation from public officials and strong support from the one East Chicago community organization. Over time coalition leadership shifted from the union to local economic development officials; the alliance then began to disintegrate over differing perspectives on what was an appropriate government role.

Several weaknesses are apparent in this effort to forge an alliance. Local union leadership played a relatively passive role, relinquished leadership over the struggle, and did not involve the membership. Given the diverse make-up of the coalition partners, and given the natural corporate subservience of local economic development officials, this became a fatal flaw. Mass turnouts at open union meetings show that many members were willing to get involved but were never given the chance. The union at the district level was supportive but did not take the leadership of the overall campaign. At the national level the union was not involved.

The other "leg" of the coalition that the Calumet Project relies upon to build a social movement is the community. The one church-based community organization in the city — the United Citizens Organization (UCO) — supported the effort, but was limited in what it could offer. It publicized the campaign and mobilized a limited number of activists to attend public meetings but either could not or did not develop a mass activism about the issue. A few religious figures participated through their UCO connection, but the religious community played no major role in the campaign.

Press coverage was extensive, so public awareness was high. Although no polls were taken, it is likely that support for the effort was high but "soft" within the larger community. This case illustrates the pitfalls for labor and community forces relying on general good will and broad coalitions with public officials in the absence of strong organization and mobilization of key constituencies. Since neither the "labor" nor the "community" leg of the labor-community coalition was strongly activated, the less reliable partners in the larger alliance eventually dominated the effort. These were the public officials. Only the local Congressman was willing to play an independent role without being forced to. Mere media campaigns, or good ideas, are not enough for organizations calling for a change in "business as usual." The Blaw-Knox campaign foundered due to insufficient grass roots organization and mobilization.

In the Combustion Engineering case, the labor-community forces were less successful than in the Blaw-Knox case. Saving the plant was next to impossible, so mass mobilization of either displaced workers or community residents was unlikely. A limited campaign concerning corporate responsibility occurred, but it was not a social movement. Union officials and Calumet Project personnel attempted to forge an alliance with city officials, but discussion took place within private or semi-private arenas, not in the streets or in an open meeting. Once again, the congressman intervened to aid the labor-community forces but not because a broader alliance was forged.

The Stratojac case involved very little building of alliances. The effort to reopen the plant never progressed to the point where alliances were necessary. The union local did mobilize its own membership for the preliminary meetings exploring the ESOP option, but no wider mobilization of forces was attempted. The only external "alliance" was the brief attempt to ally with the Hammond mayor in a search for a new owner. But overall, the case was more an attempt to explore the possibility of self-help through an ESOP than it was a campaign to force government officials into activism. Circumstances made the latter next to impossible.

The LTV Hammond case is an example of full-scale mobilization and alliance-building. The foundation of the campaign was activation of the union leadership and membership, which, in turn, organized support from the political community. Although the leadership of the AOC was always dissatisfied with the magnitude of active membership support, they were much more successful than most undertaking a similar effort.

The rather effective alliance supporting the effort to reopen the mill was wide after it had developed over a period of time: the displaced workers, the union structure, the congressman, the mayor, the city's only community organization, much of the local labor movement, and peripherally a number of local businesses having personal or commercial ties with the displaced workers. Extensive press coverage and numerous letters to the editor in local newspapers meant general public awareness and support were also high.

Several factors account for the success of the alliance-building: (1) high quality leadership, (2) good problem definition with an appealing plan of action, (3) time for the coalition to mature and develop, and (4) lack of effective counter-organizing. The alliance was strong enough to force anything short of "radical" steps challenging the normal way to do business.

But a *direct* challenge to LTV's private property rights was beyond the limit of what was permissible. The struggle escalated to the point where this was raised and in fact was the only way the worker and community goal (a reopened mill) was possible. Hammond officials talked militantly, but they blinked before the company did. However, the ultimate failure to reopen the mill should not detract from the remarkable alliance that the Calumet Project/AOC forces were able to construct and activate.

The LaSalle example also exhibits skillful construction of alliances and mobilization of political support. The union local mobilized internally and developed an active committee structure, which made it an effective instrument for outreach efforts. Their alliance with the congressman and city officials was sealed quickly and publicly. When the mayor wavered from the Calumet Project/union program by attempting to start a "bidding war," he was quickly brought back into line. Two features distinguish this campaign: first, a tenuous "alliance" was even forged with public officials in the "rival" city over the undesirability of a bidding war. Second, community support came exclusively through Calumet Project involvement; overall the community played a smaller independent role here than in earlier cases.

Public officials played the role they were asked to; they were not asked to undertake implicitly or explicitly "radical" actions, unlike the LTV case. The alliance between labor-community and political officials was solid, sufficient, not overly demanding on the politicians, and victorious.

Several themes about alliance building and mobilization emerge. *First, the Calumet Project and its allies were most successful when the union and the displaced workers initially mobilized internally and maintained an independent and leading role in external alliances.* This is only natural: other allies lack the same degree of moral legitimacy, as large a stake in the outcome, the same unrelenting focus on job preservation, or the will to carry through.

Second, *widespread press coverage and public sympathy is not enough:* it must be backed up by political muscle and a vigilance over public officials. Established institutions like the Chamber of Commerce can rely on less activist methods but not those challenging established corporate power rather than wielding it.

Third, *compared to other individuals or organizations, political officials are ultimately the most powerful allies for labor-community groups.* This is not surprising: political legitimacy and decision-making power exceeds that of virtually all private institutions or individuals except those that are exceedingly wealthy. Thus, the political structure is the natural, and potentially accessible, point from which to challenge corporate power.

Fourth, *alliances develop better if there is a lengthy period of time for them to be cemented in struggle* (LTV Hammond) *or if previous struggles have paved the way* (LaSalle). Prior efforts add to success if they are well chosen campaigns, not demoralizing exercises in futility. Labor-community coalitions must be in it for the long haul and must build incrementally, if they are serious. Starting from a disadvantaged position — both in resources and in status quo legitimacy — left populist labor-community groups have few shortcuts to success.

Following from this, a fifth theme is that *building alliances and mobilizing broad constituencies works best when the common goal seems to be both realistically achievable and highly desirable to the constituencies involved.* When saving or reopening the plant appeared unrealistic (Combustion Engineering, Stratojac) or when the goal was narrowed to something less significant than job preservation (e.g., retraining funds, "punishing" a company for past misbehavior, etc.), significant alliances never developed. The best alliances (LTV Hammond, LaSalle) focused on goals that were widely seen as achievable and critically important. Of course, it is the task of groups like the Calumet Project to constantly widen the public and political sense of what is important and achievable.

And finally, a sixth theme that emerges is that of *corporate dominance of the local constellation of alliances and political structures.* Corporate interests already have the web of connections and longer-term working arrangements necessary to make their alliances largely informal routine exercises of corporate hegemony. Therefore corporations have little need for additional organizations or mobilizations to defend themselves against labor or community adversaries, beyond what they routinely have. At the deeper ideological and institutional level, they strongly dominate. Labor-community groups must pick their battles and issues carefully, must organize winable battles within the existing environment, and must battle to win a more secure and "legitimate" role than they have at present.

The Significance of Labor-Community Coalitions

Two theoretical contexts can help us analyze the significance of these cases. One is the resource mobilization framework from the social movement literature.[4] This approach "examines the variety of resources that must be mobilized, the linkages of social movements to other groups, the dependence of movements upon third parties for success, and the tactics used by authorities to control or incorporate movements."[5] Resources can be either internal (social networks, shared identity, etc.) or external (media coverage, donations, use of influence, etc.)

Thus broadly conceptualized, the analyses in previous chapters fit within this framework. But we can also use it to look at the "big picture"; what are the possibilities and limitations of labor-community coalitions? The concluding section of this chapter addresses this question.

Prior to this, an additional perspective helps to illuminate other aspects of these cases. These cases concern working class organizations and working-class communities opposing employers, usually multinational corporations, making the class conflict perspective relevant.[6] In particular, I will focus on the issue of "class capacities": do labor-community coalitions and struggles increase the ability (capacities) of the U.S. working class and its institutions (primarily unions) to wield power?[7] Related to this is the issue of "class" vs. "community": do "populist" community struggles like this weaken and dilute class awareness and class power for workers, or can they aid working class capacities?[8]

Class capacities can be either structural or organizational. Structural capacities include those relationships within a class that weaken or strengthen its solidarity. For workers in northwest Indiana one major structural weakness is the historical racism built into both work site job patterns and community residential patterns. Union seniority rules and a government consent decree from the 1960s have somewhat lessened the power of work site racial divisions, but the heavily segregated housing patterns noted in chapter 1 have damaged working-class solidarity in the community. The cases in this volume do not contain examples of internal racial conflicts destroying a union's ability to act: unions in northwest Indiana are among the most integrated institutions in the region, and despite problems they are not strongly racked with internal racial conflict. Nevertheless, the political "Balkanization" that flows directly from housing segregation hurt the struggles by usually restricting political alliance building to the political structures of the city containing the plant. Each campaign was fought city by city. Workers residing outside the plant's city were limited in their ability to utilize political connections to aid the struggle. Racism damages the class capacities of the working class, even when this is not immediately apparent.

Organizationally, working class capacities depend primarily on unions. Unions have been in decline for some time, a fact that has been heavily documented and analyzed.[9] The question raised by these cases is whether unions would gain power through involvement with labor-community coalitions and their struggles.

The evidence indicates that unions do empower themselves by such alliances. In each case the union was unable to have influence through strictly traditional labor-management channels; the Calumet Project coalitions enhanced both strategic options and resources to achieve power.

Fears that community-based struggles will undermine class-based forms of organization by promoting an "enclave consciousness"[10] are not borne out in these plant closing cases. Rather, as Joan Fitzgerald shows in an analysis of Pittsburgh-area plant closing struggles,[11] "community based" struggles need not be "community *defined*" struggles that fragment the working class or promote competition between workers. Rather, these community struggles strengthened class identity and solidarity.

This conclusion accords with both historical and contemporary evidence. Historically U.S. unions benefited from supportive local environments even in times of hostile national trends, as evidenced by the works of Herbert Gutman and a number of his followers.[12] In the 1980s union attempts to build coalitions within the community expanded greatly.[13] Community alliances have also played an important role in some of the most innovative union organizing drives in decades.[14] Some union advocates propose "community unionism" for the future direction of the U.S. labor movement.[15]

Community alliances will not solve all of the labor movement's problems. For that, many changes would be necessary, some beyond the immediate control of unions. But community coalitions could be important local grass roots complements to national initiatives.

There is also an additional internal benefit: activation of the union membership. *Most labor-community coalitions cannot work effectively unless the union actively involves secondary levels of leadership and the membership.* They require an informed and active membership, as demonstrated by the most effective coalitions in these case studies (LTV bar mill, LaSalle Steel). If it is true that unions benefit from a more active and involved membership (and I think it is), labor-community coalitions help accomplish that.

Do they also work in the larger sense? Can they make significant gains for workers and working-class communities, given present conditions?

The cases do not provide a completely unambiguous answer; a short review of previous literature on similar movements may provide a useful context.

Examining plant closing struggles in the Pittsburgh area, Sidney Plotkin and William Scheuerman argue that such attempts amount to little more than "a sad political footnote to the decline of the steel industry in America."[16] Ann Markusen, while giving more credence to local efforts, agrees: "the evidence is rather compelling that national and international forces beyond the grasp of local governments are important determinants of jobs loss."[17] Dale Hathaway concludes from his study of Pittsburgh area plant closing struggles that workers learn "it is futile to fight decisions of the corporate elite."[18]

On a broader canvas, well-known writers on social movements reinforce the pessimism. Susan and Norman Fainstein argue that new employment patterns, racial and ethnic divisions, and the triumph of conservative ideology make significant social movements unlikely in the present era.[19] And in their well-known book *Poor People's Movements* Frances Fox Piven and Richard Cloward conclude that spontaneous disruptive outbursts can marginally improve the lives of the lower classes, but more sustained or institutional redistribution of power is next to impossible.

These cases do not universally end in defeat, so they provide some counter to the above pessimism. However, it is important to acknowledge the limitations of the labor-community coalition approach. First, it is indisputable that the globalization of the U.S. economy has removed much corporate decision making from the local to national and international arenas. Therefore, the insecure economic environment facing industrial communities can only be altered through national and even international policies and institutions aimed to ensure greater economic security and job stability.

Given this, what is the point of regional or local community-based efforts to gain more influence? Are they hopeless? I don't think so.

There are two ways in which these struggles can strengthen the influence of workers and the local community. First, they help communities to claim and exert the limited power that *is* available but usually not used because it is not insistently asserted. Second, they may provide important pressure for *national* changes in public policy, if they spread.

While they won't change global economic forces, these struggles can give workers and local communities a small degree of bargaining power with corporations. The bargaining power is constrained by three conditions that must be present.

First, the market forces on the corporation cannot be so overpowering that alternative courses of action are effectively eliminated. The Combustion Engineering and Stratojac workers faced market forces and timing circumstances making a campaign to save the plant impractical. In contrast, LaSalle Steel could make choices; alternatives were possible within the market context. So workers and the community could exert influence.

Second, the target company must be susceptible to pressure from resources the local labor-community coalition can control. It must depend on either the political good will of local public officials, positive relations with the local press, nonantagonistic relations with its local workforce, local consumers, or on other manifestations of positive local public opinion or other local factors. Both the LTV bar mill and LaSalle Steel cases illustrate how these potential sources of power might be used — in one of the two cases successfully.

Third, labor and community forces must organize to overcome potential divisions within their ranks and must struggle hard to achieve the common goal of job retention/community economic stability. Such unity is hard to achieve,[20] but is possible.

Beyond the issue of immediate bargaining power or immediate gains is the question of national impact. Local struggles can and do contribute to changes in national public policy if they grow and spread.

Early warning of plant closings provides an instructive parallel. From the late 1970s throughout the 1980s the United States labor movement and local community activists agitated for national and state laws, and local ordinances requiring companies to provide advance notice of a plant closure. By the latter half of the 1980s it appeared that very little had been accomplished: virtually no new state laws, no national law, and, at most, a half dozen local ordinances, themselves seldom enforced and frequently declared unconstitutional. Yet the activism did not abate; over thirty states had legislative proposals introduced.

By 1988 the local activism had so changed public opinion that Congress passed the WARN (Worker Adjustment, Retraining, and Notification) Act mandating sixty days notice for all establishments with over one hundred employees. Advised that public opinion favored the bill by well over 70%, President Reagan chose not to veto it despite his opposition because he feared a veto would hurt George Bush's presidential campaign.

Social legislation with a working-class or populist orientation usually becomes law only after such activism has forced it onto the agenda. Likewise, the national public policy changes needed to enhance local community and worker security in an age of capital mobility and international finance are unlikely unless the type of activism described in this book continues and spreads throughout the country.

Nevertheless, don't these cases support the pessimistic conclusion that struggle is usually hopeless? Most campaigns were lost: plants were not saved and jobs were not preserved. Only a departmental relocation was prevented. The direct pay off in jobs saved has been small but not altogether absent.

But the question may be too narrowly phrased. If the question is, "Do campaigns against plant closings save the plant?" the answer is, "Usually not." If the question is, "Do plant closing struggles improve the situation of the affected workforce?" the answer is, "Usually yes." Generalizations are risky, but it seems that well-conceived and carefully conducted plant closing campaigns frequently result in immediate improvements for the displaced workers. Under pressure, the company and/or government agencies provide additional assistance (retraining, job search assistance, etc.). The workers become more assertive; they demand more, become more aware of, apply for more, and take advantage of more programs that are available. Except for Blaw-Knox, all cases contained in this volume resulted in such immediate gains for the displaced workers.

Beyond immediate gains to the directly displaced workers, additional benefits become apparent. Plants were closed in a more environmentally responsible manner than would otherwise have been likely (Combustion Engineering, LTV bar mill). Local government obtained an unusually favorable tax settlement with a bankrupt firm (LTV). Local government improved its oversight of a public subsidy program (Combustion Engineering). On a larger scale, public concern focused more sharply on plant closings and their detrimental impact. Public officials in northwest Indiana became more responsive to the victims of plant closings.

Plant closing campaigns should also be judged by longer term consequences such as attitudinal and institutional changes.[21] By this measure the cases provide grounds for optimism.

It is important not to exaggerate the degree to which plant closing struggles have transformed northwest Indiana attitudes or institutions. No new permanent government structures have been created to bolster labor and community influence in economic decisions vital to the region. Attitudes have been altered somewhat (it is hard to document this in the absence of comparative public opinion polls), but neither labor nor (non-business) community voices are yet considered significant players in economic decision making for the region. The point is not that changes have been massive, but that they have occurred. This in itself is a significant achievement for a group as poor in resources as the Calumet Project.

Nevertheless, pessimists are correct that plant closing struggles, on an individual plant-by-plant basis, are not significant: most will be lost and the occasional victories will not effect enough jobs to have a major impact on the fate of either the U.S. labor movement or industrial communities. Taken individually, plant closing struggles are too narrowly focused.

But the labor-community coalition approach, applied to both plant closing situations and broader public policy issues, holds promise. The Calumet Project has moved well beyond individual plant closing struggles in much of its recent work, although it also continues to carry out campaigns around individual plants. Impressive results have been achieved in controlling corporate abuse of public subsidies.

From the evidence of these cases, my defense of the labor-community coalition approach is a qualified one. Local activism to contest plant closings has severe limitations: it requires a movement to broader policy issues, and only national public policy changes can effectively address many of the forces making shutdowns common. Therefore, local activism must be put in the context of other efforts around the country. Is such activism beginning to put issues onto the national agenda? Or are Calumet Project struggles isolated events with little or no connection to events elsewhere?

Labor-community coalition activism has grown enormously in the 1980s. A recent book is composed entirely of examples from around the country.[22] But such coalition efforts are relatively undeveloped and are not the norm. An embryonic national movement may be taking shape, but if so it is in its infancy.

The Calumet Project belongs to a national umbrella organization of similar groups around the country: the Federation for Industrial Retention and Renewal (FIRR). FIRR, composed of about thirty organizations around the country, is headquartered in Chicago with a staff of three employees. Since its inception in 1988, FIRR has grown from an initial grouping of fifteen organizations to its present size.[23]

As an organization FIRR attempts both to assist individual affiliates in local campaigns and organization building and to develop national programs to influence public policy at the federal level. It also has targeted areas of the country for regional organizing efforts. It was active in building a regional Economic Justice Network in the Southeast composed of thirty-five groups (three of them members of FIRR) and two California networks: the Silicon Valley Toxics Coalition and the California Network for a New Economy (fifty organizations).

Recent national issues which FIRR has focused on include monitoring and improving plant closing legislation, trade policy, military conversion to peacetime production, curbing corporate abuse of public subsidies, and economic planning for environmentally sustainable development. Its actual impact on these issues varies greatly, depending on the influence and interest of its affiliates and the larger constituencies it wishes to help galvanize into action. Most affiliates work on issues of their own choosing.

Plant closing legislation work has consisted of education and organizing about the national plant closing law (WARN) and its accompanying law (EDWAA) providing for assistance to dislocated workers. FIRR and some of its affiliates have done much to expose both the usefulness and the limitations of these laws, to aid workers to use the laws to their advantage, and to push for reform to make the laws more meaningful.

Work on trade policy has centered on the North American Free Trade Agreement (NAFTA) and the maquiladoras in Mexico. Cross-border contacts, labor and environmental protection, and justice issues for maquila workers have been areas of focus.

Military conversion work centers on planning for conversion coupled with pro-worker adjustment policies. Conversion campaigns have been difficult, but FIRR affiliates have been involved in a number of them.

Curbing corporate abuse of public subsidies is an area of Calumet Project work: it has won local and state legislation unprecedented throughout the nation.[24] FIRR is involved in similar work in other parts of the country.

Economic planning for environmentally sustainable development is a relatively new area of work. Preliminary work is being done by the Chicago-based Center for Neighborhood Technology and the Silicon Valley Toxics Coalition.

FIRR's resources are inadequate to accomplish all its goals. Therefore, it attempts to systematically link up with and to stimulate into action two potential allies it sees as having a larger political base: organized labor and the social justice movement within the religious community.

FIRR affiliates vary widely in organizational structure, goals, and stability. A few are little more than educational groups that conduct education on a specific issue, such as conversion from military to peacetime production; others have more developed labor and/or community roots and wider programmatic areas of work. A few are strictly volunteer organizations, but most have permanent staff and a budget.

Affiliates can be classified into three types: (1) technical assistance groups offering expertise to local activist groups; (2) labor-community coalitions, such as the Calumet Project; and (3) mass membership organizations. Notable technical assistance groups include the Chicago-based Midwest Center for Labor Research (MCLR) and the Boston-based ICA Group. MCLR provides research for unions and activist organizations and publishes the activist-oriented *Labor Research Review*. The ICA

Group is probably the premier organization in the country with technical expertise in employee ownership buyouts.

Outstanding FIRR labor-community coalitions include the Tennessee Industrial Renewal Network (TIRN), the Naugatuck Valley Project in Connecticut, the Merrimack Valley Project in Massachusetts, and the Calumet Project. TIRN is a Knoxville-based group working in industrial development, worker justice, environmental, antiplant closing, and other issues. The Naugatuck Valley Project and the Merrimack Valley Project are classic Saul Alinsky–style organizations with the distinctive feature of having a primary focus on industrial job retention. Both were founded by the same individual, an unusually effective community organizer with training in the Alinsky tradition of organizing.[25]

FIRR mass membership organizations include La Mujer Obrera in El Paso, Texas, and the Piedmont Peace Project in North Carolina. La Mujer Obrera has seven hundred members, virtually all of them Latina women. It runs a workers center to train women in leadership skills and works on opposing sweatshops and developing a pro-worker garment industry development plan in its area. The Piedmont Peace Project has fought plant shutdowns and addresses other progressive issues.

One FIRR affiliate is a government entity. The Steel Valley Authority (SVA) grew out of plant closing struggles in the Pittsburgh area in the 1980s. It engages in economic development activities from a pro-labor perspective and has governmental legitimacy and powers (such as the right to use eminent domain powers) unlike all other FIRR groups.

The overall impression one gets from observing FIRR as a national organization is of a struggling, fitfully growing, unevenly developed, and rather embryonic national movement of modest but not entirely insignificant proportions.[26] I do not believe that either the organization or the social movement it represents will collapse and disappear in the near future. From a resource mobilization perspective, it is unlikely to develop into a "mass" movement such as the civil rights movement in the 1960s or the CIO organizing drive of the 1930s, but neither is it a "flash-in-the-pan" phenomenon with few capabilities.

From both the class capacities and the resource mobilization perspective, the case studies in this volume offer evidence for a mild optimism. The Calumet Project has been a qualified success at achieving results that strengthen working-class power; it has also developed a limited but real ability to mobilize diverse resources by systematically developing its base and its links to sources of power.

What of the future? Will labor-community coalitions and/or struggles over job security and local economic stability continue to grow? Much depends on the economic performance and political posture of the United States in the near future. Trends from the 1980s point in the direction of continued activism.

If economic restructuring continues to reduce domestic industrial employment and to shift it away from urban industrial settings, resistance to plant closings and labor-community alliances are likely. If national political solutions are not forthcoming, as they were not in the 1980s, local activism can be expected to fill the vacuum and force national attention to the problem. Even a more activist national stance, as some expected from the Clinton presidency, could encourage local activism rather than dampen it.

On the other hand, economic and political trends could conspire to kill the type of activity related in this book. A sudden turn to economic prosperity that reached even the industrial heartland, or comprehensive national political solutions developed without widespread public agitation or input, might singly or together stamp out the activism represented by the Calumet Project and its counterparts. But I find neither to be likely in the near future.

These case studies illustrate a direction that would be beneficial to the United States labor movement, should it choose to pursue this course. Likewise it would benefit industrial communities and move them on a path to greater security. The degree to which unions and community activists will choose to pursue this direction remains to be seen.

If unions choose to ignore labor-community coalition-building as one important task in the remainder of the 1990s, they underrate a most important potential strength. They also cut off one vital avenue for membership activation. If community activists in industrial communities fail to seek out union allies in their struggles for community welfare, they ignore a potential ally of some importance. Plant closings are one type of situation illustrating common interests. Many other unifying issues exist, but they will only be found if they are forged in common struggle.

NOTES

PREFACE

1. Other published results of my research in these topics include, "Union Battles Against Plant Closings: Case Study Evidence and Policy Implications," *Policy Studies Journal,* Vol. 18, No. 2, Winter 1989–90, pp. 382–95; (coauthored with Lynn Feekin), "Early Warning of Plant Closings: Issues and Prospects," *Labor Studies Journal,* Vol. 16, No. 4, Winter 1991, pp. 20–33; (coauthored with Lynn Feekin), "For the Public Good: Calumet Project organizes for labor and community-based economic development," *Labor Research Review #19,* Vol. XI, No. 1, Fall 1992, pp. 14–29; chapters 7 and 10 of Charles Craypo and Bruce Nissen, eds., *Grand Designs: the Impact of Corporate Strategies on Workers, Unions, and Communities,* (Ithaca, NY: ILR Press, 1993); and "Combating Plant Closings in the Era of the Transnational Corporation," in Lawrence Flood, ed., *Unions and Public Policy: The New Economy, Law and Democratic Politics,* (New York: Greenwood Press, 1995).

CHAPTER 1. INTRODUCTION

1. A selected bibliography of 820 articles or books on plant closings published prior to 1986 is Harold E. Way and Carla Weiss, *Plant Closings: a Selected Bibliography of Materials Published through 1985* (Ithaca, NY: Martin P. Catherwood Library, NYSSILR, Cornell University, September 1987). An update through 1990 is Carla Weiss, *Plant Closings: a Selected Bibliography of Materials Published 1986–1990* (Ithaca, NY: ILR Press, 1991). More recent citations are easily available through both paper and computerized data base services.

2. For book length examples of the literature, see Thomas G. Fuechtmann, *Steeples and Stacks: Religion and Steel Crisis in Youngstown* (New York: Cambridge University Press, 1989); Staughton Lynd, *The Fight Against Shutdowns: Youngstown's Steel Mill Closings* (San Pedro, CA: Singlejack Books, 1983); and Dale Hathaway, *Can Workers Have a Voice?* (University Park, PA: The Pennsylvania State University Press, 1993).

3. Unless otherwise indicated, statistics cited in the following paragraphs are taken from Donald A. Coffin, "The Northwest Indiana Economy in Recent Historical Perspective," *Northwest Indiana Business Conditions,* Vol. 1, No. 1 (November 1992), pp. 2–9.

4. Census data figures in this and the following paragraphs are taken from two sources: Indiana Employment and Training Services, Gary-Hammond PMSA branch, *The Gary-Hammond PMSA in Review;* and Thomas M. Gannon, S.J., *The*

People of Northwest Indiana: Demographic Changes and Challenges, 1970–1990 (East Chicago, IN: Heartland Center, Winter 1992).

5. See U.S. General Accounting Office, *Plant Closings: Information on Advance Notice and Assistance to Dislocated Workers*, 17 April 1987 (GAO-HRD-87-86BR); and Sharon P. Brown, "How often do workers receive advance notice of layoffs?," *Monthly Labor Review*, June 1987, pp. 13–17.

6. For a discussion of the benefits and drawbacks of advance notice, see U.S. Congress, Office of Technology Assessment, *Plant Closing: Advance Notice and Rapid Response–Special Report*, September 1986 (OTA-ITE-321).

7. A number of the studies and arguments are collected in Paul D. Staudohar and Holly E. Brown, *Deindustrialization and Plant Closure* (Lexington, MA: Lexington Books, 1987); See also Ronald G. Ehrenberg and George H. Jakubson, *Advance Notice Provisions in Plant Closing Legislation* (Kalamazoo, MI: W.E. Upjohn Institute, 1988); and Nancy Folbre, Julia Leighton, and Melissa Roderick, "Plant Closings and their Regulation in Maine, 1971–1982," *Industrial and Labor Relations Review*, Vol. 37, No. 2 (January 1984), pp. 195–96.

8. For example, see Richard B. McKenzie, *Fugitive Industry: the Economics and Politics of Deindustrialization* (Cambridge, MA: Ballinger, 1984). McKenzie has also edited a book in a similar vein: *Plant Closings: Public or Private Choices?* (Washington, D.C.: Cato Institute, 1984).

9. For further information see David C. Ranney, "Manufacturing Job Loss and Early Warning Indicators," *Journal of Planning Literature*, Vol. 3, No. 1 (Winter 1988), pp. 22–35; Greg LeRoy, et al., *Early Warning Manual Against Plant Closings* (Chicago: Midwest Center for Labor Research, 1986); and U.S. Department of Commerce, Economic Development Administration, *Early Warning Information Systems for Business Retention*, September 1980.

10. See Lynn Feekin and Bruce Nissen, "Early Warning of Plant Closings: Issues and Prospects," *Labor Studies Journal*, Vol. 16, No. 4, pp. 20–33.

11. Marie Howland, *Plant Closings and Worker Displacement: The Regional Issues* (Kalamazoo, MI: W. E. Upjohn Institute for Employment Research, 1988), p. 154; Richard B. Freeman and Morris M. Kleiner, "Do Unions Make Enterprises Insolvent?" Working Paper No. 4797 (Cambridge, MA: National Bureau of Economic Research, 1994).

12. Howland, pp. 152–54.

13. The literature on this topic is large. Typical examples include Barry Bluestone and Bennett Harrison, *The Deindustrialization of America* and Robert Reich, *The Next American Frontier*.

14. See Howland, chapter 3.

15. For examples of this literature, see Stanley S. Reynolds, "Plant Closings and Exit Behaviour in Declining Industries," *Economica*, Vol. 55 (1988), pp. 493–503; Mary E. Deily, "Investment Activity and the Exit Decision," *The Review of Economics and Statistics*, Vol. 70 (1988), pp. 595–602; Mary E. Deily, "Exit Barriers in the Steel Industry," *Economic Review*, Federal Reserve Bank of Cleveland, Vol. 24, No. 1 (1988), pp. 10–18; Michael D. Whinston, "Exit with multi-

plant firms," *RAND Journal of Economics,* Vol. 19 (1988), pp. 493–503; C. W. F. Baden-Fuller, "Exit from Declining Industries and the Case of Steel Castings," *The Economic Journal,* Vol. 99 (December 1989), pp. 949–61; Pankaj Ghemawat and Barry Nalebuff, "The Devolution of Declining Industries," *The Quarterly Journal of Economics,* Vol. 105 (February 1990), pp. 167–86; Marvin B. Lieberman, "Exit from declining industries: "shakeout" or "stakeout?" *RAND Journal of Economics,* Vol. 21 (1990), pp. 538–54; and Mary E. Deily, "Exit Strategies and Plant Closing Decisions: The Case of Steel," *RAND Journal of Economics,* Vol. 22, No. 2 (Summer 1991), pp. 250–63.

16. See John Portz, *The Politics of Plant Closings* (Lawrence, KS: University Press of Kansas, 1990), especially chapter 1.

17. This threefold distinction is taken from the discussion by John Portz in *The Politics of Plant Closings* (Lawrence, KS: The University Press of Kansas, 1990), pp. 23–25.

18. "LRR FOCUS: Calumet Project for Industrial Jobs," *Labor Research Review #19* (Fall 1992), p. 17.

19. In doing so, I follow the excellent example set by Cynthia Deitch and Robert Erickson in "'Save Dorothy': A Political Response to Structural Change in the Steel Industry" in Raymond M. Lee, ed., *Redundancy, Layoffs and Plant Closures* (Wolfeboro, NH: Croom Helm, 1989), pp. 241–79.

20. A good introduction to resource mobilization theory is Mayer N. Zald and John D. McCarthy, eds., *The Dynamics of Social Movements* (Lanham, MD: University Press of America, 1988).

21. See Erik Olin Wright, *Class, Crisis and the State* (London: New Left Books, 1978), and Jerry Lembcke, *Capitalist Development and Class Capacities* (New York: Greenwood Press, 1988) for examples of this literature.

CHAPTER 2. MILITARY CONVERSION AND THE SHUTDOWN OF THE BLAW-KNOX STEEL FOUNDRY

1. Information on the history of the Blaw-Knox foundry is from Arthur D. Little, *Reuse of the Blaw-Knox Castings and Machining Mill,* June 1985, pp. II-1 and II-2.

2. "Blaw-Knox Likes East Chicago Location," Hammond *Times,* 9 November 1969.

3. *Ibid.*

4. White Consolidated *Annual Reports,* 1967, 1974, 1979.

5. White Consolidated *Annual Reports,* 1983, 1977.

6. White Consolidated *Annual Report,* 1983, pp. 3,7.

7. White Consolidated *Annual Report,* 1983, pp. 4, 6, 8, 10.

8. "Blaw-Knox Likes East Chicago Location," Hammond *Times,* 9 November 1969.

9. Arthur D. Little, *Reuse of the Blaw-Knox Castings and Machining Mill,* June 1985, p. II-2.

10. "White Will Sell Machinery, Steel Processing Subsidiaries," *American Metal Markets/Metalworking News,* 7 May 1984.

11. White Consolidated Industries, "Annual Meeting Review," in *First Quarter Report 1984.*

12. Buck Martin memo, September 1984.

13. Nancy Winkley, "Steelworkers fight to keep foundry open," Gary *Post-Tribune,* 12 October 1984.

14. "White Consolidated Operating Earnings Fell Sharply in Quarter," *Wall Street Journal,* 25 October 1984. In addition to the Blaw-Knox Foundry and Mill Machinery Company, which included the East Chicago foundry and three other facilities in West Virginia and Pittsburgh, White Consolidated was selling Blaw-Knox Food & Chemical Equipment, Blaw-Knox Equipment (steel mill equipment), Aetna-Standard (steel mill equipment), AFT-Davidson (printing equipment), Bullard Castings (foundry), Duraloy (castings and tubing), and R-P&C Valve (valves and controls). All of these companies accounted for about $200 million in yearly sales, approximately 9.5 percent of WCI's total.

15. Nancy Winkley, "East Chicago plant up for sale," Gary *Post-Tribune,* 25 October 1984.

16. *Ibid.*

17.Nancy J. Winkley, "State aid sought to study Blaw-Knox options," Gary *Post-Tribune,* 3 December 1984.

18. Nancy J. Winkley, "Massachusetts firm picked to study Blaw-Knox," Gary *Post Tribune,* 12 February 1985.

19. Nancy J. Winkley, "Blaw-Knox's future may be in smaller castings," Gary *Post-Tribune,* 4 May 1985.

20. *Ibid.*

21. All ex-managers interviewed for this study requested anonymity. The interviews occurred during Fall 1989 and Fall 1994.

22. Fall 1989 interview with ex-manager at East Chicago Blaw-Knox facility.

23. Lynn Strong interview, Fall 1989.

24. Fall 1989 interview with ex-manager of Blaw-Knox facility at East Chicago.

25. I am indebted to Lynn Feekin, Director of the Calumet Project, for making these figures available to me.

26. Total asset and book value figures are from the Lehman Bros. prospectus.

27. All information on the feasibility study is from Arthur D. Little, *Reuse of the Blaw-Knox Castings and Machining Mill,* June 1985. News reports on the findings of the study include Nancy J. Winkley, "Consulting firm reports heavy losses for area if Blaw-Knox closes," Gary *Post-Tribune,* 21 July 1985; Nancy J. Winkley, $24 million needed to convert Blaw-Knox," Gary *Post-Tribune,* 21 July 1985; Stephen P. Dinnen, "Study says mill must change," Hammond *Times,* 21 July 1985; Lauri Giesen, "Extensive Changes Could Save Blaw-Knox Foundry,"

American Metal Markets/Metal Working News, 5 August 1985; and Paul Merrion, "Study paints bleak picture for Blaw-Knox," *Crain's Chicago Business,* 19 August 1985.

28. These estimates are similar to those in the Lehman Bros. prospectus, which states: "With the end of the armor contract, the division will be faced with the task of building commercial casting sales to a profitable level. . . In order to do so, the division estimates initial capital expenditures of $8 million to $11 million over 5 years are required to transform the #2 foundry into a state-of-the-art small castings operation."

29. Nancy J. Winkley, "$24 million needed to convert Blaw-Knox," Gary *Post-Tribune,* 21 July 1985.

30. All of the following goals, scenarios, and suggestions taken from "What Are We Going to Do About Blaw-Knox?" a two-page memo in the author's possession.

31. The threat of eminent domain had been successfully employed by New Bedford, Massachusetts, in a widely publicized case involving the Morse Cutting Tool plant owned by Gulf and Western. See Barbara Doherty, *The Struggle to Save Morse Cutting Tool.* (North Dartmouth, Ma.: Southeastern Massachusetts University Labor Education Center, n.d.)

32. Letter from Reverend Vincent McCutcheon to John Artis, 5 September 1985.

33. Interview, Fall 1989. (Interviewee requested anonymity; see footnote 21)

34. Nancy J. Winkley, "Blaw-Knox foundry sold to private investors," Gary *Post-Tribune,* 28 September 1985.

35. *Ibid.*

36. Mark Hornung, "Casting firm's new owners eye retooling," *Crain's Chicago Business,* 7 October 1985.

37. Stephen P. Dinnen, "Blaw-Knox outlook mixed," Hammond *Times,* 10 November 1985.

38. These figures and the wage data are from U.S. Department of Labor, Bureau of Labor Statistics, *Industry Wage Survey: Iron and Steel Foundries October 1986,* February 1988 (Bulletin 2291), pp. 4, 68.

39. "Exhibit I–Employee Draft" — draft letter in author's possession.

40. "Exhibit II–Taxpayer" — draft letter in author's possession.

41. "Exhibit III–Petition" — draft petition in author's possession.

42. David Moberg, "Hooked on Tanks," *The Progressive,* September 1986, p. 32.

43. *Ibid.*

44. *Ibid.*

45. On 26 June 1986, Army Undersecretary James Ambrose replied to an inquiry from Congressman Peter Visclosky by noting that any further work would be "intended, in any case, to give Blaw Knox 'running room', if possible. Thus, I do not understand why Blaw Knox would advise commercial customers that their needs cannot be met. The proposal we are considering does not match, nor can

it, the total capacity Blaw Knox has." Undersecretary Ambrose was puzzled by Blaw-Knox's claim to Congressman Visclosky because he assumed the company was being truthful to him in representing its conversion efforts, specifically that conversion was being hindered by uncertainty over government intentions. In reality the company never intended to convert, but had to conceal this fact from the Congressman in order to get his help in obtaining more tank orders.

46. The Army Material Command had responded to the pressure by recommending 210 more tanks even though the need for them was questionable. Army Undersecretary James Ambrose refused to carry this recommendation to Congress, however. (Letter to Congressman Peter Visclosky from Blaw-Knox Chief Executive Officer Robert J. Tomsich.)

47. Interview, Fall 1989. (Interviewee requested anonymity; see footnote 21).

48. This paragraph is taken from Chris Isidore, "Underfunded Blaw-Knox pension terminated," Gary *Post-Tribune*, 31 January 1992.

49. Anonymous interview with ex-managers of East Chicago Blaw-Knox facility, Fall 1994.

50. This was true of the state's two Republican senators and the city's Democratic mayor. It was less true of Democratic Congressman Peter Visclosky, who, although he held the conventional business climate perspective, was also willing to push an independent worker/community viewpoint. He strongly urged corporate officials in writing to make themselves more accountable to the workers and community. No other politician was willing to do this.

CHAPTER 3. PUBLIC SUBSIDY ABUSE AT THE COMBUSTION ENGINEERING PLANT

1. Information on the earlier years taken from "The East Chicago Story," in the June 1951 issue (Vol. 1, No. 6) of *Combustion Topics;* an undated one page handout entitled "Combustion Engineering, Inc.–East Chicago Plant"; and a handwritten one page fact sheet on the plant signed and dated: Fred T. Grady, Administrator Personnel, 10-13–69. All are available from the East Chicago Historical Society and the East Chicago room at the East Chicago Public Library.

2. Handwritten memo (East Chicago Historical Society) by Fred T. Grady, Administrative Personnel Officer, 10-13-69. See also "Twin City Plant Sets Retraining," Gary *Post-Tribune*, 27 March 1964; "Plant Ends Pay Talks in Shutdown," Gary *Post-Tribune*, 16 April 1964.

3. See "Plant Operations Growing Rapidly," Hammond *Times*, 15 January 1967; "'67 Busiest Ever," Hammond *Times*, 14 January 1968.

4. See "Union Set for Strike," Hammond *Times*, 1 June 1969; and "Strikers OK New Pact," Hammond *Times*, 2 June 1969.

5. The 1972 strike account taken from: "Talks set in East Chicago plant strike," Gary *Post-Tribune*, 7 July 1972; "Strikers Weighing C-E Offer," Gary *Post-Tri-*

bune, 14 July 1972; "Negotiations at East Chicago firm break down," Gary *Post-Tribune,* 21 July 1972; "USW strike shuts plant," Hammond *Times,* 26 May 1972; "Combustion Strike Enters Third Day," Hammond *Times,* 28 May 1972; "Strikers Forced to Move," Hammond *Times,* 8 June 1972; "Steel Talks Resume," Hammond *Times,* 16 July 1972; "Combustion Votes Work," Hammond *Times,* 18 July 1972; "Dispute Worsens in 9-Week Strike," Hammond *Times,* 27 July 1972; "Talks Cancel USW Session," Hammond *Times,* 28 July 1972; and "Steelworkers Laud Combustion Pact," Hammond *Times,* 30 July 1972.

6. Account of the 1972–75 years taken from: "Combustion Faces a Busy Schedule," Hammond *Times,* 14 January 1973; "Bad News is Good for Firm," Hammond *Times,* 13 January 1974; "$6 Million Plant Set," Hammond *Times,* 12 January 1975; and "$5 million update set by firm," Gary *Post-Tribune,* 25 February 1975.

7. Compare "$6 Million Plant Set," Hammond *Times,* 12 January 1975, with "$5 million update set by firm," Gary *Post-Tribune,* 25 February 1975.

8. "Combustion Pact Ends Stoppage," Hammond *Times,* 5 July 1975.

9. "350 Strike at E.C. Firm," Hammond *Times,* 31 May 1978; "E.C. Workers Stay Out," Hammond *Times,* 1 June 1978; "Strike at E.C. Company 'Long'," Hammond *Times,* 4 June 1978.

10. "Wage Talks Will Resume," Hammond *Times,* 11 September 1978.

11. "East Chicago strike called test of wills," Gary *Post-Tribune,* 9 August 1978.

12. Daniel Rosenheim, "Strike at Combustion To Be 'Long, Difficult'," Hammond *Times,* 18 June 1978.

13. "Wage Talks Resume," Hammond *Times,* 11 September 1978; "Pact Ends Job Action," Hammond *Times,* 14 September 1978; "Steelworkers Accept Pact," Hammond *Times,* 19 September 1978; and "USWA's Cost Aid In Effect," Hammond *Times,* 21 September 1978.

14. Jack Bixeman interview, 19 February 1990. Bixeman was manager of industrial relations at the plant throughout the 1970s up until 1985.

15. Dave Brebner interview, 8 February 1990; Paul Roznawski interview, 19 February 1990; Jack Bixeman interview, 19 February 1990. Brebner was a union grievance representative; Roznawski was the union local vice president.

16. "Energy crisis boom time for East Chicago plant," Gary *Post-Tribune,* 15 February 1981.

17. Jack Bixeman interview, 19 February 1990.

18. Information from interviews of both ex-management and ex-union people, all of whom requested anonymity. Ex-union members also claimed that at least some of the eight managers were engaged in widespread organized stealing from the company. Hourly workers, concerned about this wrongdoing and the future of the plant, had contacted corporate headquarters and had aided in detective work that provided extremely strong circumstantial evidence of the managers' culpability, according to my informants. Claiming that the proof was not ironclad, the company had coaxed and forced the managers out through a combination of

"golden parachute" retirement provisions and an ultimatum to leave. However, none of this became public knowledge, and none of my management contacts ever referred to these events. Whether my hourly worker informants were telling me the truth is thus impossible to verify. It is also impossible to know if this episode played any role in the subsequent corporate decision to close the East Chicago plant. What is clear is that the thievery ring, if it actually existed, was an additional factor leading to extreme instability in management ranks in the last few years of the plant.

19. James Kane, "New contract gives E. C. plant a chance," Hammond *Times*, 2 November 1984.

20. Jack Bixeman interview, 19 February 1990.

21. All the following information on earlier shutdown planning taken from Jack Bixeman interview, 19 February 1990.

22. James Kane, "New management style begins new era at plant," Hammond *Times*, 28 January 1985.

23. *Ibid.*

24. *Ibid.*

25. Dave Brebner interview, 8 February 1990.

26. East Chicago Economic Development Commission documents relating to IRB loan to Combustion Engineering, dated 4 August 1986, prepared by Joseph Costanza.

27. Combustion Engineering *Annual Reports,* 1978–1986.

28. *Ibid.*

29. *U.S. Industrial Outlook 1986,* p. 25-5.

30. Combustion Engineering *Annual Report 1985,* p. 47.

31. "Combustion Engineering: Can High Tech Cure One of the Recession's Walking Wounded?" *Business Week,* 30 July 1984, p. 84.

32. James R. Norman, "Playing a Numbers Game to Avoid a Write-Off," *Business Week,* 17 September 1986, p. 68.

33. Robert McGough, "From dirt to glamour and mixed reviews," *Forbes,* 23 March 1987, p. 112.

34. *Ibid.,* p. 116.

35. Frank W. Campanella and Richard Rescigno, "Steam in the Boiler: Combustion Engineering is Geared for a Comeback," *Forbes,* 17 March 1986, p. 31.

36. Combustion Engineering SEC Form 10-Q, 31 March 1986, p. 8.

37. *U.S. Industrial Outlook 1987,* p. 25-1.

38. Dave Brebner interview, 8 February 1990.

39. For further information on "early warning systems," see Lynn Feekin and Bruce Nissen, "Early Warning of Plant Closings: Issues and Prospects," *Labor Studies Journal,* Vol. 16, No. 4 (Winter 1991), pp. 20–33.

40. Information in this paragraph taken from handwritten notes of the 28 May meeting by Calumet Project staff.

41. Stephen P. Dinnen, "Changing market could close plant," Hammond *Times*, 30 May 1986.

42. Nancy Winkley, "Groups urge probe of closing company's bond," Gary *Post-Tribune*, 15 July 1986; James Kane, "Combustion bond approval eyed," Hammond *Times*, 15 July 1986.

43. Richard Bryant, "Firm to repay unused loan," Hammond *Times*, 19 July 1986.

44. "Statement of Mr. William Shelton, President of USWA Local 1386, Monday, 21 July 1986 to the Economic Development Commission of the city of East Chicago."

45. "Statement of Mr. Thomas DuBois, Calumet Project for Industrial Jobs, Monday, 21 July 1986 to the Economic Development Commission of the City of East Chicago."

46. Marsha Hahney, "East Chicago considering early payback on bond," Gary *Post-Tribune*, 24 July 1986; Lauri Giesen, "Bond Probe at Combustion Urged by USW," *American Metal Market/Metalworking News*, 28 July 1986.

47. Richard Bryant, "E.C. faces economic crisis," Hammond *Times*, 22 July 1986.

48. Information in the following paragraphs taken from East Chicago EDC documents, dated 4 August 1986, prepared by Joseph E. Costanza.

49. In a letter to Costanza dated 2 July 1986, Feekin noted a similar legal case in Chicago and a New Haven, Connecticut, ordinance requiring corporate accountability in exchange for development benefits. Feekin questioned whether there had been any "chilling" effect in these cases.

50. A summary of the Playskool case is contained in David Fasenfest, "Cui Bono?" in Charles Craypo and Bruce Nissen, eds., *Grand Designs: The Corporate Assault on Workers, Unions, and Communities* (Ithaca, NY: ILR Press, 1993). An interesting analysis of Playskool is Robert Giloth and Robert Mier, "Democratic populism in the USA: The Case of Playskool and Chicago," in *Cities: an International Quarterly on Urban Policy* (London), February 1986, pp. 72–74. A very good account is also contained in Robert Giloth and Susan Rosenblum, "How to Fight Plant Closings," in *Social Policy*, 17 (Winter 1987), pp. 20–26.

51. In fact, a legal precedent in a similar case was established shortly thereafter. Diamond Tool in Duluth, Minnesota, was forced by court action to remain operating in the city because of an IRB commitment. For details, see the David Fasenfest article referred to in endnote 50.

52. Letter from Thomas H. Geoghegan, attorney at law offices of Leon M. Despres, Chicago, to Nancy Jones dated 17 September 1986. (Copy in the author's possession).

53. Tom Knightly, "Workers gather as plant closing nears," Gary *Post-Tribune*, 26 August 1986.

54. Visclosky letter of 26 August 1986. (Copy in author's personal possession.)

55. Campbell letter of 29 August 1986. (Copy in author's personal possession.)

56. Visclosky letter of 17 September 1986. (Copy in the author's personal possession.)

57. Union officials later stated that this was only achieved because outside pressure from the Calumet Project and the Congressman improved their bargaining position. (Brebner interview, 8 February 1990.)

58. Campbell letter, 25 September 1986 (Copy in the author's personal possession).

59. "Engineering Co. designs some 'extended' benefits," Hammond *Times,* 27 September 1986.

60. Ex-workers related numerous tales to me alleging incompetent running of the operations. It is said that production schedules would be scribbled out on an envelope just prior to plantwide management meetings because permanent or more accurate records were not even kept. This lack of professionalism plus the alleged corruption referred to in endnote 18 led workers to allege "mismanagement." Management sources I interviewed saw it differently: they saw no major mismanagement and thought that corporate headquarters had always looked unfavorably on East Chicago, perhaps because its management team had come "up from the ranks," rather than through the college training route.

61. "Two Fortune 500 Companies Consolidating, Expanding in Wellsville, N.Y.," *Industrial Development and Site Selection Handbook,* July/August 1987, pp. 26–27.

62. On 21 November 1986, President William Shelton of the ex-local wrote a heartfelt letter of thanks to Calumet Project staffers Lynn Feekin and Tom DuBois, stating, "We can't begin to thank you enough for the seemingly endless hours of work and research that your project donated to our people. Without your insight and resources we would not have been able to secure the additional plant closing benefits that we did. With plant closings becoming more frequent in our area, your project is proving to be a very important tool in securing benefits for the workers who have spent their lives building these Companies. Although most of our employees have gone onto other jobs or retraining opportunities, the spirit of your strength and determination will go with us."

63. "Two Fortune 500 Companies Consolidating, Expanding in Wellsville, N.Y.," *Industrial Development and Site Selection Handbook,* July/August 1987, p. 27.

CHAPTER 4. SUCCESSORSHIP AND MANAGERIAL COMPETENCE AT THE STRATOJAC PLANT

1. Phyllis Jordan interview, 29 March 1990.

2. A long-time worker and union official estimated that 21 of the twenty-five workers in the cutting room were female in 1985; all 125 sewing room workers were female; all thirty-five pressing room employees were female; and all eight press room workers were female (Phyllis Jordan interview, 29 March 1990).

3. Collective bargaining agreement between Winer Manufacturing Company and United Garment Workers Local 256, 1 January 1984.

4. All of the information in this and the following paragraphs is taken from interviews with a number of ex-employees of Stratojac.

5. My account of Sakin is based on interviews with those who knew him while he was at Stratojac. Because of the extremely unfavorable picture painted of him, nobody was willing to be quoted by name for fear of a lawsuit. However, I can state that my informants fall within the general categories of ex-employees, ex-management personnel, ex-creditors, ex-board members, etc. The picture from all sources is uniform and unfavorable.

6. James Kane, "Stratojac Corp. moves plant to New York," Hammond *Times*, 14 December 1985.

7. Nancy Banks, "Employees notified of plant closing," Hammond *Times*, 18 December 1985.

8. James Kane, "Stratojac Corp. moves plant to New York," Hammond *Times*, 14 December 1985.

9. Tom Knightly and Bob Ashley, "Plant closing shocked investors," Gary *Post-Tribune*, 27 April 1986.

10. Douglas E. Landon, "State URA may buy, lease Casual Craft," *The Recorder* (Amsterdam, New York), 17 December 1985; Douglas E. Landon, "UDC grant clears the way for Stratojac to move to Amsterdam," *The Recorder* (Amsterdam, New York), 31 December 1985.

11. Douglas E. Landon, "New firm loses one, win another financial aid plan," *The Recorder* (Amsterdam, New York), 17 January 1986.

12. Douglas E. Landon, "Stratojac gets a tax break from Amsterdam council," *The Recorder* (Amsterdam, New York), 22 January 1986.

13. Douglas E. Landon, "New Amsterdam manufacturer explains reasons for move here," *The Recorder* (Amsterdam, New York), 21 January 1986.

14. *Ibid.*

15. Phyllis Jordan interview; Barbara Alicea interview; interviews with ex-management people who wish to remain anonymous.

16. Lynn Feekin interview, 7 April 1990.

17. Tim Cavanaugh, "Creditors Force Firm Into Bankruptcy," *Capital District Business Review* (Albany, New York), Vol. 15, No. 51 (3 April 1989).

18. Jeannine Mundy, "Stratojac shifts production to Casualcraft facility," *Daily News Record,* 25 January 1986; "Stratojac's new facility now fully operational," *Daily News Record,* 5 May 1986; "Stratojac gears up area operations," *Capital District Business Review* (Albany, New York), 7 July 1986.

19. Douglas E. Landon, "Stratojac receives low marks from Indiana," *The Recorder* (Amsterdam, New York), 26 February 1986.

20. *Ibid.* At the time, virtually none of the workers had been reemployed.

21. Lynn Feekin interview.

22. Douglas E. Landon, "UDC, Stratojac reach agreement for $2 million," *The Recorder* (Amsterdam, New York), 19 May 1986.

23. "Stratojac's new facility now fully operational," *Daily News Record,* 5 May 1986.

24. "Committee takes over at Stratojac as Sakin exits," *Daily News Record,* 23 October 1986.

25. The information in this and the following four paragraphs is taken from notes by Calumet Project staffers from numerous meetings and telephone calls in January through March 1986.

26. Phyllis Jordan interview.

27. Undated press release on the meeting issued by the union local.

28. James Kane, "Ex-employees eye purchase," Hammond *Times,* 21 March 1986.

29. "Workers want plant reopened," Hammond *Times,* 2 May 1986.

30. 19 June 1986 letter from Barbara Alicea to Hammond Mayor Thomas McDermott; 20 June 1986 letter from McDermott to Alicea. (Copies in the author's possession.)

31. Phyllis Jordan interview; Barbara Alicea interview.

32. 6 August 1986 letter from United Garment Workers Local 256 Vice President Audrey Harris to all former employees of the Stratojac Corporation. (Copy in the author's possession.)

33. Lynn Feekin interview.

34. Tim Cavanaugh, "Stratojac Seeks Time From Creditors to Restructure Debt of More Than $7 M," *Capital District Business Review* (Albany, New York), vol. 15, no. 30 (7 November 1988).

35. *Ibid.*

36. Bryan Doherty, "Stratojac expected to ask for time to reorganize," *Daily News Record,* 28 March 1989.

37. "Stratojac files to switch its case to chapter 11," *Daily News Record,* 28 April 1989.

38. "Ailing Stratojac expects OK on bid for more time," *Capital District Business Review* (Albany, New York), 7 May 1989.

39. "Stratojac Gets Offer of $150,000 For Assets," *Daily News Record,* 2 June 1989; Tim Cavanaugh, "Stratojac to Sell Its Assets to Pay Off Creditors," *Capital District Business Review* (Albany, New York), Vol. 16, no. 9 (18 June 1989).

40. "Alliance buys marks, assets of Stratojac," *Daily News Record,* 7 July 1989.

41. Tim Cavanaugh, "NYC Company Pays $225,000 for Apparel Name," *Capital District Business Review* (Albany, New York), vol. 16, no. 14 (23 July 1989).

42. Fran Brown, "A dream on the block," *The Recorder* (Amsterdam, New York), 25 October 1989.

43. Fran Brown, "Stratojac, UDC battle over equipment," *The Recorder* (Amsterdam, New York), 26 October 1989.

44. All market information in the following paragraphs is collected from Pierre Dui of the Commerce Department's Office of Textiles and Apparel in a telephone interview conducted 9 May 1990.

45. *U.S. Industrial Outlook 1989*, p. 41-2.

46. Robert Schall, "Converting Family-Owned Businesses to Employee-Owned Firms: Experience of the Center for Community Self-Help," paper delivered to the Democratic Ownership Working Group Conference on Retiring Owners, June 1989; cited in Midwest Center for Labor Research, *Intervening With Aging Owners to Save Industrial Jobs: A National Survey of Literature and Practice and a Preliminary Assessment of Successorship Needs and Plans of Chicago's Aging Manufacturing Entrepreneurs,* a report prepared for the Strategic Planning Committee of the Economic Development Commission of Chicago, August 1989, p. 24.

CHAPTER 5. STRUGGLE TO REOPEN THE HAMMOND LTV STEEL BAR MILL

1. The history and current information on the Hammond LTV bar mill in the following paragraphs is taken from "Plant Closing Profile: LTV/Hammond Cold Drawn Bar," pp. 62–66 in Calumet Project for Industrial Jobs, *A Study of Hammond Economic Development for the Common Council of Hammond, Indiana* (14 December 1987) and two unpublished documents used by the Calumet Project as working papers during the campaign to reopen the plant. Information in the bargaining history in the 1980s from an interview with Jerry Brown, 5 August 1990.

2. Figures on imports and on market conditions taken from Calumet Project charts used in the course of developing a campaign to reopen the plant. The original source is the American Iron and Steel Institute (AISI).

3. Letter dated 20 February 1987 from Chester Smithers to USWA District 31 Director Jack Parton. (Copy in the author's possession.)

4. Letter dated 6 March 1987 from Chester Smithers to USWA District 31 Director Jack Parton. (Copy in the author's possession.)

5. Letter dated 2 June 1978 from Jack Parton to Chester Smithers. (Copy in the author's possession.)

6. Letter dated 5 May 1987 from Thomas McDermott to David Hoag. (Copy in the author's possession.)

7. Letter dated 30 April 1987 from Peter Visclosky to David Hoag. (Copy in the author's possession.)

8. Calumet Project, *A Study of Hammond Economic Development for the Common Council of Hammond, Indiana* (14 December 1987), p. 64.

9. Letter dated 8 May 1987 from John Lichtenstein of Locker Associates to Jack Parton, USWA District 31 director and James W. Smith, assistant to the president, USWA. (Copy in the author's possession.)

10. Letter dated 20 August 1986 from Woodruff Imberman to Jack Parton. (Copy in the author's possession.)

11. Letter dated 6 July 1987 from Woodruff Imberman to Lynn Feekin. (Copy in the author's possession.)

12. Letter dated 14 July 1987 from Chester Smithers to LTV President David Hoag. (Copy in the author's possession.)

13. See letter dated 17 September 1987 from Lynn Feekin to LTV's George Henning (copy in the author's possession) and subsequent letter from Dan Broughton (business analyst with the Midwest Center for Labor Research who was assisting the Calumet Project) to LTV's Francis Mangano (28 September 1987).

14. Letter dated 31 July 1987 from LTV Vice President A. C. Tremain to Chester Smithers (copy in the author's possession); Paul Hohl, "Group Seeks to Reopen LTV's Hammond Bar Mill," *American Metal Markets,* 28 September 1987.

15. Interview with Jerry Brown, 5 August 1990.

16. Letter dated 30 July 1987 from D. I. Williams, Union Drawn Vice President for Finance and Administration, to the Calumet Project for Industrial Jobs. (Copy in the author's possession.)

17. Letter dated 16 June 1987 from Chester Smithers to Jack Parton. (Copy in the author's possession.)

18. Letter dated 27 July 1987 (cover memo dated 18 August) from Jack Parton to Chester Smithers. (Copy in the author's possession.)

19. For contrasting coverage of the event, see Cynthia Ogorek, "Support Requested for plant," Hammond *Times,* 25 September 1987 and Barry Saunders, "LTV workers; Don't move equipment," Gary *Post-Tribune,* 25 September 1987. See also Paul Hohl, "Group Seeks to Reopen LTV's Hammond Bar Mill," *American Metal Markets,* 28 September 1987.

20. Steve Walsh, "Resolution calls for lien on LTV plant equipment," Gary *Post-Tribune,* 29 September 1987; Sharon Bohling, "Council backs employee buyout effort," Hammond *Times,* 29 September 1987.

21. Nancy Winkley, "Group stalled in LTV buyout bid," Gary *Post-Tribune,* 29 September 1987.

22. Letter dated 1 October 1987 from LTV Asset Sales General Manager Francis P. Mangano to Union Draw Steel President R. F. Hawkins. (Copy in the author's possession.)

23. Letter dated 6 October 1987 from Peter Visclosky to David Hoag. (Copy in the author's possession.)

24. Letter dated 3 November 1987 from David Hoag to Peter Visclosky. (Copy in the author's possession.)

25. See Deborah Squiers and Paul Hohl, "Plant Seen as Valueless if LTV Sells Drawbench," *American Metal Markets,* 2 November 1987.

26. Press release dated 23 October 1987: "LTV Breaks Promises to Hammond Workers." (Copy in author's possession.)

27. Bob Kostanczuk, "Talk on Hammond plant encourages union official," Gary *Post-Tribune,* 13 November 1987.

28. Cynthia Ogorek and James Kane, "Ex-LTV workers push plant sale," Hammond *Times,* 13 November 1987.

29. Interview with Lynn Feekin, Fall 1989.

30. Paul Hohl, "LTV Moves to Shift Bar Equipment," *American Metal Markets,* 24 November 1987.

31. Terms of the agreement taken from LTV letter to USWA Local 6518 President Chester Smithers, dated 23 November 1987. (Copy in the author's possession.)

32. Paul Hohl, "LTV, Union Reach Agreement On Course for Hammond Plant," *American Metal Markets,* 25 November 1987.

33. Lynn Feekin interview, Fall 1989.

34. Brian Bremmer, "Hopes dim for LTV mill here as would-be buyer departs," *Crain's Chicago Business,* 7 December 1987.

35. Letter dated 17 December 19878 from Jerry Brown to Thomas McDermott; letter dated 22 December 1987 from Thomas McDermott to LTV General Assets Manager George Henning. (Copies in the author's possession.)

36. Nancy Winkley, "LTV plant sale may stir suit, pickets," Gary *Post-Tribune,* 13 January 1988.

37. *Ibid.*

38. Letter dated 22 January 1988 from George Henning to Thomas McDermott. (Copy in the author's possession.)

39. Nancy Winkley, "LTV sells bar plant equipment," Gary *Post-Tribune,* 15 July 1988. Information in this and previous paragraphs also taken from Sharon Bohling, "Former workers offer look at plant-buying efforts," Hammond *Times,* 14 June 1988; "Former workers trying to sell LTV plant, Gary *Post-Tribune,* 20 June 1988; Nancy Winkley, "Mayor holds to bar-plant sale plan," Gary *Post-Tribune,* 1 July 1988.

40. Jerry Brown interview, 5 August 1990. Later press accounts state that Metal-Matic had fifty truckloads of equipment stored in the plant.

41. Chris Isidore, "Hazardous wastes found at closed LTV steel mill," Gary *Post-Tribune,* 3 November 1988.

42. Sandra Guy and Phillip Wieland, "Sale talks on bar plant," Hammond *Times,* 29 November 1988. See also Chris Isidore, "PCBs on property stall LTV mill sale," Gary *Post-Tribune,* 30 November 1988.

43. *Ibid.*

44. Chris Isidore, "Bar mill menace spreads," Gary *Post-Tribune,* 12 January 1989. See also Richard Bryant, "Site Report 'devastating'," Hammond *Times,* 12 January 1989.

45. "LTV Deserves Praise For Being a Good Neighbor," a handout distributed at the 12 January 1989 public meeting. (Copy in the author's possession.)

46. Chris Isidore, "LTV cleanup will take longer," Gary *Post-Tribune,* 4 March 1989.

47. Nancy Pieters, "Ex-LTV workers ask sale details," Hammond *Times,* 25 May 1991; Robin Biesen, "2 move to open former factory," Gary *Post-Tribune,* [313-?] May 1991.

48. Jerry Brown interview, 5 August 1990.

49. On Youngstown plant closing struggles, see Thomas Fuechtmann, *Steeple and Stacks: Religion and Steel Crisis in Youngstown* (New York: Cambridge University Press, 1989), pp. 186–94. For Pittsburgh struggles, see Dale Hathaway, *Can Workers Have a Voice?* (University Park, PA: The Pennsylvania State University Press, 1993), and William Serrin, *Homestead: the Glory and Tragedy of an American Steel Town* (New York: Random House, 1992).

50. Jerry Brown interview, 5 August 1990.

51. *Ibid.*

52. *Ibid.*

53. *Ibid.*

54. For an account of this struggle, see Bruce Nissen and Lynn Feekin, "For the Public Good: Calumet Project organizes for labor and community-based economic development," *Labor Research Review #19* (Fall 1992), pp. 15–29. See also the following chapter.

CHAPTER 6. PREVENTING A DEPARTMENT RELOCATION AT THE LASALLE STEEL PLANT

1. All information on the early years of LaSalle Steel taken from *LaSalle Steel Courier,* 50th Anniversary Souvenir Edition (1962), and "LaSalle Steel Company, 1912–1987" a report produced by Winslow Studios for LaSalle's 75th Anniversary celebration.

2. "Quanex restructuring steel firm debt package," Gary *Post-Tribune,* 18 January 1983; "Quanex agrees to Buy Assets of LaSalle Steel for Total of $52 Million," *Wall Street Journal,* 16 November 1981.

3. Information on LaSalle's market share and employment taken from a Calumet Project document relating the contents of a 14 September 1985 interview with Darell Wilson, president of the Progressive Steelworkers Union.

4. *1987 Quanex Annual Report,* p. 5.

5. *1991 Quanex Annual Report,* p. 4.

6. *Quanex 1990 Proxy Statement,* p. 12.

7. Information on the strike issues and the strike vote taken from: Phillip Britt, "LaSalle workers strike over pensions," Hammond *Times,* 15 February 1990; Chris Isidore, "Strike shuts LaSalle Steel plant," Gary *Post-Tribune,* 16 February 1990; Phillip Britt, "Steelworkers to vote on wage increase," Hammond *Times,* 17 February 1990; Chris Isidore, "Union, LaSalle Steel confident about vote," Gary *Post-Tribune,* 17 February 1990; Phillip Britt, "Quantex (sp) LaSalle Steel pensions questioned," Hammond *Times,* 18 February 1990; Tracey Maple and Phillip Britt, "Determination drives strikers at LaSalle," Hammond *Times,* 19 February 1990; Jean Marie Brown, "LaSalle contract is rejected," Gary *Post-Tribune,* 19 February 1990; and

Karen Snelling, "No end in sight in steel strike," Gary *Post-Tribune*, 10 February 1990.

8. Jean Marie Brown, "LaSalle contract is rejected," Gary *Post-Tribune*, 19 February 1990.

9. Phillip Britt, "Quantex [sp] LaSalle Steel pensions questioned," Hammond *Times*, 18 February 1990.

10. Karen Snelling, "No end in sight in steel strike," Gary *Post-Tribune*, 10 February 1990.

11. I am indebted to Kerry Taylor for this information. Taylor interviewed LaSalle workers for a paper written for a college class taught by me.

12. "Quanex LaSalle union rejects offer," Gary *Post-Tribune*, 13 March 1990; Phillip Britt, "New Quanex LaSalle offer rejected," Hammond *Times*, 13 March 1990.

13. Settlement terms taken from Phillip Britt, "Steelworkers end walkout," Hammond *Times*, 20 March 1990; Chris Isidore, "Striking steelworkers return," Gary *Post-Tribune*, 10 March 1990.

14. 16 November 1990 letter from Richard Treder to Zed Rixie. (Copy in the author's possession.)

15. 26 November 1990 letter from Zed Rixie to Richard Treder. (Copy in the author's possession.)

16. 30 November 1990 letter from Richard Treder to Zed Rixie. (Copy in the author's possession.)

17. 25 November 1990 letter from Larry Sutton, Daniel Colon, and Larry Partain to Carl E. Pfeiffer. (Copy in the author's possession.)

18. 3 December 1990 letter from Carl E. Pfeiffer to Larry Sutton, Daniel Colon, and Larry Partain. (Copy in the author's possession.)

19. Nancy Pieters, "Steelworkers fear LaSalle Steel will close," Hammond *Times*, 7 December 1990.

20. Laura Viani, "Steelworker union seeks info on LaSalle's plans for its grinding division," *American Metal Market,* 10 December 1990.

21. Chris Isidore, "Meeting on LaSalle move," Gary *Post-Tribune,* 7 December 1990.

22. Nancy Pieters, "LaSalle Steel withdraws closing notice," Hammond *Times*, 9 December 1990. See also, Nancy Pieters, "Impact of plant closings goes beyond numbers," in the same issue.

23. Phil Britt, "Support grows to keep LaSalle from moving," Hammond *Times*, 11 December 1990.

24. 11 December 1990 letter from Zed Rixie to Tom McDermott. (Copy in the author's possession.)

25. 20 December 1990 letter from Charles Pettersen to Carl Pfeiffer. (Copy in the author's possession.)

26. 4 January 1991 letter from Carl Pfeiffer to Charles Pettersen. (Copy in the author's possession.)

27. Information on this meeting obtained from notes taken by Calumet Project Director Lynn Feekin, who attended.

28. 25 January 1991 letter from Richard Treder to Zed Rixie. (Copy in the author's possessio.n)

29. My summary is taken from the document itself, titled, "Save Jobs at LaSalle Steel in Hammond." (Copy in the author's possession.)

30. Phillip Britt, "Labor group examining ways to keep LaSalle jobs," Hammond *Times*, 13 February 1991.

31. See, for example, Chris Isidore, "Quanex planning move to Frankfort," Gary *Post-Tribune*, 13 February 1991; Nancy Pieters, "LaSalle may yet move grinding unit," Hammond *Times*, 13 February 1991.

32. Editorial: "Big pay cuts aren't the best way," Hammond *Times*, 14 February 1991.

33. Nancy Pieters, "Group blasts LaSalle steel on tax abatement," Hammond *Times*, 15 February 1991.

34. Nancy Pieters, "Group blasts LaSalle Steel on tax abatement," Hammond *Times*, 15 February 1991.

35. 20 February 1991 letter from Richard Treder to LaSalle employees, retirees, and friends. (Copy in the author's possession.)

36. Letter to the editor: "LaSalle sees move as cure for company," Hammond *Times*, 21 February 1991.

37. Nancy Pieters, "Quanex: LaSalle's health comes first," Hammond *Times*, 21 February 1991.

39. 25 February 1991 letter from Robert A. Markovich to Richard W. Treder. (Copy in the author's possession.)

40. 25 February 1991 letter from Robert A. Markovich to the Frankfort City Council. (Copy in the author's possession.)

41. 26 February 1991 letter from Thomas M. McDermott to Richard W. Treder. (Copy in the author's possession.)

42. Howard W. Hewitt, "Plant relocation causing stir," Frankfort *Times*, 2 March 1991.

43. "Appeal to steel firm planned," Gary *Post-Tribune*, 26 February 1991.

44. Debra Gruszecki, "Council eyes steps to stop LaSalle plans," Hammond *Times*, 26 February 1991.

45. Nancy Pieters, "Grinding department moving plans on hold," Hammond *Times*, 6 March 1991.

46. Chris Isidore, "LaSalle Steel putting move on hold," Gary *Post-Tribune*, 6 March 1991.

47. Nancy Pieters, "Grinding department moving plans on hold," Hammond *Times*, 6 March 1991.

48. Chris Isidore, "LaSalle Steel putting move on hold," Gary *Post-Tribune*, 6 March 1991.

49. Kerry Taylor, "They fought for their jobs — and won," Gary *Post-Tribune*, 28 February 1993.

50. *1991 Quanex Annual Report,* p. 13.

51. *1992 Quanex Annual Report,* pp. 12, 13.

52. 25 February 1993 News Release: "Quanex results show steel tubes and bars improved, aluminum lagging," p. 1.

53. Undated Calumet Project document entitled, "Victory at LaSalle." The document was written by Lynn Feekin, Calumet Project Director.

54. An interesting exploration of this issue is *Labor Research Review #14* (Vol. VIII, No. 2, Fall 1989). Book-length criticisms of the effect of cooperative programs on unions include Mike Parker, *Inside the Circle: a Union Guide to QWL* (Boston: South End Press, 1985) and Donald Wells, *Empty Promises: Quality of Working Life Programs and the Labor Movement* (New York: Monthly Review Press, 1987). A positive portrayal is given in Barry Bluestone and Irving Bluestone, *Negotiating the Future: a Labor Perspective on American Business* (New York: Basic Books, 1992).

CHAPTER 7. COMPARING THE CASES: CRITICAL FACTORS

1. Marie Howland, *Plant Closings and Worker Displacement: The Regional Issues* (Kalamazoo, MI: W. E. Upjohn Institute, 1988), p. 153.

2. Market figures in this paragraph taken from *1987 U.S. Industrial Outlook* (Washington, D.C.: U.S. Department of Commerce), p. 17-7.

3. See Marie Howland, *Plant Closings and Worker Displacement: the Regional Issues* (Kalamazoo, MI: W.E. Upjohn Institute, 1988), p. 158.

4. For a discussion, see *1987 U.S. Industrial Outlook,* p. 17-7.

5. All figures on capacity utilization taken from Board of Governors of the Federal Reserve System, *Industrial Production and Capacity Utilization: Historical Data and Source and Description Information,* 1990 revision.

6. All data on the Combustion Engineering product market taken from 1987 *U.S. Industrial Outlook,* p. 25-1 and *1988 U.S. Industrial Outlook,* p. 27-1.

7. All import figures in this paragraph taken from *1987 U.S. Industrial Outlook,* p. 25-3.

8. Board of Governors of the Federal Reserve System, *Industrial Production and Capacity Utilization: G.17 (419) Historical Data and Source and Description Information,* 1990 revision.

9. Profit data taken from Dun and Bradstreet, *Industry Norms and Key Business Ratios.*

10. All market data and imports data in this and the following paragraphs taken from *1989 U.S. Industrial Outlook,* p. 41-2, *1990 U.S. Industrial Outlook,* p. 35-3, and *1993 U.S. Industrial Outlook,* p. 32-2.

11. Capacity utilization figures taken from Board of Governors of the Federal Reserve System, *Industrial Production and Capacity Utilization: G 17 (419) Historical Data and Source and Description Information,* 1990 revision.

12. Profit data taken from Dun and Bradstreet, *Industry Norms and Key Business Ratios*, relevant years.

13. Market and import data in the following paragraphs taken from *1989 U.S. Industrial Outlook*, p. 17-1; *1990 U.S. Industrial Outlook*, p. 16-1; and *1991 U.S. Industrial Outlook*, p. 15-3.

14. Capacity utilization figures taken from Board of Governors of the Federal Reserve System, *Industrial Production and Capacity Utilization: G.17 (419) Historical Data and Source and Description Information*, 1990 revision.

15. Profit figures taken from Dun and Bradstreet, *Industry Norms and Key Business Ratios*, relevant years.

16. See Marie Howland, *Plant Closings and Worker Displacement: The Regional Issues* (Kalamazoo, MI: W. E. Upjohn Institute, 1988). See also Doreen Massey and Richard Meegan, *The Anatomy of Job Loss*, (New York: Methuen Press, 1982).

17. For a discussion of socially responsible corporate behavior in a plant closing situation, see Archie B. Carroll, "When Business Closes Down: Social Responsibilities and Management Actions," *California Management Review* 26, no. 2 (winter 1984), pp. 125–39; reprinted as "Management's Social Responsibilities" in Paul D. Staudohar and Holly E. Brown, *Deindustrialization and Plant Closure* (Lexington, MA: Lexington Books, 1987), pp. 167–81.

18. One attempt to do this is the Steel Valley Authority (SVA) in the Monongahela Valley near Pittsburgh. For information on the SVA see Mike Stout, "Reindustrialization from Below: The Steel Valley Authority," *Labor Research Review* #9 (Fall 1986), pp. 19–33; chapter 5 in John Portz, *The Politics of Plant Closings* (Lawrence: University Press of Kansas, 1990); and Tom Croft, "Achieving City Pride: Labor, community and the private sector bake a new idea in ownership," *Labor Research Review* #19, (Fall 1992), pp. 1–13.

CHAPTER 8. PROBLEM DEFINITION, ALLIANCE FORMATION, MOBILIZATION, AND THE SIGNIFICANCE OF LABOR COMMUNITY COALITIONS

1. John Portz, *The Politics of Plant Closings* (Lawrence: University Press of Kansas, 1990), p. 139.

2. I am indebted to David Fasenfest of Purdue University and Laura Reese of Eastern Michigan University for the following ideas on the market paradigm. See "Measuring the Effects of Local Economic Development Policy: Considering Social Outcomes," a paper presented to the Urban Affairs Association Annual Meeting, Indianapolis, Indiana, 21–24 April 1993.

3. Charles Craypo and Bruce Nissen, "The Impact of Corporate Strategies," chapter 11 in Craypo and Nissen, *Grand Designs: the Impact of Corporate Strategies on Workers, Unions, and Communities* (Ithaca, NY: ILR Press, 1993), p. 246.

The stakeholder rights language is being used increasingly by the U.S. labor movement in recent years. See Patricia A. Greenfield and Julie Graham, "Workers, Communities, and Industrial Prosperity: An Emerging Language of Rights," *Employee Responsibilities and Rights Journal* (forthcoming).

4. See William A. Gamson, *Strategy of Social Protest* (Homewood, IL: Dorsey, 1975); Anthony Oberschall, *Social Conflict and Social Movements* (Englewood Cliffs, NJ: Prentice Hall, 1973); Charles Tilly, *From Mobilization to Revolution* (Reading, MA: Addison-Wesley, 1978); and Mayer N. Zald and John D. McCarthy, eds., *The Dynamics of Social Movements: Resource Mobilization, Social Control, and Tactics* (Lanham, MD: University Press of America, 1988).

5. Mayer N. Zald and John D. McCarthy, "Introduction," in Zald and McCarthy, eds., *The Dynamics of Social Movements*, p. 1.

6. The literature here is voluminous, going back to Marx and many varieties of socialist and radical thought. In the following I confine the discussion to the "class capacities" question and to related debates concerning "class" vs. "community."

7. For more on the "class capacities" question, see Erik Olin Wright, *Class, Crisis and the State* (London: New Left Books, 1978) and Jerry Lembcke, *Capitalist Development and Class Capacities* (Westport, CT: Greenwood Press, 1988).

8. For an interesting introduction to this debate, see Joseph M. Kling and Prudence S. Posner, eds., *Dilemmas of Activism: Class, Community, and the Politics of Local Mobilization* (Philadelphia: Temple University Press, 1990).

9. The literature is too large to cite here. Useful book-length studies are Michael Goldfield, *The Decline of Organized Labor in the United States* (Chicago: University of Chicago Press, 1987), and Thomas Kochan, ed., *Choices and Challenges Facing American Labor* (Cambridge, MA: MIT Press, 1985). See also Seymour Martin Lipset, *Unions in Transition* (San Francisco: Institute for Contemporary Studies, 1986); Bruce Nissen, *U.S. Labor Relations 1945–1989: Accommodation and Conflict* (New York: Garland Publishing, 1990), and Gordon L. Clark, *Unions and Communities Under Siege: American Communities and the Crisis of Organized Labor* (New York: Cambridge University Press, 1989).

10. The phrase is from Sidney Plotkin, "Enclave Consciousness and Neighborhood Activism," in Kling and Posner, eds., *The Dilemmas of Activism*.

11. See Joan Fitzgerald, "Class as community: the new dynamics of social change," *Environment and Planning D: Society and Space*, Vol. 9 (1991), pp. 117–28.

12. For a general introduction to Gutman's historical work, see *Work, Culture, and Society in Industrializing America*. Many other recent works in labor history scholarship explore the same theme.

13. Many types of labor-community coalition efforts are detailed in Brecher and Costello, *Building Bridges: the Emerging Alliance of Labor and Community*.

14. The "Justice for Janitors" campaigns of the Service Employees International Union (SEIU) have achieved unusually large victories under normally improbable circumstances by employing a "social movement" approach involving community alliances. For an introduction to this topic, see Stephen Lerner, "Let's

Get Moving: Labor's survival depends on organizing industry-wide for justice and power," *Labor Research Review #18* (Fall/Winter 1991–92), pp. 1–16.

15. See Andy Banks, "The Power and Promise of Community Unionism," *Labor Research Review #18* (Fall/Winter 1991–92), pp. 17–32.

16. Sidney Plotkin and William E. Scheuerman, "Two Roads Left: Strategies of Resistance to Plant Closings in the Monongahela Valley," chapter 8 in Kling and Posner, eds., *Dilemmas of Activism.*

17. Ann R. Markusen, "Planning for Industrial Decline: Lessons from Steel Communities," *Journal of Planning Education and Research,* Vol. 7, No. 3 (1987), p. 181.

18. Dale Hathaway, *Can workers Have a Voice? The Politics of Deindustrialization in Pittsburgh* (University Park: The Pennsylvania State University Press, 1993), p. 215.

19. Susan S. Fainstein and Norman I. Fainstein, "Economic Restructuring and the Rise of Urban Social Movements," *Urban Affairs Quarterly,* Vol. 21, No. 2 (December 1985), pp. 187–206.

20. This is one of the themes of Gordon L. Clark, *Unions and Communities Under Siege* (Cambridge: Cambridge University Press, 1989).

21. Joan Fitzgerald and Louise Simmons make this same point in "From Consumption to Production: Labor Participation in Grass-Roots Movements in Pittsburgh and Hartford," *Urban Affairs Quarterly,* Vol. 26, No. 4, (June 1991), pp. 512–31.

22. See Jeremy Brecher and Tim Costello, *Building Bridges: the Emerging Alliance of Labor and Community* (New York: Monthly Review Press, 1990).

23. Much of the information on FIRR in this and the following paragraphs obtained from an 9 August 1993 interview with Jim Benn, the Executive Director of FIRR.

24. See Lynn Feekin and Bruce Nissen, "For the Public Good: Calumet Project organizes for labor and community-based economic development," *Labor Research Review #19* (Fall 1992), pp. 15–29. Another account is contained in Bruce Nissen, "Successful Labor-Community Coalition-Building," chapter 10 in Charles Craypo and Bruce Nissen, eds., *Grand Designs: the Effect of Corporate Strategies on Workers, Unions, and Communities* (Ithaca, NY: Cornell University ILR Press, 1993).

25. On the Merrimack Valley Project, see George Packer, "Down in the Valley," *The Nation,* 27 June 1994, pp. 900–04.

26. As a board member of the Calumet Project, I have had occasion to attend most FIRR national and midwest regional meetings, in addition to studying its newsletter and written materials.

SELECTED BIBLIOGRAPHY

Addison, John T., and Pedro Portugal. "The Effect of Advance Notification of Plant Closings on Unemployment," *Industrial and Labor Relations Review,* Vol. 41, No. 1 (October 1987), pp. 3–16.

Baden-Fuller, C. W. F. "Exit From Declining Industries and the Case of Steel Castings," *The Economic Journal,* Vol. 99 (December 1989), pp. 949–61.

Banks, Andy. "The Power and Promise of Community Unionism," *Labor Research Review #18,* Vol. X, No. 2 (Fall/Winter 1991–92), pp. 17–32.

———, and Jack Metzgar. "Participating in Management: Union Organizing on a New Terrain," *Labor Research Review #14,* Vol. VIII, No. 2 (Fall 1989), pp. 1–55.

Bluestone, Barry, and Bennett Harrison. *The Deindustrialization of America.* New York: Basic Books, 1982.

———, and Irving Bluestone. *Negotiating the Future: a Labor Perspective on American Business.* New York: Basic Books, 1992.

Brecher, Jeremy, and Tim Costello. *Building Bridges: the Emerging Alliance of Labor and Community.* New York: Monthly Review Press, 1990.

Brown, Sharon P. "How often do workers receive advance notice of layoffs?" *Monthly Labor Review,* June 1987, pp. 13–17.

Bureau of National Affairs. *Plant Closings: The Complete Resource Guide.* Washington, D.C.: Bureau of National Affairs, 1988.

Buss, Terry F., and F. Stevens Redburn. *Mass Unemployment: Plant Closings and Community Mental Health.* Beverly Hills, CA: Sage Publications, 1983.

———. *Shutdown at Youngstown: Public Policy for Mass Unemployment.* Albany, NY: SUNY Press, 1983.

Calumet Project for Industrial Jobs. *Preventing Plant Closings in Northwest Indiana: A Public Policy Program for Action.* East Chicago, IN: The Calumet Project for Industrial Jobs, November 1989.

Carroll, Archie B. "When Business Closes Down: Social Responsibilities and Management Actions," *California Management Review,* Vol. 26, No. 2 (Winter 1984), pp. 125–39.

Castells, Manuel. *The City and the Grassroots.* Berkeley: University of California Press, 1983.

Clark, Gordon. *Unions and Communities Under Siege: American Communities and the Crisis of Organized Labor.* New York: Cambridge University Press, 1989.

Coffin, Donald. "The Northwest Indiana Economy in Recent Historical Perspective," *Northwest Indiana Business Conditions,* Vol. 1, No. 1 (November 1992), pp. 2–9.

Craypo, Charles, and Bruce Nissen, eds. *Grand Designs: the Impact of Corporate Strategies on Workers, Unions and Communities.* Ithaca, NY: ILR Press, 1993.

Croft, Tom. "Achieving City Pride: Labor, community and private sector bake a new idea in ownership," *Labor Research Review #19,* Vol. XI, No. 1, pp. 1–13.

Cummings, Scott, ed. *Business Elites and Urban Development.* Albany, NY: SUNY Press, 1988.

Deily, Mary E. "Exit Barriers in the Steel Industry," *Economic Review* (Federal Reserve Bank of Cleveland), Vol. 24, No. 1 (1988), pp. 10–18.

———. "Investment Activity and the Exit Decision," *The Review of Economics and Statistics,* Vol. 70 (1988), pp. 595–602.

———. "Exit Strategies and Plant Closing Decisions: The Case of Steel," *Rand Journal of Economics,* Vol. 22, No. 2 (Summer 1991), pp. 250–63.

Deitch, Cynthia and Robert Erickson. "'Save Dorothy': A Political Response to Structural Change in the Steel Industry," in Raymond M. Lee, ed. *Redundancy, Layoffs and Plant Closures.* Wolfeboro, NH: Croom Helm, 1987, pp. 241–79.

Doherty, Barbara. *The Struggle to Save Morse Cutting Tool.* North Dartmouth: Southeastern Massachusetts University Labor Education Center, n.d.

Ehrenberg, Ronald G., and George H. Jakubson. *Advance Notice Provision in Plant Closing Legislation.* Kalamzaoo, MI: W. E. Upjohn Institute, 1988.

Fainstein, Susan S., and Norman I. Fainstein. "Economic Restructuring and the Rise of Urban Social Movements," *Urban Affairs Quarterly,* Vol. 21, No. 2 (December 1985), pp. 187–206.

Fasenfest, David. "Cui Bono?" in Charles Craypo and Bruce Nissen, eds. *Grand Designs: The Impact of Corporate Strategies on Workers, Unions and Communities.* Ithaca, NY: ILR Press, 1993, pp. 119–37.

Feekin, Lynn, and Bruce Nissen. "Early Warning of Plant Closings: Issues and Prospect," *Labor Studies Journal,* Vol. 16, No. 4 (Winter 1991), pp. 20–33.

Fitzgerald, Joan. "Class as community: the new dynamics of social change," *Environment and Planning D: Society and Space,* Vol. 9 (1991), pp. 117–28.

———, and Louise Simmons. "From Consumption to Production: Labor Participation in Grass-Roots Movements in Pittsburgh and Hartford," *Urban Affairs Quarterly,* Vol. 26, No. 4 (June 1991), pp. 512–31.

Folbre, Nancy, Julia Leighton, and Melissa Roderick, "Plant Closings and their Regulation in Maine, 1971–1982," *Industrial and Labor Relations Review,* Vol. 37, No. 2 (January 1984), pp. 185–96.

Freeman, Richard B., and Morris M. Kleiner, "Do Unions Make Enterprises Insolvent?" *National Bureau of Economic Research,* Working Paper No. 4797 (1994).

Fuechtmann, Thomas G. *Steeples and Stacks: Religion and Steel Crisis in Youngstown.* New York: Cambridge University Press, 1989.

Gamson, William A. *Strategy of Social Protest.* Homewood, IL: Dorsey, 1975.

Gannon, Thomas M. *The People of Northwest Indiana: Demographic Changes and Challenges, 1970–1990.* East Chicago, IN: Heartland Center, Winter 1992.

Gearhart, Paul F. *Saving Plants and Jobs: Union-Management Negotiations in the Context of Threatened Plant Closing.* Kalamazoo, MI: W. E. Upjohn Institute, 1987.

Ghemawat, Pankaj, and Barry Nalebuff. "The Devolution of Declining Industries," *The Quarterly Journal of Economics,* Vol. 105 (1990), pp. 167–86.

Giloth, Robert, and Robert Mier. "Democratic populism in the USA: The Case of Playskool and Chicago," *Cities: an International Quarterly on Urban Policy* (London), February 1986, pp. 72–74.

Giloth, Robert, and Susan Rosenblum. "How to Fight Plant Closings," *Social Policy,* Vol. 17 (Winter 1987), pp. 20–26.

Goldfield, Michael. *The Decline of Organized Labor in the United States.* Chicago: University of Chicago Press, 1987.

Gordus, Jeanne Prial, Paul Jarley, and Louis A. Ferman. *Plant Closings and Economic Dislocation.* Kalamzaoo, MI: W. E. Upjohn Institute, 1981.

Greenfield, Patricia, and Julie Graham, "Workers, Communities, and Industrial Prosperity: An Emerging Language of Rights," *Employee Responsibilities and Rights Journal* (forthcoming).

Gutman, Herbert G. *Work, Culture & Society in Industrializing America*. New York: Alfred A. Knopf, 1976.

———. *Power and Culture: Essays on the American Working Class*. New York: The New Press, 1987.

Haas, Gilda. *Plant Closures: Myths, Realities and Responses*. Boston: South End Press, 1985.

Harrison, Bennett, and Barry Bluestone. *The Great U-Turn: Corporate Restructuring and the Polarizing of America*. New York: Basic Books, 1988.

Hathaway, Dale. *Can Workers Have a Voice? The Politics of Deindustrialization in Pittsburgh*. University Park: Pennsylvania University Press, 1993.

Hecksher, Charles. *The New Unionism*. New York: Basic Books, 1989.

Hoerr, John P. *And the Wolf Finally Came: the Decline of the American Steel Industry*. Pittsburgh: University of Pittsburgh Press, 1988.

Howland, Marie. *Plant Closings and Worker Displacement: The Regional Issues*. Kalamazoo, MI: W. E. Upjohn Institute, 1988.

Hudson, Ray, and David Sadler. "Region, class, and the politics of steel closures in the European Community," *Environment and Planning D: Society and Space,* Vol. 1 (1983), pp. 405–28.

Indiana Employment and Training Services, Gary-Hammond PMSA branch. *The Gary-Hammond PMSA in Review.*

Kling, Joseph M., and Prudence S. Posner, eds. *Dilemmas of Activism: Class, Community, and the Politics of Local Mobilization*. Philadelphia: Temple University Press, 1990.

Kochan, Thomas, ed. *Choices and Challenges Facing American Labor*. Cambridge, MA: MIT Press, 1985.

———, Harry Katz and Robert B. McKersie. *The Transformation of American Industrial Relations*. New York: Basic Books, 1986.

Lee, Raymond M., ed. *Redundancy, Layoffs and Plant Closures*. Wolfeboro, NH: Croom Helm, 1987.

Lembcke, Jerry. *Capitalist Development and Class Capacities*. Westport, CT: Greenwood Press, 1988.

LeRoy, Greg. *Early Warning Manual Against Plant Closings*. Chicago: Midwest Center for Labor Research, 1986.

Lieberman, Marvin B. "Exit from declining industries: 'shakeout' or 'stakeout?'" *RAND Journal of Economics,* Vol. 21, No. 4 (Winter 1990), pp. 538–54.

Lipset, Seymour Martin, ed. *Unions in Transition.* San Francisco: Institute for Contemporary Studies, 1986.

Lynd, Staughton, *The Fight Against Shutdowns: Youngstown's Steel Mill Closings.* San Pedro, CA: Singlejack Books, 1983.

MacKenzie, Richard B. *Fugitive Industry: the Economics and Politics of Deindustrialization.* Cambridge, MA: Ballinger, 1984.

———, ed. *Plant Closings: Public or Private Choices?* Washington, DC: Cato Institute, 1984.

Markusen, Ann R. "Planning for Industrial Decline: Lessons from Steel Communities," *Journal of Planning Education and Research,* Vol. 7, No. 3 (1987), pp. 173–84.

Massey, Doreen, and Richard Meegan. *The Anatomy of Job Loss.* New York: Methuen Press, 1982.

Metzgar, Jack. "Plant Shutdowns and Worker Response: The Case of Johnstown, Pa.," *Socialist Review,* Vol. X (Sept.–Oct. 1980), pp.9–49.

Midwest Center for Labor Research. *Intervening with Aging Owners to Save Industrial Jobs: A National Survey of Literature and Practice and a Preliminary Assessment of Successorship Needs and Plans of Chicago's Aging Manufacturing Entrepreneurs.* Report prepared for the Strategic Planning Committee of the Economic Development Commission of Chicago, August 1989.

National Lawyers Guild. *Plant Closings and Runaway Industries: Strategies for Labor.* Washington, DC: National Labor Law Center, 1981.

Nissen, Bruce. "Union Battles Against Plant Closings: Case Study Evidence and Policy Implications," *Policy Studies Journal,* Vol. 18, No. 2 (Winter 1989–90), pp. 382-95.

———, ed. *U.S. Labor Relations 1945–1989: Accommodation and Conflict.* New York: Garland Publishing, 1990.

———, and Lynn Feekin. "For the Public Good: Calumet Project organizes for labor and community-based economic development," *Labor Research Review,* Vol. XI, No. 1 (Fall 1992), pp. 14–29.

———. "Successful Labor-Community coalition Building," in Charles Craypo and Bruce Nissen, eds. *Grand Designs: the Impact of Corporate Strategies on Workers, Unions and Communities.* Ithaca, NY: ILR Press, 1993, pp. 209–23

————. "Combating Plant Closings in the Era of the Transnational Corporation," in Lawrence Flood, ed., *Unions and Public Policy: The New Economy, Law and Democratic Politics*. New York: Greenwood Press, 1995.

Obserschall, Anthony. *Social Conflict and Social Movements*. Englewood Cliffs, NJ: Prentice Hall, 1973.

Packer, George. "Down in the Valley: a Community Fights Hard Times," *The Nation*, Vol. 258, No. 25 (June 27, 1994), pp. 900–4.

Pappas, Gregory. *The Magic City*. Ithaca, NY: Cornell University Press, 1989.

Parker, Mike. *Inside the Circle: a Union Guide to QWL*. Boston: South End Press, 1985.

"Participating in Management," *Labor Research Review* #14, Vol. VIII, No. 2 (Fall 1989).

Perrucci, Carolyn, Robert Perrucci, Dena B. Targ, and Harry R. Targ. *Plant Closings: International Context and Social Costs*. Hawthorne, NY: Aldine de Gruyter, 1988.

Piven, Frances Fox, and Richard A. Cloward. *Poor People's Movements: Why They Succeed, How They Fail*. New York: Pantheon Books, 1977.

Portz, John. *The Politics of Plant Closings*. Lawrence: University Press of Kansas, 1990.

Raines, John C., Lenora E. Berson, and David McI. Gracie, eds. *Community and Capital in conflict: Plant Closings and Job Loss*. Philadelphia: Temple University Press, 1982.

Ranney, David C., "Manufacturing Job Loss and Early Warning Indicators," *Journal of Planning Literature*, Vol. 3, No. 1 (Winter 1988), pp. 22–25.

Reich, Robert. *The Next American Frontier: A Provocative Program for Economic Renewal*. New York: Times Books, 1983

Reynolds, Stanley S. "Plant Closings and Exit Behaviour in Declining Industries," *Economica*, Vol. 55 (1988), pp. 493–503.

Rothstein, Lawrence E. *Plant Closings: Power, Politics, and Workers*. Dover, MA: Auburn House, 1986.

Scott, Allen J., and Michael Storper, eds. *Production, Work, and Territory: The Geographical Anatomy of Industrial Capitalism*. Boston: Allen & Unwin, 1986.

Serrin, William. *Homestead: The Glory and Tragedy of an American Steel Town*. New York: Times Books, 1992.

Sheehan, Michael F. "Plant Closings and the Community: The Instrumental Value of Public Enterprise in Countering Corporate Flight," *The American Journal of Economics and Sociology,* Vol. 44 No. 4 (October 1985), pp. 423–33.

Staudohar, Paul D., and Holly E. Brown, eds. *Deindustrialization and Plant Closure.* Lexington, MA: Lexington Books, 1987.

Stern, Robert N., K. Haydn Wood, and Tove Helland Hammer. *Employee Ownership in Plant Shutdowns: Prospects for Employment Stability.* Kalamzaoo, MI: W. E. Upjohn Institute, 1979.

Stout, Mike. "Reindustrialization from Below: The Steel Valley Authority," *Labor Research Review #9,* Vol. V, No. 2 (Fall 1986), pp. 1–13.

Tennessee Industrial Renewal Network. *Taking Charge! A Hands-On Guide to Dealing with the Threat of Plant Closings and Supporting Laid-Off Workers.* Knoxville: Tennessee Industrial Renewal Network, n.d.

Tilly, Charles. *From Mobilization to Revolution.* Reading, MA: Addison-Wesley, 1978.

U.S. Congress Office of Technology Assessment, *Plant Closing: Advance Notice and Rapid Response–Special Report,* September 1986 (OTA-ITE-321).

U.S. Department of Commerce, Economic Development Administration. *Early Warning Information Systems for Business Retention,* September 1980.

U.S. General Accounting Office, *Plant Closings: Information on Advance Notice and Assistance to Dislocated Workers,* 17 April 1987 (GAO-HRD-87-86BR).

Way, Harold E., and Carla Weiss. *Plant Closings: a Selected Bibliography of Materials Published through 1985.* Ithaca, NY: Martin P. Catherwood Library, NYSSILR, Cornell University, September 1987.

Weiss, Carla. *Plant Closings: a Selected Bibliography of Materials Published 1986–1990.* Ithaca, NY: ILR Press, 1991.

Wells, Donald. *Empty Promises: Quality of Working Life Programs and the Labor Movement.* New York: Monthly Review Press, 1987.

Whinston, Michael D. "Exit with multiplant firms," *RAND Journal of Economics,* Vol. 19, No. 4 (Winter 1988), pp. 568–88.

Woolfston, Charles, and John Foster. *Track Record: The Story of the Caterpillar Occupation.* New York: Verso, 1988.

Wright, Erik Olin. *Class, Crisis and the State*. London: New Left Books, 1978.

Zald, Mayer N., and John D. McCarthy, eds. *The Dynamics of Social Movements*. Lanham, MD: University Press of America, 1988.

Zipp, John F., and Katherine E. Lane. "Plant Closings and Control Over the Workplace," *Work and Occupations*, Vol. 14, No. 1 (February 1987), pp. 62–87.